THE STAGES OF LIFE

Is personality 'in the genes'?
Do our infant experiences matter, even though we can't remember them?
Why do patterns repeat within the lives of individuals and families?

The Stages of Life provides answers to these and other intriguing questions, and presents a refreshingly readable introduction to human development from birth to death. The book synthesises those theories and research findings that are most helpful in explaining the paradoxes and complexities of human personality and human problems.

The book provides a thought-provoking discussion of several important topics, including:

*   how personality evolves in response to both genetic and social influences;
*   how individuals differ and what this means for them; and
*   how some problems tend to develop at particular stages of the life course, from early childhood through to midlife and old age.

Throughout the book, Hugh Crago relates both 'nature' and 'nurture' to the challenges individuals must face from early childhood through to old age. He draws attention to often-ignored clinical findings about 'cross-generational repetition' in families, and shows how recent developments in epigenetics may supply an explanation for such mysterious phenomena.

Written without jargon, and full of new and provocative ideas, the book will be of great interest to students of counselling, psychotherapy and developmental psychology, and it also has much to offer the general reader. With its engaging examples from history, literature and the author's experiences, readers will find that *The Stages of Life* illuminates puzzles in their own lives and opens a road to self-acceptance.

Hugh Crago is Adjunct Fellow in the School of Social Sciences and Psychology at Western Sydney University, Australia.

Praise for Hugh Crago's recent *Entranced by Story*

'A book of extraordinary scope and ambition'
— Ralf Thiede in *Children's Literature Association Quarterly*

'Crago's ground-breaking book has all that one expects of a visionary work'
— Mateusz Mareki in *International Journal of Children's Literature Research*

'Reading the book is like listening to an experienced and entertaining guide'
— Wolfgang Loth in *Zeitschrift für Systemische Therapie und Beratung*

THE STAGES OF LIFE

Personalities and patterns in human emotional development

Hugh Crago

Routledge
Taylor & Francis Group

LONDON AND NEW YORK

First published 2017
by Routledge
2 Park Square, Milton Park, Abingdon, Oxon OX14 4RN

and by Routledge
711 Third Avenue, New York, NY 10017

Routledge is an imprint of the Taylor & Francis Group, an informa business

© 2017 Hugh Crago

British Library Cataloguing in Publication Data
A catalogue record for this book is available from the British Library

Library of Congress Cataloging in Publication Data
Names: Crago, Hugh, 1946– author.
Title: The stages of life: personalities and patterns in human emotional
development / Hugh Crago.
Description: Abingdon, Oxon; New York, NY: Routledge, 2016. |
Includes index.
Identifiers: LCCN 2015050386 | ISBN 9781138923867 (hardback) |
ISBN 9781138923898 (pbk.)
Subjects: LCSH: Developmental psychology. | Personality. | Emotions. |
Life cycle, Human—Psychological aspects.
Classification: LCC BF713.C695 2016 | DDC 155—dc23
LC record available at http://lccn.loc.gov/2015050386

ISBN: 978-1-138-92386-7 (hbk)
ISBN: 978-1-138-92389-8 (pbk)
ISBN: 978-1-315-68470-3 (ebk)

Typeset in Bembo
by Keystroke, Station Road, Codsall, Wolverhampton

CONTENTS

PREFACE

The Stages of Life is a substantial revision and updating of my 1999 book, *A Circle Unbroken*. I introduced that book in the following way:

> How do we become who we are? Is personality 'in the genes'? Does our childhood dictate the future course of our lives? Can parents make or break their children? Can we change? Do we have choice?
>
> In attempting to change ourselves, we often run up against powerful forces which we do not fully understand. It helps to know what parts of our personalities are 'hard wired' by genetic heritage, and what parts are open to modification through introspection and conscious decisions to be different. It helps to know whether or not we can 'delete' things in our existing personalities, or only add new capabilities and roles. It helps to know roughly what we can expect to experience at various stages of our life journey. These are the things I have tried to lay out in this book.

As you can see, *A Circle Unbroken* was primarily addressed to the general reader, although I hoped that it might also be of use to students of counselling and psychotherapy. While I still expect that general readers will find the *The Stages of Life* interesting and approachable, I have expanded key aspects to make it more useful to students. I've updated research findings, supplied fuller references and included detailed new material on epigenetics, temperament, attachment and the structure of the brain. I have expanded my coverage of common problems that may afflict individuals at different stages in the lifespan, and examine why these conditions occur when they do. Apart from trainee counsellors and psychotherapists, I hope that *The Stages of Life* will supply a 'big picture' of lifespan development for clinical, educational and counselling psychologists, supplementing the evidence-based, detail-focused texts with which they will be familiar.

I have tried to present a coherent map of how a child's genetically shaped temperament may interact with its environment to produce not only its individual personality, but also (in some cases) potential problems. The notion that some human beings might be 'hard wired' for anxiety, shyness, sensitivity or impulsivity was unpopular with experts throughout most of the last century. Students of human development, along with most parents and teachers, wanted to believe that every child could grow up to be confident, outgoing, resilient and sensible. But a mass of evidence from researchers over the past 50 years, marginalised at first, has forced us to acknowledge that some personality traits *are* genetically linked, and *do* constrain the ways that our personalities eventually develop – albeit with some room for modification. Since I wrote *A Circle Unbroken*, science has greatly expanded our understanding of the way that particular genes in a child elicit ('pull') particular responses from their environment, or (to put it the other way around, but equally correctly) how particular aspects of a child's environment *enable the expression* of genes that might not otherwise come 'on-line'. These developments lay to rest the old 'nature versus nurture' debates. *Both* its genetic heritage *and* the way a child is parented must necessarily be involved in shaping that child's later personality. Unsurprisingly, however, the proponents of attachment theory have ignored or downplayed the importance of a child's genetically influenced temperament, while researchers of temperament have downplayed or even dismissed attachment. Both these approaches embody important parts of the truth, and in *The Stages of Life* I have attempted to give due weight to both.

Equally importantly, our understanding of the human brain has expanded exponentially in the last 20 years. Neurological advances have made it clear that the 'emotional brain' evolved long before the 'thinking brain'. We humans are prone to act impulsively on the basis of our feelings because most of us are (at least some of the time) under the sway of the older parts of our brains – the brain stem and the limbic system – which we share with forms of life that evolved aeons before humans did. Our knowledge of the 'new brain' – the cerebral cortex, with its two hemispheres – has also expanded. Contrary to what used to be taught in developmental psychology courses, the maturation of the cortex is not complete by late adolescence. Human brains do not function at full capacity until the mid-thirties, and the final stages of brain maturation may not occur until even later, perhaps as late as the mid-fifties. Among other things, this helps to explain why young people are so prone to risk-taking behaviour, convinced that 'those warnings don't apply to me!' It also underwrites the belief that 'wisdom' (as opposed to 'knowledge' or 'skill') tends to develop only in the latter half of our lives – the result of accumulated experiences, interacting with the very gradual maturation of the brain. It is not too much to claim that neurological exploration has actually established a 'brain basis' for some of the most fundamental principles of psychotherapy – Freud's 'conscious' and 'unconscious', for example – principles which for most of the last century were regarded by mainstream psychology as unscientific and impossible to prove. Psychoanalytic theory now has a neurological foundation, and there *is* a dynamic push-pull between one part of our minds and another, except that the real conflict may be between the survival-governed, instinctive, holistic right hemisphere of the cerebral cortex, and the rational, reflective, analytic left hemisphere!

Counsellors and therapists need to know how human beings typically grow and change across the lifespan – but in a way that emphasises continuities as well as changes. Rather than mastering every physiological detail of early childhood language development, puberty, menopause or dementia, they need to know how each stage of life is likely to *feel* to an individual who is going through it. When I wrote *A Circle Unbroken* I was in my early fifties. My chapter on old age was written 'from the outside, looking in'. Now, closing on 70, I have a surer sense of what ageing is actually like. I know how declining bodily capacities can affect the way I think, feel and see the world. Yet I am the same person, with the same virtues and deficits as I have always had – although somewhat softened, I trust, by experience and personal psychotherapy.

Adolescents and adults can tell us directly about their experience, but we must infer the experience of infants, toddlers and even some older children from observing what they *do* (typically, their play) instead of relying on what they *say*. In *The Stages of Life*, I have drawn on as wide a range of evidence as possible to provide accounts of how children and adults *experience* their lives, and like many others before me, have supplemented scientific findings with evidence from art, literature and music, because creative individuals are capable of conveying experiences that are not readily expressible in language. I've made many references to biographies of individuals (politicians, musicians, soldiers, scientists, performers, writers) because counsellors and therapists need a sense of individual uniqueness – how the developmental changes that *all* human beings go through have impacted upon *this particular person*, at this particular time in history.

While concentrating on how human beings develop in a contemporary Western context, I've tried to make readers aware of how some things might be very different in other cultural contexts, or at other times in history. One culture's 'healthy and desirable' development can be another culture's 'dysfunction' – and, notoriously, one culture's 'crazy person' can be another culture's shaman or spiritual healer. As temperament scholar Jerome Kagan points out, genetic differences between ethnic groups can also make a contribution to their values, philosophies, behaviour – even to the kinds of drugs they may prefer, or their propensity for suicide.

As I've already anticipated, *The Stages of Life* seeks to offer its readers a 'big picture' of human development – one in which individuals are viewed *in context*. Relational contexts – how each of us interacts with significant others in our lives – are vital for understanding the growth of personality and for appreciating the potential for greater or lesser degrees of 'pathology' within individuals. 'Pathology' is a medical term meaning 'disease' or 'illness'; however, the Greek word from which it was formed (we know it in English as 'pathos') signified 'suffering' or even 'emotion' in general. In the West, we see problem behaviour as located within individuals, but that behaviour develops in interaction with other individuals – inevitably, they 'suffer' along with the 'disordered' individual – and is maintained by the behaviours of others towards them. That is the core insight offered by family systems theory, which has made an important and often-overlooked contribution to our understanding of human behaviour from the 1960s onwards.

Early family therapy, informed by the widespread use of genograms (family trees that mapped emotional and behavioural traits as well as emotional bonds and conflicts), showed how patterns of personality and behaviour that appeared incomprehensible in individuals often made sense in the context of their extended families. The combination of repeated genes and repeated enculturation into particular attitudes and values made for a powerful template which, over time, would produce 'repeats' of the same situation across the generations. Ironically, family therapy rapidly abandoned these disturbing insights in favour of more optimistic theoretical paradigms that promised 'magical' change, and substituted professional cleverness for the challenge of developing empathy with confused, shamed or angry family members. I make this judgement advisedly, for 30 years ago I too began my counselling career by substituting cleverness for wisdom!

The view taken in this book is that personality is a 'package', each personality type having its basis in a genetically influenced 'temperament' (weakened or intensified by its environment) and each type exhibiting potential 'strengths' and 'weaknesses'. Each personality type includes healthy, well-functioning individuals at one end of its range, and disturbed, impaired or 'dysfunctional' individuals at the other – most of us, most of the time, are somewhere in between these two extremes. Most of us can function at our best when we feel safe and comfortable. When subjected to extremes of fear, pain or unjust treatment, we are far more likely to display our more dysfunctional propensities.

The current well-intentioned push to 'normalise' depression and anxiety disorders via widely quoted statistics such as 'One in four adults will experience mental illness at least once during their lives', actually makes it harder, not easier, for the average person to grasp what true mental illness might actually feel like. There is a world of difference between 'feeling down' for a few weeks in response to a painful loss or shock, and a depression so pervasive that the affected individual cannot even get out of bed in the morning to go to the toilet, let alone go to work. Too many of us revert to concepts like 'will power' or 'positive thinking' when dealing with such states: 'She's not crazy, she's just using that behaviour to manipulate you', 'Take a good look at yourself, mate – there's plenty of people in this world worse off than you!' That 'logical' advice might serve as a wake-up call to people like us, but it is totally unhelpful when we are dealing with those who truly struggle to stay 'in their right mind'.

I have arranged *The Stages of Life* in the obvious way, in chapters that proceed through the human lifespan from birth to death. However, most chapters also look forward to later developments and backward to earlier developmental phases, so not everything that is relevant to a particular period of life will be found in the chapter formally assigned to that period. This is quite deliberate on my part. *The Stages of Life* is designed to be *read*, not 'quarried' for little nuggets of information that can then be transposed into an academic assignment! The book presents an *argument*; it offers a particular perspective which is best appreciated by reading chapters as wholes, and (better still) all the chapters in sequence. So what is my perspective?

Human development is often portrayed as a linear process, a journey from its starting point (birth) to its destination (death), but human emotional lives are circular and self-echoing: patterns set up in infancy still influence us in adult relationships; midlife crises resemble the 'acting out' of troubled adolescents. Our most vivid memories of our childhoods may come to us when, in the grip of dementia, we have lost our ability to remember what happened to us only minutes earlier. In the realm of feelings and relationships, what Freud called the 'repetition compulsion' holds sway to an extent that most of us find very uncomfortable to contemplate. If I have emphasised these aspects in this book, it is to offer some correction to the emphasis of most courses and textbooks on linear 'change' across the lifespan – to remind readers, and especially those intending to be psychotherapists, that *continuity*, as well as change, is key to how we as human beings experience our lives.

In providing endnotes to *The Stages of Life*, I have been guided by my years of experience as a university teacher of both human development and counselling. I know that only a small minority of students will read beyond their set texts and assigned readings. I recognise that many students today, brought up in the computer age, find reading lengthy documents challenging. So I have avoided loading the text with bracketed references (Harvard, APA) as is the current academic norm – such references simply slow readers down and break the flow of the writing. My notes are provided via numbered endnotes to each chapter, and these have been kept to a necessary minimum. My preference is for a clear, simple style that contains no unnecessary jargon, and explains the technical terms that it does use. Wisdom is different from 'cleverness' – something many academics fail to realise.

For my authorities, I have searched out those experts who have not only mastered the scientific literature in their particular field, but who also know how to write accessibly about complex matters. I favour experts who can 'see the big picture', whose theories make sense of diverse phenomena (including phenomena outside of their own disciplines). For this reason my endnotes cite *books* as well as *articles*, and a number of these books are included again in the 'Further reading' list at the end. Whole books may strike a student as daunting, but they do enable authors to present big, complex subjects in a meaningful and coherent way, and are more likely to embody the enduring truths that research has uncovered, instead of the confusion of claims and counter-claims that 'cutting edge' research (published in journals) tends to present.

I am well aware that today's university students are told that 'if a reference is more than five years old, it's out of date'. This may well be true in the hard sciences, but when we come to the human sciences, it is a less reliable guide, and in the field of counselling and psychotherapy, it can be positively misleading. Books on psychotherapy do not date nearly as rapidly as those on medicine or neurology, because their subject – human beings – does not change at a fundamental level. Yes, we now have digital social media, but have the latter altered anything fundamental in human nature? I doubt it. Yes, we have new therapeutic 'modalities' and approaches, hundreds of them – but how 'different' are they really? In my years as a therapist, I've seen Psychodrama, Gestalt Therapy, Neurolinguistic Programming, Family Therapy, Cognitive Behaviour Therapy, Eye Movement Desensitisation and Reprocessing, Narrative Therapy and Mindfulness (among others) generate wild excitement among practitioners, along with wild claims of success in addressing a wide range of human problems. In time, the wild excitement nearly always subsides into more muted claims and more realistic expectations. This 'manic-depressive' curve has also applied to 'wonder drugs' (from Freud's early faith in cocaine to the more recent overvaluation of Prozac). This should alert us to the fact that therapeutic models have a lot in common with religions – charismatic founders, passionate disciples, 'evil' heresies and damaging schisms (splits) are typical of both. So I have recommended books (and some articles) that contain the fundamental principles that are a better guide to good practice than the latest brand of counselling that 'everybody's talking about'. Trainee counsellors and therapists are often bewildered by the different models and theories presented to them – each with its own specialised terminology – and instructors fail to help them see the important common principles that lie behind the confusing differences. Though psychoanalytic theory is the source of many of these principles, I have deliberately avoided reproducing the mystifying jargon that some analytic writers continue to use, despite the confusions it can cause (ask a roomful of analysts how 'countertransference' differs from 'projective identification' and you'll see what I mean).

Finally, I have aimed for a balance between evidence-based 'hard science' and the kind of speculation that we need if science is to progress. Sometimes careful data-gathering may explode speculative theories that sound intuitively correct, but that doesn't mean all speculation should be abandoned. I have included in *The Stages of Life* material that is frankly conjectural, and if no references are supplied for such material, readers can assume that the conclusions are my own. I have also summarised developmental findings sup-porting propositions that would otherwise seem hard to credit, or counter-intuitive. A sense of *wonder* is vital to human endeavour, in the sciences as well as in the realm of human thoughts and feelings, and it is my hope that *The Stages of Life* may inspire or rekindle wonder in at least some of those who read it. The story of human life from birth to death is a moving and dramatic one, and I trust that some of its joy, along with its inevitable sadness and ironies, are conveyed here.

Hugh Crago, Blackheath NSW Australia, 2015

Our birth is but a sleep and a forgetting:
The Soul that rises with us, our life's Star,
Hath had elsewhere its setting
And cometh from afar:
Not in entire forgetfulness,
And not in utter nakedness,
But trailing clouds of glory do we come
From God, who is our home:
Heaven lies about us in our infancy!
Shades of the prison-house begin to close
Upon the growing Boy,
But he beholds the light and whence it flows,
He sees it in his joy;
The Youth, who daily from the East
Must travel, still is Nature's Priest,
And by the vision splendid
Is on his way attended;
At length the Man perceives it die away,
And fade into the light of common day.

William Wordsworth, from 'Ode on Intimations of
Immortality from Recollections of Early Childhood'
(early version first published Poems in Two Volumes, *1807,*
later revised in its present form, 1815).

1

THE END AND THE BEGINNING

'A sleep and a forgetting'

Birth is life's first great journey, its first great transition, yet we remember nothing of it. 'Our birth is but a sleep and a forgetting', wrote the English poet William Wordsworth[1]: he meant that we 'forget' or blot out, as in sleep, the (heavenly) experiences that preceded our birth. Human life is full of paradoxes, but there is none more dramatic than this one, that the epic of our journey from the womb to the world is a story we cannot tell, because we did not possess language when it happened. Medicine and developmental psychology tell us only what can be observed and monitored from the outside. On the great subject of what birth might actually have *felt* like for the baby, the textbooks fall silent because no baby has ever been able to tell us.[2] We must rely on reconstructions – attempts to sense through the mind and body of an adult what a wordless, selfless being might once have felt. Some have attempted to reconstruct birth experiences intellectually – arguing backwards from the dreams and fantasies of adults as reported in psychoanalysis. Others have claimed to simulate the bodily experiences of birth – or something like them – through special breathing or even the use of hallucinogenic drugs.[3] Either way, though, we can never be sure where memory ends and fantasy begins. But we have another potential source of information about the experience of birth, perhaps more trustworthy because it does not claim to be about birth at all. This source can be found in music, literature and art. Creative artists are, among other things, abnormally sensitive to the world around them, and retain vivid memories of childhood experiences that most of us have forgotten. In the terminology we'll introduce in Chapter 2, they have 'thin boundaries'. They, if anyone, ought to be able to draw from the depths of the well, even though they may not realise what they are doing.

In the prelude to his opera *Rheingold*, Richard Wagner thought he was composing a musical portrait of the river Rhine, a hymn to the primeval force of Nature. But what I hear in his music is a re-creation of birth: deep, throbbing bass notes, barely audible at first, slow, quiet arpeggios that begin to ripple upwards through the serene darkness, gradually gaining speed and increasing to full force in a great orchestral crescendo, after which the music falls away, and in the sudden silence can be heard the lilting of women's voices. For Wagner, three river-spirits called Rhinemaidens are singing a hymn of praise to the watery world in which they live, but for me, the chorus of their song sounds like a lullaby. Is this how a baby named Richard once experienced his coming into the world, 39 years before he wrote those notes? We can never know, we can never prove it, yet it is possible. What we are dealing with are sense impressions only, felt by the body and registered in the infant's brain at birth. A newborn has no verbal language, and consequently no 'thought' as we understand it, so these memories are not like later memories, which we reflect upon, talk to ourselves about, deliberately conjure up and elaborate upon. They are simply *there*, some-how. It is these sensory memories – of increasing urgency, of sudden relief from pressure, of comforting, high-pitched sounds – that Wagner's prelude re-creates. And research shows us that a newborn baby responds to its mother's voice, and to her smell, even before it can recognise her face.[4] Indeed, we know that babies respond to voices while still in the womb.

Enid Blyton, who was the most popular British children's author of her time (for very good reasons, which we shall explore later), once confessed that she had experienced a vision while in the dentist's chair, under the influence of laughing gas:

> I found myself (apparently bodiless but still firmly myself) being drawn through space at a speed so great that I thought I must be going at the pace of light itself. I seemed to be going through vibrating waves of light, and thought I must be passing many suns and many universes . . . Finally, after a long, incredibly long journey in an incredibly short time, I arrived somewhere. This Somewhere was, as far as I could make out, in my dazed and amazed state, a place of wonderful light (not daylight or sunlight) – and I saw, or knew, that there were Beings there – no shape, nothing tangible – but I knew they were great and holy and ineffable. Then I knew that I was going to hear the secret of Everything – and Everything was going to be explained to me, simply, and with the utmost lucidity. I was overjoyed – filled with wonder and delight. I knew the reasons behind existence, time, space, evil, goodness, pain – and I rejoiced, and marvelled that no-one had guessed such things before . . .[5]

Blyton describes this as a sort of mystic vision, but does it not remind us of something else? 'Being drawn through space' at a great speed, 'going through vibrating waves', emerging into a 'place of wonderful light' inhabited by huge creatures who seem all-knowing and all-powerful? Many other descriptions of out-of-body experiences, some drug-induced, some not, resemble Blyton's.

In many of them there is a journey through vast spaces, a sense of being pulled along or carried along by a force outside oneself, an emergence into a place of light. Intriguingly, a similar (though not identical) pattern typifies descriptions of the so-called Near Death Experience (NDE).[6]

In 1918, Lt Colonel George Patton, under murderous enemy fire in France, looked up and 'saw' in the clouds above him images of his Patton ancestors, many of whom had fought in the Civil War 50 years before. He felt that he knew what was required of him. He charged forward with a few volunteers, and was wounded. While lying waiting to be evacuated, he wrote later that he was:

> overwhelmed by a deep feeling of warmth and peace and comfort, and of love. I knew profoundly death was related to life; how unimportant the change-over was; how ever-lasting the soul – and the love was all around me, like a subdued light.[7]

Like Blyton's vision, NDEs are normally construed in spiritual terms – passing through the 'shadow of death', reaching heaven, meeting angels or departed loved ones – yet could it be that the experience of passing from life somehow triggers buried memories of that other great passage which hardly any of us can remember? Such speculations cannot ever be proved, yet, as we will see, human emotional life is so pattern-governed, so mysteriously circular and self-echoing, that the end may well resonate with the beginning.

The first migration

The Genesis story of the Garden of Eden distils some of the impressions human-kind may have unconsciously stored about the experience of birth. Adam and Eve live in mindless bliss, in total harmony with the rest of Creation. There is no strife, no work, no pain, no sex and no procreation. When the first woman and the first man eat the fruit of the Tree of Knowledge (consciousness?), they lose their paradise. They must clothe their nakedness in order to endure the heat and cold of the world outside the Garden (outside the womb?); they must work hard in order to feed themselves (as a baby must learn to breathe through its lungs and suck with its mouth, instead of being nourished automatically through the umbilical cord?); they can reproduce themselves, but now Eve must bleed monthly as the price of being fertile, and suffer pain in order to bear children. Conflict, suffering and struggle enter the world when humankind becomes conscious of death.

The Genesis story helps us to isolate the key elements that make birth both similar to, and different from, the transitions that we will all experience later in life. First, birth is *involuntary*. A baby does not decide to be born, or instigate the process (although no doubt its biochemistry participates in the 'decision', signaling to its mother's body that it is time for parturition to begin). When musicians like Wagner and writers like Blyton conjure up a powerful sense of being carried along on rippling, endless waves, I suspect they are reflecting their early experience of being totally under the control of the muscular contractions that propel a baby down the birth canal. That first experience will reproduce itself many times later in life. It recurs when a child is placed in the car seat and driven to a totally new place, or is carried effortlessly in an elevator up or down a great department store or shopping mall. It is re-created in the sense of euphoria and freedom adults often experience as their plane lifts off, or their train gathers speed towards a distant destination. Maybe all of our excitement (and fear?) about travel has its roots here. And perhaps it is significant that so many human stories – from the Sumerian *Epic of Gilgamesh* to *The Lord of the Rings* – involve the hero or heroine in a long, hard, frightening journey on the way to the fulfilment of a quest.[8]

Birth marks the end of the phase of human life that is (so far as we know) totally involuntary, and begins that part of life where we must, like Adam, work to live – the part of life where we must, like Eve, feel unpleasure as part of *knowing* that we live. In the womb, we are nourished, contained and protected without having to ask for it. With our birth, gaps appear in the seamless walls of our world: discomfort, frustration and longing enter our lives. A baby learns to want only by *not* having; deprivation is how we learn about desire. For most of us, then, birth is the beginning of the great lesson of lack and loss, the first great mourning, with which all later losses must surely reverberate. And it is the first of many migrations, large and small.

What else can we say about the first migration? It involves a *movement from a largely unchanging world to one that is constantly changing*. Of course, a baby in the womb is not shielded from all change: its own body is growing and developing; minute chemical variations in its mother's blood impact upon it. It is affected by her panic, and perhaps her joy, as extra adrenalin reaches its own veins from hers[9]; for at least the final three months, the baby can hear sounds from beyond the walls of the womb; it can sense gross motions and can make its own presence felt forcibly with kicks and shoves as it adjusts to a more comfortable position, and gradually outgrows its warm, fluid world. But all of these changes, real as they are, are nothing compared with the rate and magnitude of the changes that a baby will encounter as soon as it emerges from its mother's body.

Relative to that, the world of the womb seems (at least to us adults) one of endless sameness. Perhaps that is why the folklore of many peoples contains stories of a Fairy Hill or some other underground (or underwater) world, where the light is neither that of sun nor moon, where there are no seasons to mark the passing of time, where a thousand years are as a day. It may be significant, too, that in the tales, these magical worlds are places of endless feasting and dancing – effortless gratification, eternal holiday. For when we emerge from the womb, pleasure becomes less predictable, and gratification something that we often have to strive for rather than something that is simply there. And there is yet another paradox, for if there is only pleasure, then pleasure has no meaning: we recognise joy only by contrast with pain. Life involves pain, and so pleasure becomes possible: what came before in that safe, warm, unchanging world may seem bliss by contrast with the uncertainty of now, but it was not experienced as bliss then. We were not 'happy' in the womb: we simply *were*. To become conscious of pleasure or pain, we have to acquire a capacity to examine, to *think about* our own experience – and this capacity has not yet developed. We are in a state akin to that of an animal. In myths and the folktales, humans who find themselves visitors in the Otherworld are not usually tempted to stay there. The time-less realm strikes them as alien, boring or even frightening. If, like Persephone in the Greek myth, they are foolish enough to eat the food of the Underworld, they may be trapped there, but most mortals manage to escape. Having left the womb, they know that they cannot go back, ever. In *Peter Pan*, Wendy realises what Peter never does: that to stay in Neverland is to condemn herself to an enthralling, endless game which simply goes round and round in a circle, and leads nowhere.

So it is not that life in the womb is really as changeless as we imagine it to have been; rather, what seems to happen is that, having been forced out of the womb into something very different, we *idealise* our first world, now for-gotten, into a Paradise, a Fairy Realm, a Neverland, and magnify the dangers and difficulties of our new life by comparison. Human beings tend to remember most vividly whatever happens right at the beginning of any new experience, something that psychologists call the 'primacy effect': why would birth be an exception? Those first impressions can shape our view of all that happens after. So perhaps what happens as a result of birth is that we begin to register *difference*, and once having done so, we do not stop, ever. All of human knowledge is constructed by noticing differences: between black and white, hot and cold, pleasure and pain, 'us' and 'them'. And on these simple foundations we erect our complex, sophisticated structures of thought and belief.

But the noticing of difference is also the bane of human existence. Our thought-world is founded upon a tendency to see things as polar opposites and to attach a moral value to each – *either* you are a 'good person' *or* a 'bad person' – and our gradually developing capacity to modify stark black and white into shades of grey never fully catches up. Even highly intelligent, highly rational scientists and philosophers are as much governed as the rest of us by either/or thinking, at least in their intimate relationships and deep assumptions. It is either/or thinking which produces the idealisation of life in the womb as contrasted with what comes after; which convinces us of 'my country, right or wrong'; which feeds the heroin addict's conviction that life without daily hits would be grey, depressing and purposeless. It is either/or thinking which persuades some men that if their partner is temporarily absorbed in a new baby, then she cannot any longer love *them*. It is either/or thinking which persuades some mothers that if their son is serious about his fiancée, then he cannot have any love left for *her*. And, as we shall see in the next chapter, it is either/or thinking which results in human beings insisting that babies are either hard wired for a given personality (which they can never change) or born as blank slates to be written on by life (and will therefore be totally the product of the chances of their upbringing). Neither is true. When human life is the subject, then either/or must always yield to both/and. In our next chapter, we'll see how the actual structure of the human brain gives us 'either-or thinking', while also permitting us a more unified, holistic way of understanding the world.

Oneness and separateness

Conventionally, we think of birth as the beginning of life: of course sentient life exists long before birth, that nobody would deny, but when we are born, when we *physically* separate from our mothers, we begin to live in a new way, a way which forces on us the potential for emotional as well as physical separateness. Having grown, for nine long months, within another body, we must now start to experience ourselves as apart, alone, cut off. Because baby humans will take long years to reach the maturity that puppies and kittens reach in a matter of months, human evolution arranges for us to continue to *feel* part of our mothers even after birth – psychoanalytic researcher Margaret Mahler called this 'normal symbiosis'.[10] At least, so we hypothesise, since nobody can tell us for sure that it was so. Again, our best evidence for that infant feeling of oneness with mother comes from certain types of experience in adulthood, which we do not normally think of in connection with infancy, although once we do, the connection is blindingly obvious.

The early stages of sexual love often involve, for short spaces of time, a sense of intense oneness between the lovers, as if each becomes the other's 'baby'. (Lovers' talk allows them to actually refer to each other as 'baby', but there is a taboo on the reciprocal 'Mum' or 'Mummy'). Lovers speak of 'belonging to' one another, merging, 'becoming one'. They are not speaking only of the act of sexual intercourse, but of a feeling that spills over, for a time, into every moment of their joint lives. When lovers are forced to be apart, they feel the separateness acutely. In the 1920s, aspiring politician Tom Mosley and his wife Cimmie (Cynthia Asquith) exchanged notes and letters in 'baby language' that astounds us with its lack of boundaries, the pronouns so intertwined that it is often hard to know who is addressing whom ('His own darling Moo Moo, Does so miss her . . . All love in world from adoring Her Fellow').[11] The Righteous Brothers' 1960s classic 'Unchained Melody' is a hymn to infant longing, cast as a lover's cry of passion. '"Nellie", says Cathy in Emily Bronte's *Wuthering Heights*, "*I am* Heathcliff"'.

And so it is, we guess, with mother and baby. An awareness of separateness makes oneness all the more sweet, the more longed-for. Held safe by mother's arms, surrounded by the warmth of her flesh, the smell of her skin and her milk, a baby feels, not what it once felt in the womb, but something close to it. Now, we guess, bliss can be experienced, because it can be contrasted with lying alone, deprived of the comfort of a mother's embrace, cold, perhaps, or wetly uncomfortable, or hungry. An infant knows separateness through unpleasure, as it knows pleasure through unseparateness. Both experiences resonate through the experience of sexual love. Yet while an infant clings close for its own survival, and experiences joy in that very closeness, it must also learn to tolerate being alone, learn to enjoy its independence and its mastery. That tension between fusion and separateness, between attachment and individuation, is one of the great propelling forces of human life, not only in infancy and early childhood, but throughout the lifespan. To stay in the womb beyond our appointed time is, in effect, to die: we must leave it in order to live, but by leaving it, we appoint our own death just as surely as we would if we had stayed. Perhaps it is no wonder that birth is something we need to forget.

'Not in entire forgetfulness . . .'

And that brings us back to our point of departure: the great enforced migration of birth is *something we cannot remember*. There is a profound significance to that. In later life, the majority of people can recall very little from the period before they were three or four years old. When Sigmund Freud evolved his concept of the 'unconscious' (the word itself existed long before he made it a centre-piece of his theory) he was intuitively aware that there were layers of memory to which the conscious mind of an adult, or even a school-aged child, had no access. He hypothesised that a young child's ideas about unacceptable impulses (for example, to destroy the world, or to 'marry' its mother or father) would be 'repressed' – that is, sent down into the unconscious, so that they would not compromise the child's day-to-day sense of being 'good'. Freud knew that people sometimes told themselves things like, 'I mustn't think that' and surmised that something similar would occur in the first years of life – except that true repression, in his view, occurred *automatically*, without conscious thought or intention. Still today psychoanalysts speak of 'unthinkable thoughts' or 'feelings that we cannot tolerate' at a conscious level. As adults we push away such thoughts and feelings in order to get on with living – sometimes this is functional, sometimes it is not.

More than a century later, we possess knowledge of the human brain that Freud (who had originally intended to be a neurologist himself) could only have dreamed about. In the light of what we know today, we can see a substantial basis for Freud's theory of an 'unconscious mind' – but at the same time, science suggests some ways in which Freud's understanding was incorrect, or incomplete. We now know that the organ called the amygdala – part of the 'limbic system', the sub-cortical layer of the brain which we share with other mammals – does indeed 'store memories' from our first 12 to 18 months after birth ('store' is a convenient expression, though not a strictly accurate one; however, it will do for now). These earliest memories are not encoded in language, because a child has no *verbal* language at this stage. Rather, the memories are retained in the form of neural pathways that represent body sensations – for example, constriction, breathlessness, excitement, discomfort and so on. As a child's brain continues to evolve, and the speech function begins to develop, another sub-cortical organ called the hippocampus matures and starts to share the function of storing memories. These memories, unlike the earlier amygdala-based ones, are encoded in *language*, and are thus more accessible to conscious recall – and to modification (see Chapter 3). So, by the third year of life, a child begins to have 'memories' of the kind we adults would recognise. '*Daddy, remember when we went shopping and I fell over and got hurt?*' These memories take precedence over the earlier, body-based ones, and we have no reason to be conscious of the latter until something in our later lives 'triggers' them, bringing back a sudden, vivid sense experience, often linked with details of place that are difficult to explain otherwise than as something stored by the amygdala in our earliest, pre-verbal period.

The arrival

Consider migration, as experienced consciously by older children and adults. What happens when people move to a new country, thousands of miles from their birthplace? Their first days in the new place are bewildering, even frightening, and they are bombarded with new sights, sounds and smells; typically, they cannot understand what is being said to them, do not know their way around, do not even know, sometimes, what to ask for. Artist and illustrator Shaun Tan, whose father came to Australia from Malaysia in 1960, conveys the migrant experience in his masterly graphic novel *The Arrival*, a book that, significantly, is completely wordless. Everything that happens as his protagonist arrives in a fantastic city (like, and yet totally unlike, the New York to which so many hundreds of thousands migrated from Europe in the early years of the twentieth century) has to be figured out by readers as they turn through the mysterious, sepia-tinted pages of *The Arrival*; much remains unfathomable to the end. In this way, Tan puts *us*, his readers, in the position of being 'strangers in a strange land', trying to understand, reaching out tentatively for what is familiar among so much that is alien and incomprehensible.[12]

What happens when migrants have established themselves more firmly in their new country? Some cling to the customs, language and thought-patterns of their homeland. They maintain frequent communication with relatives there and, if they can afford it, travel back regularly to renew their links. In their adopted country, they may even choose to live in a closed community, speaking only to those from the same background, refusing to learn the new language, insisting that their children follow the 'old ways'. Other migrants do almost the opposite. They cut themselves off aggressively, putting all their energies into their new life, learning the new language, re-creating themselves – and their children – on the new model. The first kind of migrant is likely to idealise the homeland, the second kind to denigrate it, although of course many find a middle way.

At the two extremes, however, what happens in migration is a kind of amnesia. Whether the decision to do so was voluntary or forced, living in the new place automatically weakens the links with the old: it cannot do otherwise. The harder migrants try to preserve the connection, the more they falsify the realities of their new existence. And though they themselves can preserve their memories of the former place, their memories are memories of a time which is going to correspond less and less to present realities in the land of their birth. So they end up falsifying it too. Their children, born in the new country, or at least growing up there, can at best share their parents' memories incompletely. Loyalty may compel them to mouth the same sentiments, but the experiences of the homeland are not there to lend solidity to the words and customs. And so, in the second generation after migration, or certainly by the third, all *experience-based* memory of the homeland will have been lost, bringing the first type of migrant family around, full circle, to the experience of the second type, who begin with denial and cut-off. In both families, as offspring grow to adulthood without ever having known the old place, real memory is replaced by 'cultural memory' – something deliberately fostered in imagination. Yet apart from these consciously worked-up beliefs and images of the country-of-origin, something else lives on within the generation who have never seen it. Whether their parents and grandparents talked obsessively of the 'old country', or whether they never mentioned it at all, it will have left its invisible traces. Family members will continue to behave, to feel, even to think, as their ancestors did, *but without knowing it*.

A 30-year-old woman complains of depression and a persistent feeling of guilt and pessimism. She believes these feelings are located 'in her' and have nothing to do with anyone or anything else. Conventionally, she would be diagnosed as suffering from a depressive illness. Yet look at the wider picture: her grandparents emigrated to Canada from the Ukraine before she was born. She has never been to the Ukraine and, apart from a certain degree of pride in her heritage, does not see herself as Ukrainian or care greatly about what happens there. Her grandparents talked little about the old life, but she does know that her grandfather held a position of rank and status during the German occupation and was forced to flee, first to Germany and later to north America, when the tide turned against Hitler's armies. 'They lost everything', she says. Indeed they did, and in many ways, her own thoughts have been shaped by that loss, as her own inexplicable guilt has been shaped by the experience of grandparents who were on 'the wrong side' during the war. Her grandfather shot no Jews, but he was part of a regime that condoned it. He is dead now, and it does not occur to her to ask her parents about him. She is alone with feelings and convictions that she did not ask for, feelings and convictions that are in a real sense family memories, yet memories that transmit themselves below the level of consciousness. She absorbed them unasked while she was growing up, and now they are part of her. Her invisible legacy has intensified her depression, and given it a very particular form, which simply does not make sense if you do not know what happened 60 or 70 years ago. Indeed, her potential for depression might never have been *activated* had it not been for the 'repressed memories' her family bequeathed her. It is only when she realises that her obscure but powerful sense of loss and guilt owes its existence to this forgotten history that she begins a long process of learning to value herself for who she is, instead of constantly punishing herself for sins that were never hers.

In just this way, I suspect, all of us are affected by the long-forgotten migration of birth: affected without our being aware of it. Theories about the influence of the 'birth trauma' on later personality and psychopathology have long been unfashionable, and are still not taken seriously in mainstream psychology. Yet logically, it is hard to justify the position that birth has little or no effect on the evolving child. Every *later* transition affects us, often very powerfully: so why not this first and most dramatic one?[13]

Beyond the broad, general features we have been discussing, each of us experiences a different birth, and the specifics of our personal mode of entry to the world will surely modify or intensify those features of birth which we would expect to hold good for everyone. Some babies are born easily, after a short labour, and with no complications; others are delayed well beyond their due time; some become stuck in the birth canal, and must be sucked or pulled out artificially; still others must be 'from their mother's womb untimely ripp'd' as Shakespeare put it in *Macbeth*. The umbilical cord, and the placenta, behave in different ways in different births. We can be born oxygen-starved (as I am told I was) or jaundiced, or affected by the drugs given to our mothers. We may need to be rotated before we can emerge naturally. It would be surprising, indeed, if such a range of complications and potential traumas did not also leave their traces on the individual's later personality; folk wisdom, as preserved by women and by midwives, has always intimated that they do. In our century, the tendency has been to turn away from such lore and dismiss it as unscientific. Much of it undoubtedly *is* unscientific, at least in the sense of being anecdotal and based in naturalistic observation, and any personality theory readily becomes self-fulfilling – we all tend to notice the evidence that seems to prove our position and to overlook the evidence that seems to undermine it. Yet isn't it just as unscientific to dismiss out of hand observations that have repeatedly been made, without subjecting them to proper scrutiny?

Consider a young woman who described her years as a child in a small rural town as 'stifling', who voluntarily chose to leave home at 16 and live in a large city where she feels more accepted and under no 'pressure' to conform. Throughout her young adulthood she found making big decisions difficult, resulting in long periods of feeling 'stuck'. This young woman's language expresses clear and consistent themes of confinement, the wish to escape, the difficulty of doing so, and the longing for separateness and individual space. Should it surprise us that as a baby she became stuck in the birth canal and had to be extracted with a suction device? Or is that 'just a coincidence'? Might it not be, as psychoanalysts have long maintained, that the kind of language we use, the metaphors that we unconsciously adopt, might offer subtle indications of the ways that, very early in life, we learned to organise our experiences? What does it mean that we humans traverse our life paths without conscious memories

of the earliest and most formative parts of them? Could it be that this is responsible for such phenomena as *déjà vu*? For much of our longing for a 'something'
that we can never quite define? For our idea of a 'soul', a 'spirit' quite separate
from our physical body?[14]

In such ways – simple and complex, trivial and huge – the experience of
birth seems to reverberate throughout all our lives. But, individual differences
aside, I have hypothesised that birth is a transition from relative sameness to the
awareness of change and difference; from unrecognised, unconscious bliss
to conscious awareness of alternating pleasure and pain; from unrecognised
subservience to dawning consciousness of agency and will. *And we cannot remember
it.* To the extent that we have 'slept and forgotten' our pre-birth existence, then
birth is also about giving up (or being given up on). Birth is the death of
the existence that precedes it; simultaneously, it is the beginning of a new kind
of existence – one which will, many years later (if we are permitted to live out
our allotted span) eventually lead to another death.

Notes

1 William Wordsworth's 'Ode: Intimations of Immortality From Recollections of
Early Childhood' (originally published in *Poems in Two Volumes*, 1807: line 58).

2 Typical of website summaries intended for about-to-be parents is Donna Christiano's
'A Baby's View of Birth' (www.parents.com; accessed 29 May 2015). It covers the
following topics: 'How does his head fit through there? How does baby breathe?
How does baby stay warm? What can he hear and see?' Under the heading 'Does he feel
pain?' the author comments, 'If pain does register with a baby, some experts liken it
to a feeling of being gradually squeezed. "It's hard to say what a baby senses", says
Dr Auerbach, ". . . It's possible that the baby's pain may be what it feels like to squeeze
through a tight space, such as the feeling of compression you get when you try to crawl
under a fence"'.

3 See Stanislas Groff, *Realms of the Human Unconscious: Observations from LSD Research*,
NY, Viking, 1975. Such work, though fascinating, is open to the objection that those
who claim to be 'reliving' their birth while under the influence of LSD may simply have
been *inventing* 'memories' based on what they, as mature adults, have read and learned
about birth.

4 The newborn's sensory abilities and its capacity to distinguish its mother from others
from very early in life is ably summarised in Douglas Davies, *Child Development:
A Practitioner's Guide*, 2nd Edn, NY/London, Guilford, 2004: 142–145.

5 See Barbara Stoney, *Enid Blyton: The Biography*, 2nd Edn, London, Hodder & Stoughton,
1992: 224–225 [first edition published 1974]. The quotation was originally published
in Peter McKellar's *Imagination and Thinking*, NY, Basic Books, 1957.

6 See Yvonne Kason and Teri Degler, *A Farther Shore: How Near-death and Other
Extraordinary Experiences Can Change Ordinary Lives*, NY, Harper Collins, 1994; more
scientific papers on the NDE are regularly published in *The Journal of Near-death
Experiences*.

7 See Carlo d'Este, *A Genius for War: A Life of General George S. Patton*, London,
HarperCollins, 1995: 260–261.

8 One of Christopher Booker's 'seven basic plots' is 'the Quest', which begins with the
hero or heroine in a 'constricted' place, from which he or she *must* escape, in search
of a new life and a new world, for to remain there is stasis and death. See *The Seven
Basic Plots: Why We Tell Stories*, London, Continuum, 2004: 69–86.

9 See C. Monk, 'Stress and Mood Disorders During Pregnancy: Implications for Child Development', *Psychiatric Quarterly*, 72, 4 (2001): 347–357; R. Sullivan, D. A. Wilson, J. Feldon, B. K. Yee, U. Meyer et al., The International Society for Developmental Psychobiology Annual Meeting Symposium: Impact of Early Life Experiences on Brain and Behavioral Development, *Developmental Psychobiology*, DOI 10.1002 (2006): 583–602.

10 See Margaret Mahler, Fred Pine and Anni Bergman, *The Psychological Birth of the Human Infant*, London, Karnak, 1985. [First published in the US in 1973.]

11 For examples, see Nicholas Mosley, *Rules of the Game* and *Beyond the Pale: Memoirs of Sir Oswald Mosley and Family*, London, Pimlico, 1998: 57. [*Rules of the Game* first published in 1982.] Mosley eventually became leader of the British Union of Fascists, placing himself 'beyond the pale' and ensuring that he spent the war years in prison.

12 Shaun Tan, *The Arrival*, Sydney, Lothian, 2006.

13 Echoing an earlier idea of Freud's, Otto Rank argued that the anxiety experienced by a baby in being forcibly separated from its mother's body was the earliest anxiety a human being experiences, and hence the origin of all later anxiety. (*The Trauma of Birth*, London, Kegan Paul, Trench, Trubner, 1929; republished Dover, 1994). Later, English psychoanalyst Wilfred Bion saw trauma as an inevitable part of birth, because a baby is born with very limited ability to process its perinatal sense impressions, which it will inevitably find chaotic and overwhelming. See Wilfred Bion, 'Caesura' in W. R. Bion, *Two Papers*, London, Karnak Books, 1989. Scholarly literature on these and associated topics can now be found under the headings of 'Prenatal and Perinatal Psychology', early contributions to these modern disciplines being those of Thomas R. Verney, *The Secret Life of the Unborn Child*, NY, Dell, 1988 [first published in 1981] and David Barnes Chamberlain, *Babies Remember Birth*, Los Angeles, J. P. Harcher, 1988. The term 'birth trauma' is now usually employed in medicine to refer to particular disruptions of the normal birth process, which might be expected to adversely impact the baby. Gunnel Minett, 'Where is the Trauma in Birth Trauma?' (www.breathwork-science.com; accessed 7 July 2015) reminds us that in the process of normal birth, a 'flood of hormones' protects both mother and baby from undue pain and stress.

14 See Michael R. Trimble, *The Soul in the Brain: The Cerebral Basis of Language, Art, and Belief*, Baltimore, Johns Hopkins University Press, 2007. Trimble argues that our apprehension of a 'soul' stems from the fact that primitive parts of our brains, like the amygdala, preserve experiences that continue to resonate with us, despite the fact that we cannot consciously recall them.

2

'NOT IN UTTER NAKEDNESS'

Temperament and attachment

'And not in utter nakedness'

Babies are different: any mother will tell you that. She knows that her children were individuals from the start (even in the womb one hardly moved at all, the other was always butting and kicking). But experts and professionals have taken a long time to catch up. Partly this is because so many of them have been men, who have never experienced pregnancy; but some women experts were quick to join them, for much of the last century, in the belief that a child's individuality evolves only in response to critically important interactions with its caregivers. Experts – and many parents too, especially educated, middle-class parents – *wanted* to believe in the power of early parenting to shape children's personalities, because that belief was consistent with an optimistic, individualistic view of life, in which all of us can determine our own future. We still *want* to believe that loving, well-informed parenting, excellence in pre-school care, and stimulating teaching can make up for the deficits of heredity or poverty, turn potential 'problem' children into good citizens and high achievers – and sometimes, of course, they can.

On the whole, the tide of opinion prior to modern medicine and psychology ran the opposite way. Long before the popularisation of Mendel's and Darwin's theories encouraged loose talk of a child having 'bad genes', parents spoke darkly of 'bad blood'. There was a strong tendency to attribute unruly behaviour and constitutional weakness – along with looks and talents – to ancestry, even though the mechanism by which these things were inherited was not understood: 'She privileges her grandmother', they said in the eighteenth century, where we would say that she 'takes after' her grandmother. Most parents in pre-modern societies did not worry nearly as much about the future of their children as we do, for the chances that more than half of them would survive to adulthood were pretty low. But they did wonder why children from the same family turned out so differently, despite a good upbringing (by which they usually meant a moral and disciplined upbringing). For an explanation they mostly turned to a grim determinism. God had decreed that one child was not long for this world; God had saved a second child from early death in order to 'work greatly through her'; a third child was 'sure to be hanged', for he had been born with the umbilical cord looped around his neck. Though devoid of genetic awareness, such pronouncements had the same *effect* as modern genetic determinism, in that they claimed that however hard parents and teachers tried, they were powerless against something inherent in the child's nature, something that might well be divinely decreed.

When I was a young man, I energetically argued the environmental case, and hated the idea that my genetic heritage might have anything much to do with my limits or potentials as a person (though I admitted that it had dictated my height, my prominent ears and, to a lesser degree, my intelligence and creativity). I was happy to blame my parents for whatever had gone wrong with me and was convinced that, as a parent, I would be able to do much better than they had. Having watched my own children grow to adulthood despite (as well as because of) everything their mother and I did or failed to do, I am now prepared to concede that genetics play a considerably larger role than I once wanted to believe. In my forties, ten years' investigation into patterns of personality and behaviour in my own family of origin left me convinced that I was far more a product of my genes than I — or they, for that matter — thought possible.[1] That awareness makes me no less of an individual than I have always been. But I see myself now in a genetic context broader than the one I was aware of at the age of 30, and the result is both disquieting and reassuring.

Traits that I had imagined peculiarly my own proved to be shared with relatives I had never met; two families that seemed diametrical opposites (my mother's and my father's) proved to have had a great deal more in common than I (or they) ever guessed; my most proudly self-chosen courses in life turned out to have echoed, or even exactly repeated, similar moves made by relatives before I was born. Faced with this evidence, not only from my own life, but from the lives of those who consulted me for professional help — most of whom were equally unaware of the connection between themselves and their families — I can no longer avoid a belief that genes are important, even though I know that genes alone have not produced these uncanny similarities.

So babies are born different, and this difference stems (as it must) primarily from the genetic mix they inherit. Yet to assert this is by no means to discount the influence of other factors. We can still, if we wish, blame our parents for what they did or failed to do. And my children can blame me! We shall explore how the complex relationship between genetic heritage and environment unfolds shortly. But first, we need to examine exactly what it is that babies bring with them into the world. Is a baby born with a personality, as we adults understand the term? Can we say that a child is 'born bad'? Or born a criminal, or a genius, or a leader, or a follower?

The answer to all of these questions, I believe, is 'no'. What babies are born with is not a fully fledged personality, but a bundle of genetically determined *potentials* which will confine their likely development within certain limits, but which will also offer much scope for individual variation and responsiveness to particular environments. We call this bundle of genetic potentials a 'temperament' – in music, the more tightly the strings of an instrument are wound, the higher the pitch of the note when the string is plucked or struck. The process of tuning used to be called 'tempering' (it survives in the name of J. S. Bach's famous composition, *The Well-Tempered Klavier*). The same metaphor was employed when people referred to a child as 'highly strung' (probably today parents would prefer to say 'gifted and talented'!) A child's temperament forms the *basis* for its later personality. But, as we saw in the last chapter, a newborn baby is only just beginning to experience itself as a separate being. What a baby seems to possess, rather than a personality as such, is *a set of broad, general traits.* A baby may be active or content to lie still much of the time, loud in expressing its needs or reticent, eager to encounter new things or reluctant, smile readily or rarely. Most important of all, the traits that make up infant temperament are *morally neutral.* Babies know nothing of good and bad, right and wrong – such things they will learn about in due course, but they will learn them from their environment, not from their genes. That is why no baby can be 'born evil' (or 'good' either, for that matter).

More than 50 years ago, New York psychiatrist Stella Chess, together with her husband Alexander Thomas, began a series of studies which seriously challenged the then-current belief that all babies start life roughly equal, and that the differences that emerge between them are, therefore, largely due to how they are parented. Chess and Thomas asked mothers of two- and three-month-old infants to report on the details of their baby's behaviour, and these same babies were then tracked and observed at regular intervals as they grew into adulthood. The researchers came up with a number of broad-band traits on which individual differences between infants could be detected. In all, Thomas and Chess proposed nine of these: how active the infant was; how regular and predictable the infant's feeding/sleeping/elimination cycles were ('rhythmicity'); whether the infant readily approached or predictably withdrew when presented with a new stimulus ('approach/avoidance', later conflated with 'sociability'); whether in the longer term the infant found it easy or hard to adapt to change; the amount of stimulus necessary to cause the baby to respond ('threshold of response'); how intensely the infant expressed its feelings; whether its prevailing mood was happy or sombre; how easily distractible the infant was; and how prepared it was to keep trying for something it wanted ('persistence'). Some of these characteristics did not reliably endure beyond infancy, and some infants varied from month to month in their ratings on some traits. However, when the same babies were followed through their later years, some traits, or combinations of traits, seemed particularly likely to persist – in many cases, right through into adulthood – despite the widely varied ways the children had been parented. This strongly suggested that the traits were at least partly genetic in origin.[2]

Activity level is one of the easiest temperamental traits to measure, and not surprisingly, humans share it with lower forms of life (some rats are far more active than others, almost from birth). Thomas and Chess and their associates found that extremely active infants preserved their high level of activity into childhood and, in many cases, into adulthood also. Though a high level of restlessness *could* be induced by the intrauterine environment (a baby born addicted to crack cocaine, for example), most children's activity levels seem clearly genetic in origin. Children at the extreme of high activity will probably – though not necessarily – go on to be described as 'hyperactive' (more recently Attention Deficit Hyperactivity Disorder (ADHD)). Children at the other extreme would be slow-moving and perhaps somewhat passive, at least physically. Somewhere in the middle would be those children we would simply describe as 'lively'. We shall return later to the whole question of the power of language to shape the way we view behaviour, but for the present, let's simply note that while one set of parents may call their child 'hyper' or 'uncontrollable', another child, with exactly the same level of activity, may be called 'active' or 'always on the go' by a different set of parents. The first will be seen as 'a problem', the second as 'normal'.

Sociability is also a strongly genetically linked trait. Some of the Chess and Thomas infants seemed to welcome new people into their world, and were generally unfazed by strangers. At the other extreme, some infants shrank away from unknown adults, seeming confused or intimidated. You *can* be 'born shy' – as I know well, for several of my close relatives exhibit this trait very clearly. Being born with low sociability, however, does not necessarily mean that you are going to be 'a hermit' or that you suffer from what the psychiatric texts call 'social phobia' – because different children handle their shyness in different ways, and because other temperamental traits can offset shyness. Jill Ker Conway, who tells the story of her early life on a property in rural Australia in *The Road from Coorain*, was clearly a temperamentally shy child.[3] Yet her childhood reserve did not prevent her from interacting competently in adult life with a wide range of people; in fact, she ended her academic career as President of Smith College in the United States. Jill's low sociability would have been moderated, and offset, by her temperamental trait of persistence – a trait that is almost essential if you are going to be a successful and high-achieving individual.

Temperamental shyness may nudge a child into an intense interest in his inner thoughts and feelings as a refuge from the external stimulus he finds confusing or overwhelming – but not every shy child is going to be an introvert. A classic example would be my father's father, Albert (who died when I was 18 months old). Everyone agreed that Albert had been extremely shy, and throughout his life avoided situations that would require him to meet or interact with new people. Yet he appeared to have little insight into, or interest in, his own inner world. The perfect contrast to Albert is provided by Victor, my grandfather on my mother's side, who died 16 years before I was born. An outgoing, sociable man, he enjoyed the company of others as much as Albert shunned it. Yet Victor seems to have shown no more evidence of self-reflection than Albert did.

Clearly, however, individuals who are low in sociability are less likely to become leaders than those who can easily make contact with others. Victor enjoyed the experience of command while in the army during World War One, while Albert dreaded getting up in front of the smallish congregation at his local church for the few minutes it took him to make the weekly announcements. But it is not only temperament that makes a leader. Victor's family had taught him pride and self-confidence, and his close relatives provided models of leadership in the professions; Albert's family taught him humility and self-doubt, and though there were leaders among his family too, they mostly thought of themselves (for religious reasons) as 'servants' of the community. Constantly, in the making of personality, temperamental traits interact with family values and practices, intensifying the importance of some traits, and devaluing others. This is one way in which genetic potentials get to be expressed or (conversely) not expressed ('inhibited'). Thomas and Chess came up with three 'bundles' of temperamental traits which accounted for a considerable proportion of their sample: the 'easy' baby (predictable, smiling, positive about new experiences and readily soothed if upset); the 'slow to warm up' baby (taciturn and unsmiling, wary of new experiences but able to adapt to them, given time and patience); and the 'difficult' baby (strongly reactive to new experiences, easily upset and very hard to soothe). Here, in embryo, were three potential 'personality types', it seemed.

Since Thomas and Chess's pioneering publications, other temperament studies have continued their work, tracking large samples of children through into adulthood to find out the extent to which their infant temperament might persist into later life.[4] Thomas and Chess's findings have also been modified and to some degree superseded by the research of Harvard psychologist Jerome Kagan, famous for his throwaway line to the effect that human beings come in breeds, like dogs. Needless to say, this did not endear him to his academic colleagues, nor to the public, but many years of rigorous, painstaking work has enabled him to establish two bundles of temperamental traits, two fundamental temperamental categories, which Kagan originally called the 'inhibited' and the 'uninhibited'.[5] Kagan's 'inhibited' child is fearful and avoidant towards new stimuli (which means she reacts negatively to change); sombre in mood ('serious', unsmiling) and has a low threshold for stimuli in general. Inhibited children find too much stimulus (or unfamiliar stimulus) overwhelming and protect themselves by withdrawing physically ('moving away') or protesting loudly. By contrast, Kagan's 'uninhibited' child moves towards new stimuli (including new people) with pleasure and interest, smiles a lot and takes change and challenge in her stride.

Clearly, Kagan's 'uninhibited' infants were the ones Thomas and Chess classified as 'easy babies', while Thomas and Chess's 'slow to warm up' and 'difficult' types would represent milder and more extreme versions respectively of Kagan's 'inhibited' type. Thomas and Chess's categories tell us about how *parents* view their children's behaviour and, as Kagan pointed out, parents' objectivity when reporting on their children is often questionable. Kagan's research, on the other hand, tells us about the essence of the children themselves, measuring heart rate, frequency of eye blinks and smiling, and brain activity in particular regions – for example, inhibited children proved to have more excitable amygdalas than uninhibited children. It was partly as a result of this finding that Kagan later dropped the term 'inhibited' and substituted 'high reactive' (correspondingly, 'uninhibited' has been replaced by 'low reactive'). 'Reactivity' cuts deeper than 'inhibition'. Not all reactive babies are 'inhibited' (in the usual sense of that word) but all 'inhibited' babies are reactive: 'thin skinned' in colloquial language. These babies are the ones who rapidly pick up tensions between their parents, and cry as if in sympathy. They are easily wounded by minor slights and rebuffs that 'thicker skinned' individuals would brush aside, and they tend to remember reverses and rejections for very long periods. Often, they will attempt to protect themselves from such wounds by avoiding any situation which might present an undesirable stimulus, so it is easy to see how temperamental reactivity might reinforce temperamental shyness.

Beginning in the late 1970s, Ernest Hartmann, an American psychiatrist, began researching the kinds of individuals who experienced nightmares and other sleep disorders. Over the next decade, his work expanded to become a system of classifying personalities which distinguished those with 'thin boundaries' from those with 'thick boundaries'. In many ways, his system anticipated Kagan's: Hartmann's 'thin boundaries' correspond with Thomas and Chess's 'low threshold for stimulus', the core of Kagan's reactivity.[6] In more recent publications, Kagan acknowledges that high-reactive individuals tend to be more sensitive to *all kinds* of stimulus (making them more potentially vulnerable to physical illnesses as well as to emotional distress).[7] Not surprisingly, they also have more nightmares! Conversely, individuals with Hartmann's 'thick boundaries' find it easier to screen out unwanted stimulus, and consequently are less reactive – 'easygoing', 'thick skinned'. They are generally harder to upset or insult, and quicker to forgive and forget. Almost certainly, they have less excitable amygdalas! Accordingly I have chosen to employ Hartmann's terminology in parallel with Kagan's for the rest of this book. It has the added advantage of corresponding with the folk wisdom embodied in the colloquial descriptions, 'thick skinned' and 'thin skinned'.

Like very low sociability, very high reactivity is *potentially* a source of vulnerability for the individual born with it, because a highly reactive person will register everything that happens to them more powerfully and lastingly than other people do. Having high reactivity does not predict any specific problem, but clearly, such individuals are more likely to develop disorders like anxiety or phobias. Extreme reactivity also seems to be part of the temperament that underpins both manic-depression (bipolar disorder) and borderline personality disorder. However, only in extreme cases will thin-boundaried people develop these disorders without some form of reinforcement from trauma, neglect or abuse (usually, but not necessarily, in childhood) and many will not develop such disorders at all.

Yet thin boundaries can also be a positive influence. The highly sensitive child may channel acute awareness of its own feelings into creative work, where the trait will enable it to illuminate for the rest of humanity things that most of us do not readily notice or remember. Great 'fearfulness' or sensitivity is often associated with a vivid, accurate memory for tiny details, because any stimulus that crosses the low emotional threshold of such individuals comes into sharp focus for them. Thin boundaries can facilitate leaps of imagination into other times and places – an asset for historians and novelists. High sensitivity is very useful for any who work in depth with people in emotional distress: indeed, it is the basis of what we call 'empathy'. On the other hand, therapists whose temperament predisposes them to extreme reactivity will need to inhibit the expression of their reactions in the interests of their patients.

At the other extreme of the temperamental continuum, very thick boundaries – which may in some cases mean a total *lack* of fearfulness and a total *lack* of sensitivity to the feelings of others – can be equally problematic, or equally useful. Absence of anxiety can make you a wonderful fighter pilot, for example, if you possess the other skills required – but it would also make you an effective bank robber or serial killer. The ability to remain calm and unmoved while others are in a state of panic or of high emotion can be an asset to lawyers, surgeons, ambulance officers – and stock-exchange speculators. Overly sensitive individuals could not be as effective in these professions as those who seem to be able, without effort, to remain outside of an emotional 'force field'. But the thick-boundaried individual may be oblivious of the distress he causes, and charge through life convinced of his own entitlement to do whatever he likes, regardless of the cost to others.

A person who is extremely reactive to change may also develop a heightened awareness of difference, which he can put to good effect in work or personal relationships, compared with a person who 'rolls along' with whatever changes life presents, and who may never develop much interest in, or sensitivity to, the changes themselves. On the other hand, an extremely reactive individual who is subjected to external stress and trauma – forced migration, loss of stable employment, serious illness or accident, loss of loved ones – will find it enormously difficult to bounce back, and may become depressed, angry or even violent if his immediate family or friends cannot provide a high level of stability and dependability to compensate for these losses.

The broad-brush nature of temperamental traits is a valuable corrective to our human tendency to judge harshly on the basis of too little evidence. If a child is genetically reactive, he or she will probably need more preparation for interruptions to routine, and take longer to adjust to them, than an 'easier' brother or sister would. Understanding this can help a parent to see the child's behaviour pattern *as a morally neutral whole* – neither 'good' nor 'bad' – rather than as indicating some specific problem. When an extremely reactive child screams and arches her back in response to a sudden change that she did not expect, the natural tendency of many parents is to see the child as 'angry', as somehow deliberately 'making trouble'. 'She's a punishing kid to raise!' parents may say. A moral judgement descends, which clouds the true nature of the child's behaviour.

One of the most worrying things about some parents is that they underestimate the real capacities of their infant children ('they're too young to understand') while simultaneously *overestimating* the infant's ability to 'oppose' them or 'punish' them, concepts that properly apply to the behaviour of much older children. 'She's out to get me, the wilful little thing!' says one young mother of her high-reactive baby daughter. Yes, the child is strong willed – the temperamental trait of persistence – but her will is not directed against her mother. It is directed at *protecting herself* from some behaviour that the child perceives as intrusive. Fear, rather than anger, is the emotion that underlies the apparent willfulness and contrariness of this child. Yet if the mother *believes* that her daughter is 'trouble', and responds to her accordingly, sufficiently often and sufficiently forcefully, then she will end up actively creating the very result she expects and dreads. It is not the mother's fault that she treats her child this way. It is not the baby's fault either. But the damage is done, and not easily repaired later.

Temperament and personality

The relationship between the genetically based temperamental traits we have been discussing and a fully developed personality is much like the relationship between the timber frame of a house under construction and the completed dwelling. The frame cannot tell you whether the exterior of the finished house will be made of wood, of brick, or even of glass or plastic. It cannot tell you what colour the house will be painted, or the material it will be roofed with. But it does predict the *size and shape* of the finished house, and it does indicate how its interior will be divided up into rooms. In this analogy, the exterior cladding, colouring and roofing, along with the furnishings of individual rooms, are all aspects of the 'personality', which for every individual are heavily influenced by non-genetic factors. But the frame itself, which predicts the scope and limitations of the personality, is largely temperamental. Analogies, however, only work to a certain point. A developing child is not a static structure made from inert materials, but a living, breathing, constantly changing entity. Its temperamental traits interact constantly with parental behaviour, values and expectations, and personality is, as it were, 'negotiated' rather than 'built'. Nurture, as well as nature, inevitably plays a part in determining the extent to which a child's genetic potentials are either expressed, or suppressed, as it grows into adulthood.

Thomas and Chess's 'easy' baby (low-reactive, thick-boundaried) will settle into routines well, but not be unduly disturbed when the routines are altered; she will be friendly and interested in the world around her, responding well to new people; she will gratify her parents and others by actively mastering her environment, and she will probably crawl or walk early; and though she will of course be upset sometimes, she will generally be of a sunny disposition. Such a child will also – in all probability – receive what behaviourists term 'positive reinforcement' for all of these traits, because our society sees them as desirable. Hugs, coos, exclamations of delight and other pleasant responses will probably greet this baby, making it likely that she will continue to display the traits that bring her such acclaim.

There is another scenario – less likely, but feasible nonetheless. Imagine that this same child, with the same temperamental traits, is born to (or more likely, adopted by) two shy, anxious, sensitive, 'slow to warm up' parents. Then everything may alter considerably. These parents may be puzzled and taken aback by the forthright, questing little being they have brought into their home. Her readiness to make friends with strangers scares them (what if she got abducted or abused?). Because her activity level is so much higher than theirs, they fear she may be 'hyperactive'. And when they compare her with themselves, she may perhaps seem too easygoing, even 'insincere' or 'uncaring'. How different her future may now be! These parents cannot take away her genetically given traits, but they can give them a negative *meaning*. The little girl may grow up wondering what is wrong with her, and encounter various difficulties because of this. However, her genetic endowment is a very positive one, which will probably ensure that she meets people who will balance and correct her parents' failure to understand and appreciate her personality.

Now consider a baby who is extremely active (hyperactive, possibly, by today's standards), extremely persistent, extremely reactive to change, highly expressive, fearful and sensitive. Such a child seems a textbook example of the 'thin-boundaried' category, except that this little boy is not shy, and relates easily to others. Such a child will have difficulty settling, and will want to be constantly 'on the go'. Unless his world is very orderly and routine-governed, he will tend to be seen as 'trouble'; his active exploration and persistence may bring him into contact with new places or people, which on the whole he will enjoy, but it may also lead him into danger. He will soak up praise and be elated at success, but his extreme sensitivity will mean that he will take failures and slights to heart, and his extreme expressivity may lead him to weep at the drop of a hat. Above all, large scale changes in his environment will lead him to exhibit what appears to be rage, or stubborn refusal to do what he is told. Such a child is not necessarily doomed to experience problems, but he is going to be much more challenging to care for than the first. His behaviour will demand more patience, more understanding, more flexibility and more sensitivity than the first baby's will. If he is fortunate enough to receive all or most of these things, the second baby may well grow up to live a happy, fulfilled life – but it will not be automatic. He is much more likely than the first child to grow up being punished for being 'bad', because this is the sort of response his combination of inherited traits will tend to elicit from others.

Born in 1885, young George Smith Patton – hero of the Battle of the Bulge in 1944 – exhibited just that combination of traits. However, far from regarding him as a 'problem child', George's family doted on him, and in their eyes he could do no wrong. A career in the army offered him the opportunity for constant action, combined with just the amount of predictability he needed, and he coped easily with the constant changes of location, rank and responsibility with which the military life confronted him – though not with the abrupt change from war to peace in 1919 and in 1945 (as we'll see in Chapter 8). Despite his strenuous attempt to make himself into a 'man's man', Patton retained lifelong his tearfulness and frequently behaved in anything but a conventional 'military' way. For Patton, despite his loving, indulgent upbringing, struggled lifelong with a massive fear of failure, and low self-esteem. However hard he worked to achieve his goals (persistence), every setback sent him into deep gloom. And though his family never punished him or put him down, in due course his superiors in the army did, bringing about the very thing he had feared since childhood. Patton eventually found an environment that would treat him as a 'problem child' – but that was 30 years after he had grown up and left his family.[8]

Already we can see the operation of a principle that for many years was overlooked in the whole debate about genes versus environment: more often than not, *environment tends to reinforce genetic heritage, rather than modifying or undermining it.* This is not through any conscious wish on the part of parents and caregivers. Far from it. Humans have often assumed that the things they *add* to nature – in this case, parenting – must necessarily work *against* nature: domesticate it, improve on it, even eliminate it. Yet surprisingly often, the reverse seems to occur: what nurture does is to build on and even intensify nature. To those who have, more tends to be given, and from those who have less, even that little can easily be taken away. In this seemingly paradoxical way, our upbringing often ensures that we *will* be who we genetically *could* be.

In Hans Christian Andersen's famous story 'The Tinder Box', a king is told that his daughter will one day marry a common soldier. Dismayed by the news, he acts as kings do in such tales, and shuts his daughter securely inside a copper castle in order to prevent her meeting any soldiers. But of course, the fact that the princess has been placed in maximum security is soon all over town. It reaches the ears of Andersen's soldier hero, who, with magical help, succeeds in gaining entry to the castle, and winning the princess's heart. The king's attempt to prevent a feared outcome has only ensured that it came about anyway. In the language of story, where particular characters engage in particular events, Andersen's tale symbolically conveys a general truth: that in attempting to solve problems, we often make them worse. Faced with something that seems troublesome or alarming, we naturally try to 'make it go away'. It seems far less natural or logical to attempt to *understand* what is troublesome or alarming. Yet if we adopt the first approach (make it go away) the solution itself usually becomes part of the problem – as early family therapists realised. Parents' responses to the temperamental differences in their children often exhibit the same pattern.

Consider a girl at an extreme of low sociability. As a child, she hides when strangers come to the front door and later in life she will do anything to avoid having to enter a room full of people she does not know. The majority of parents will react to this temperamental trait in either of two ways. On the one hand, they could see their daughter's shyness as normal and acceptable (usually because one of them, or even both of them, are themselves shy). 'That's just the way she is', they will say, making excuses for her, and refusing to challenge her extreme anxiety about social encounters. Such an environment encourages her shyness to continue. She may even grow up believing things like, 'Who'd want to be pushy?' or 'Being quiet means you're trustworthy and nice'. On the other hand, the girl's parents could be horrified at what they perceive as a looming problem, and make all sorts of attempts to persuade, cajole or discipline their daughter into being less shy. This is the 'make it go away' solution. Since their attempts to solve the problem draw attention to their daughter, which in itself is stressful for her, they are unlikely to succeed – but they do succeed in confirming her in the view that her shyness is 'a problem'. She feels ashamed of it, and expects to be criticised for it. So whichever attitude they take, parents' response to a temperamental trait that is potentially problematic tends to reinforce it, just as nine out of ten parents of the 'easy' baby we met earlier will tend to reinforce her easygoing, sociable nature by responding positively to it.

There is another alternative, though. Unfortunately, it is comparatively rare. The shy girl's parents may be sufficiently objective, and sufficiently caring, to offer her *both* sensitive understanding of her difficulties in meeting people *and* step-by-step encouragement to try herself out in new situations in which she can gradually gain confidence. They do not make excuses for her, but nor do they harshly impose on her expectations that she is not yet ready to live up to. They wait, patiently and caringly, while she progresses at her own pace, but they do expect progress, not simply resigned acceptance. These wise parents realise that their child is going to have difficulties in life if she continues exactly as she is. They also realise that this is neither her fault, nor theirs. They accept that she needs *both* acceptance of who she genetically is *and* encouragement to develop her own potential as far as her temperamental endowment will permit.

So where do we stand at the end of our brief survey of genetic influences on the developing individuality of the infant? We have established that a child is *not* born a 'blank slate' to be written on by family and society. Rather, each child is born with a set of potentials that means that he or she is *more likely* to develop in some directions than in others. But for any one child, the possibilities are not unlimited. The pioneering behaviourist John Watson once claimed that he could turn any child into a doctor, a lawyer, a politician, an artist or an athlete, simply by manipulating that child's environment, and rewarding 'desirable' responses to produce the desired outcome. Half a century later, a new-generation behaviourist,

B. F. Skinner, came up with a more sophisticated version of this claim in his surprisingly persuasive novel *Walden Two*. In fact, no child becomes a champion or a genius simply because its parents do their best to make it one. A favourable environment may be certainly *necessary* to allow genius or talent to develop to its full potential; but so is innate persistence – a temperamental trait – which drives the child whether or not its environment is favourably disposed. The saying that talent – whether in sport, in the arts or in politics – is 'ten per cent inspiration and 90 per cent perspiration' is not so far off the mark.

What parents and caregivers can do is to go with the flow rather than against it, recognising the range of possibilities in their child's particular temperamental combination, and providing opportunities for the child to develop flexibly within that range. Parents can also resist the temptation to make moral judgements of their infants. The genetic heritage of some children does potentially place them more at risk, more vulnerable to crises or deficits in their environment, as we have already seen: what it does not do, ever, is make them 'bad' or 'sick'.

We have examined the genetic framework of personality, and begun to look at how it can be modified by the attitudes and meanings that parents bring to the temperamental traits of their infants. We need now to focus in more depth on the ways in which an infant's first relationship – the attachment bond with its mother – may profoundly influence its way of relating to others, not just in childhood, but throughout its life. Remember that Chess and Thomas's original measures of temperament were based on mothers' reporting of their infants' behaviour at around three months. Rightly, critics objected that for any baby that had been parented for ten to 12 weeks, its genetic temperament would most likely have been influenced already by repeated interactions with its caregivers. So those studies might not have measured temperament *per se*, but rather, temperament as modified by environment, and in particular, by the type and quality of *attachment* between the baby and its primary carer.

The first relationship

Infant attachment is about *the survival of the individual*. Mammal babies (including human babies) must stay close to their mothers in order to be fed, cared for and protected from danger. Given these things, they stand a good chance of growing into adulthood and becoming capable of reproducing themselves – adult attachment is about the survival of the *species*.[9]

As we all know, human babies are extremely vulnerable at birth: they cannot yet see properly, they have little control over the movements of their bodies, they cannot walk or reach out to get what they need. They can communicate only in very limited ways – by crying, by turning away from a stimulus that they find frightening or overwhelming, by turning *towards* a stimulus – like the sound of their mother's voice – that they have learned to trust. A handful of primitive reflexes must stand for a much wider range of feelings that need expression – thus an infant's cry may mean hunger, fear, surprise . . . Yet this principle (many complex communications expressed via a single 'channel') remains key to understanding human behaviour even after we reach maturity.

The young of our species stay in a position of vulnerability for far longer than most other baby mammals. Human infants' dependence on an adult of their species is absolute. A baby's mother must learn to distinguish its 'hunger cry' from its 'fear cry', decipher what it means when the infant flexes its limbs vigorously again and again. Fortunately, most mothers do learn to read their baby's signals, and hence interpret their baby's needs correctly most of the time. To aid this process of 'attunement', evolution has ensured that babies' appealing eyes and large heads (relative to their tiny bodies) will strike adults as 'cute' and 'loveable'. Their strident cries automatically tug at our heartstrings: 'Oh the poor little thing!' we think, and want to run to the crying baby, pick it up and soothe it – even if it is someone else's. Apart from these inbuilt 'attachment generators', babies (as they develop) also figure out reliable ways of ensuring that they will gain the adult attention they need in order to live and grow – *attachment strategies*. When things go well, a baby learns that it can rely on its caregiver to provide nurturing, protection and loving attention most of the time. It will not be ignored for too long, nor will it be threatened by a caregiver's loud, angry voice; it will not be struck or shaken – in other words, it will be kept safe from danger. It turns towards its 'primary attachment figure' (usually, but not necessarily, its mother) and snuggles close to her – 'proximity seeking' in the language of Attachment Theory. Babies whose caregivers respond to them with warmth and empathy, perceiving the baby's requirements and providing them, will exhibit *secure attachment* – equating with Eric Erikson's 'basic trust'[10], a trust that will gradually transfer to the world in general – to such an extent that the securely attached child must later learn, with some pain and dismay, that not everyone can be trusted to the same extent – but this new learning will be built on a secure foundation of trust and confidence. Securely attached babies constitute 'Type B' in Mary Ainsworth's typology of attachment strategies, which we shall shortly describe in more detail. They openly express their feelings, knowing that it is safe to do so, trusting that their needs will be recognised and, where possible, met. Experts estimate that around 60 per cent of infants fall into the securely attached category.[11] Interestingly, roughly the same proportion of infants fall into Kagan's 'low-reactive' category – almost certainly making them easier to care for than high-reactive babies.[12]

In the landmark 'Strange Situation' procedure[13] that psychologist Mary Ainsworth devised to test the attachment styles of very young children, one-year-olds' mothers left the room while the child played with toys, and were temporarily replaced by a friendly stranger who attempted to engage the children in play. When the stranger left, and the mother returned, most of the babies greeted her with obvious relief and ran to her arms. But when the mother left the room a second time, and the children were alone, their distress was clear. After a short time, she returned for good, and those children later classified as securely attached (Type B), although initially distressed, settled down in response to her comforting.

A minority of children, however, treated their mother's return almost with indifference, looking around to register that she was back, but then continuing to play. These children's message to their caregivers could not be clearer: 'Why should I run to you? I don't need you! I'm fine on my own, thanks very much!' Children who exhibited this behaviour were classed by Ainsworth as *insecure-avoidant*. The *avoidant* strategy was to 'turn away' from the caregiver, almost as if to 'punish' her or 'dismiss' her. Insecure-avoidant children (Type A) formed the largest sub-group among those who were not secure – somewhere between 20–25 per cent of all those tested. They *looked* secure, because they did not exhibit much obvious emotion, and seemed confident and self-sufficient. But, thought Ainsworth, they had simply hidden their vulnerability from their mother – and, indeed, from themselves.

The next largest sub-group (around 10 per cent) behaved quite differently in the Strange Situation experiment from both the Type A and the Type B infants. These Type C infants looked anything but 'secure' in their attachment. In the Strange Situation, they openly showed their anger, kept crying and refused to be comforted even after their mothers returned to the room for the final time. Ainsworth theorised that these infants relied on displays of *feeling* to attract attention from their caregivers. It was as if the child thought, 'She's not taking any notice of me when I cry quietly, but if I cry loudly, she might' – only, of course, they had not 'reasoned' this out in any conscious way. The principle that 'negative attention is better than no attention' definitely seems to apply to this group, and not surprisingly, some of these infants will often go on to become 'uncontrollable' or 'punishing' children who get into lots of trouble with author-ity figures like teachers. Negative attention is better than no attention, right? Ainsworth believed that this strategy, which she called 'ambivalent' (because the baby alternates between clingy-dependent and angry-blaming) was adopted when the child's mother was sometimes warm and caring (at the extreme, intru-sively over-close) yet at other times distant or angry. Where the avoidantly attached child had learned that its mother's behaviour pattern was *consistent*, the ambivalently attached child had been confronted with *inconsistency*. Unable to 'figure out' its mother's behaviour, the ambivalent infant abandons *thinking* and falls back on a display of *feelings* to get at least some of the attention she needs. It works – up to a point. Sometimes mothers realise what is wrong, and give their babies what they need. But not always. Screaming babies who refuse to be comforted also attract angry yelling, or even shaking and other forms of physical abuse. 'I just needed him to shut up! I was so desperate, I shook him until he quieted down'.

Both types of insecure attachment can give rise to problems later in life. Adults whose style has remained ambivalent (Type C) are likely to have a pattern of intense but unsatisfactory relationships, which often end in anger, blaming and cut-off from the former partner. In the same way, ambivalently attached indi-viduals can find difficulty in holding jobs, and readily become dissatisfied in their work. At the high-reactive extreme of the Type C style, they may be diagnosed with borderline personality disorder – a syndrome characterised by pervasive feelings of 'flatness' or 'emptiness', impulsive actions and addictive behaviours, self-harm and rage at perceived abandonment by significant others in their lives.

By contrast, avoidantly attached adults are often high achievers, but they may suffer from depression or anxiety because they have learned too well to cut themselves off from their own feelings. Within their adult relationships, avoidants tend to distance themselves emotionally, physically or both when conflicts erupt, and their partners typically feel shut out and unable to reach them. As children, Type As learned to suppress their own feelings, and instead to pay close, anxious attention to the feelings of their caregiver, in order to 'keep in the right side of her'. It's almost as if they display towards *her* the sensitive attunement that by rights she should have showed to *them*. Seeing their caregiver looking 'down' or irritable, a Type A three-year-old will say, 'I make Mummy cup of tea?' Twenty years later they will do a 'grown up' version of the same, 'looking after' their partner and neglecting their own needs in a pattern of behaviour that is popularly known as 'co-dependent', and which also corresponds with the ACA (adult child of an alcoholic) syndrome. But a person does not need to have had an alcoholic or otherwise addicted parent to become an avoidantly attached adult. Avoidants learn to be 'strong' – the quality that adults think of as 'self-discipline'. As grown-ups, they will say things like, 'I can cope!', or, 'The only person in this world that you can really rely on is yourself!' More disturbingly, they may also say, 'What's the point of talking about how I feel? People will just think I'm a complainer!'

Interestingly, researchers of attachment and temperament have often ignored or dismissed each other's findings – another example of how even highly intel-ligent men and women can be seduced into either/or thinking by their strong conviction of the 'rightness' of their pet theory. And the research that does attempt to address the key question of how temperamental types might 'map onto' attachment strategies has not been nearly as conclusive as one might have hoped.[14] For example, commonsense might suggest that temperamentally 'shy' infants might be more likely to adopt the 'avoidant' strategy than those who were more sociable – but there appears to be no correlation. Would those children who were temperamentally 'low reactive' find it easier to hold in their feelings than others? Almost certainly. But Ainsworth's belief was that any child, even a sociable, normally expressive, adaptable 'easy baby', could adopt the avoidant strategy in response to parenting that consistently disallowed displays of anger or sadness in the child.

Temperamentally, it is a reasonable extrapolation that Thomas and Chess's 'difficult' baby (which Kagan would term 'high reactive') is born with the genetic 'bundle' most likely to ensure that it becomes an ambivalently attached child. Yet one key study indicated that the overwhelming majority of babies with this temperamental type actually ended up as *avoidantly* attached rather than ambivalently attached![15] The same study, conducted by Van den Boom in the Netherlands, also suggested that very early interventions aimed at helping mothers to soothe their high-reactive infants could achieve a disproportionately powerful effect: 68 per cent of the 'fussy', easily irritated, hard-to-soothe babies (high reactives) whose mothers received this assistance were classified as 'secure' at the end of their first year of life! Confusing and sometimes contradictory though the research findings are, it is clear that responsive, caring and patient parenting *can* make a difference, even to children of the most 'difficult' or challenging temperamental type.

We are 'born that way', but we are also 'made that way'. Those of us who have the mixed blessing of being born 'thin boundaried' – fearful, sensitive, reactive – are likely to find our path through life is more difficult than those who are born with 'thick' boundaries – confident, sociable, easygoing and flexible. Those at the temperamental extreme of high reactivity are more likely later to earn a diagnostic label. But, as we've already seen, a temperamentally low-reactive 'easy' baby could still end up insecurely attached if its parenting badly lacked the kind of positive, loving responses it needed; and a temperamentally challenged baby could still end up with a secure attachment if its parents had been able to respond flexibly and empathically to its needs instead of taking its 'difficult' behaviour as a personal attack on them.

There are at least two sources of support to a parent who is struggling with an infant. The first, and most important, comes from other family members – the child's grandparents, sometimes another relative. Such individuals can provide consistency and love that the biological parent may be unable to offer, or better still, can model this behaviour for the parent, so that she can gradually learn to provide it herself. Such in-family helpers are far from *indifferent* to the needy child, but they did not give birth to it, they do not feel 'responsible' for its difficulties, and so they are much less likely to feel blamed or hurt when the child initially rejects their help, or refuses to be comforted quickly. They 'don't take it personally', and they keep trying. They notice what works, and do more of it.

The second source of potential help is professional. Professionals who have themselves been parents, who know the heartache and the guilt and self-blame that one can feel, but who are secure in their knowledge of what every child needs, will possess a degree of objectivity somewhat like that exhibited by a relative who is not the child's biological parent. If sufficiently empathic and skillful, they too can assist troubled parents to do a better job with their 'difficult' child, or to pull back from behaviour that may create problems for a temperamentally 'easy' child. In particular, intervention in infancy, or, at least, in the pre-school years, can substantially modify the scope of the difficulties that child may later face. Intervention in middle childhood or early adolescence can help, too, especially if the attachment deficits of *both* the child *and* the main caregiver can be addressed, first separately, and then conjointly, as in Parent and Child Therapy.[16] Later intervention (in adulthood) can make a real difference, even if considerable damage occurred early in the client's life. But the earlier the damage, and the more pervasive its effects, the harder it is to modify, and that is why many adults, traumatised or neglected as children, may need years of therapy in order to func-tion better. Attachment Theory recognises something called 'earned secure' attachment – that is, that an insecure attachment style in adulthood can under some circumstances be *converted* into a secure one, as we've just seen, through therapy or through other relationships that offer the person more positive and consistent care than she or he originally experienced.

And here is the key principle: early damage occurs within the context of an attachment relationship – caregivers who fail in empathy, and thus impose their own hurt or anger on the child through misinterpreting its signals or ignoring its needs in favour of their own. That is why the correction or reversal of early damage must take place *within a relationship* also – a relationship that can provide the trust, empathy and consistency that was lacking earlier in the adult's life. Providing parents with information and 'strategies', even teaching them 'mindfulness', may seem like a good thing for professionals to do, but unless these things are provided *within the context of a trusting, empathic relationship* they will fail to be effective, or will work only for a short time. Learning new ways of behaving, or unlearning dysfunctional ones, must be done within a relationship with someone who will 'be there' no matter what, who will take you seriously, and who will not blame you or reject you even if you are 'bad'. Seduced as they are by the promise of 'quick fix' interventions that promise speedy results, politicians, social policy-makers and funding bodies have too often failed to recognise that.

Notes

1 See my study 'A Family in Time' (unpublished, 1993). I have drawn on this work for the profiles of my family members that are scattered throughout this book.

2 Alexander Thomas, Stella Chess and Herbert Birch, *Behavioural Individuality in Early Childhood*, NY, University Press, 1963; an updated version of their findings, incorp-orating new research, can be found in Alexander Thomas and Stella Chess, *The Dynamics of Psychological Development*, NY, Brunner-Mazel, 1980.

3 See Jill Ker Conway, *The Road from Coorain*, Sydney, Heinemann, 1989.

4 More recent large scale temperament studies include The Early Childhood Longitudinal Study of some 14,000 US children born in 2001; and the Australian Temperament Study of 10,000 children born in 2005 (in progress). The latter study has been publicised through a series of films (*Life at One, Life at Three, Life at Five* and so on) which track a small sample of children through their childhood. Though suggestive and often moving, the earlier films fail to clarify what 'temperament' actually is, and mostly duck the confronting issue of temperamental vulnerability.

5 Jerome Kagan (with Nancy Snidman, Doreen Arcus and J. Steven Reznik), *Galen's Prophecy: Temperament in Human Nature*, NY, Basic Books, 1994; this book gives the fullest picture of Kagan's actual research and sets it in a broad context of human thinking about 'temperament' from the ancient Greeks onwards. His more recent *The Temperamental Thread: How Genes, Culture, Time and Luck Make Us Who We Are*, NY, Dana Press, 2010, is a very clearly organised summary of the current state of temperament research, intended for non-academic readers.

6 See Ernest Hartmann, *Boundaries in the Mind: A New Psychology of Personality*, NY, Basic Books, 1990: 20–48.

7 See Kagan, 2010, op. cit.: 207.
8 Carlo D'Este, *A Genius for War: A Life of General George S. Patton*, London, HarperCollins, 1995.
9 Attachment Theory originated in the work of John Bowlby, a psychoanalytically trained British paediatrician, in the 1940s and 1950s. His trilogy, *Attachment*, London, Hogarth Press, 1969; *Separation: Anxiety and Anger*, London, Hogarth Press, 1973; and *Loss, Sadness and Depression*, NY, Basic Books, 1980, draws on biology, ethology, psycho-analysis and developmental findings to build a new theory of infant–parent bonding and its immense significance for later development. Bowlby's student and later col-league Mary Ainsworth devised the 'Strange Situation' test for attachment in infancy, and devoted her life to establishing a solid evidence base for the three types of infant attachment (A, B and C). Mary Main and her colleagues later added a fourth type, (D) – disorganised – which combines elements of both the A and C strategies, but is not, in itself, an organised 'strategy'. It occurs only in extreme situations, where the caregiver herself is either 'frightened, or frightening'.
10 See Erik H. Erikson, 'Eight Ages of Man' in his *Childhood and Society*, London, Hogarth Press, 1965: 239–261. [First published in the US in 1950.]
11 See Sophie Moullin, Jane Waldfogel and Elizabeth Washbrook, 'Baby Bonds: Parenting, Attachment and a Secure Base for Children', The Sutton Trust, 2014.
12 See Kagan, 2010, op. cit.: 201–202. Note that Kagan's figures are based on *Caucasian* infants only.
13 For a full description of the experimental design and the initial findings, see M. D. S. Ainsworth, M. C. Blehar, E. Waters and S. Wall, *Patterns of Attachment: A Psychological Study of the Strange Situation*, Hillsdale, NY, Erlbaum, 1978.
14 For a good summary of such research, see Robert Karen, *Becoming Attached: First Relationships and How They Shape Our Capacity to Love*, NY, Oxford University Press, 1998: 289–312. [First published by Warner Books in 1994.]
15 See D. C. Van den Boom, 'The Influence of Temperament and Mothering on Attachment and Exploration: An Experimental Manipulation of Sensitive Responsiveness among Lower-Class Mothers with Irritable Infants', *Child Development*, 65, 5 (October, 1994): 1457–1477.
16 Parent and Infant Therapy was evolved by New Zealand psychologist Heather Chambers, and is described in Jackie Amos, Simon Beal and Gareth Furber, 'Parent and Child Therapy (PACT) in Action: An Attachment-based Intervention for a Six Year Old with a Dual Diagnosis', *Australian and New Zealand Journal of Family Therapy*, 28, 2 (2007): 61–70. Of course this is only one approach to early intervention to address attachment difficulties, and there are many others, but it appears to be particularly useful where parent and child are struggling with a badly disrupted attachment bond.

3

'HEAVEN LIES ABOUT US IN OUR INFANCY'

The pre-school years

Our first world

In my mind lives a scene I *believe* I once experienced. I am sitting on a porch, in sunlight, with steps leading down to a grassy lawn. There is nothing else, except a sense of this being something intensely special and satisfying. My parents told me that when I was very small, we lived in a house in the Sydney suburb of Lindfield. Is this 'close-up' an image from that time? Might this have been my first-ever venture outside the house on my own? I'll never know for sure.

Children are perfectly capable of creating mental images based on their parents' stories, and then believing that these images constitute their own memories – a version of 'false memory syndrome'. Once we have seen photographs (and now, movies recorded on smart phones) of our own early childhoods, these 'official' images tend to replace whatever vague memories we possessed before. Similarly, when we read a novel, many of us form shadowy mental pictures of the characters or settings – perhaps based on people we know, or places we have been. Yet when we see a movie or TV series based on the same novel, our original images are nearly always supplanted by images based on the movie. However readers of Margaret Mitchell's best seller *Gone with the Wind* might have imagined Scarlett O'Hara, after 1939 she looked like Vivien Leigh – and however today's readers might have pictured Harry Potter, he is now, for all time, Daniel Radcliffe.[1] So it is difficult to be sure quite which 'memories' of our early childhoods are truly authentic. Some guidelines do exist to help us with this task, however.

For most of us, conscious memories begin around 18 months of age, as we begin to learn to speak. Typically, the earliest memories to survive are of places (like mine), incidents without context or (as we saw in the last chapter) simply feelings – perhaps associated with a place, an object or a person. These early memories are like random scenes: they do not form part of a coherent story that has a beginning, a middle and an end. We may not be sure what their significance actually was, or why our brains have preserved them. The little memory of my own that I described earlier fits these criteria, so I feel reasonably certain that it is genuinely mine, and not based on later, parent-influenced information. Compare a photograph taken when I was about the same age (myself in the back garden, holding a flower but looking solemn). My father jokingly wrote 'Hugh: glum' on it, and my unsmiling expression clearly meant something to him, but I have no memory whatsoever of the occasion on which that photograph was taken, or of whatever it was that had made me 'glum'. Of course, I could not have seen my facial expression from the outside (as the photograph shows it) but research does indicate that most of our older memories tend to be 'observer memories', where we ourselves are seen 'from outside', as in my 'sitting on the porch' image, whereas more recent events tend to be remembered as 'field memories' – in which we do not see *ourselves*, but rather, see *what we would have seen at the time*.[2] Our early memories may well have begun as 'stories in the first person' (seen through our eyes) but our brains later shifted them into the 'third person' – as our ability to imagine ourselves 'from the outside' developed (which, as we'll see later in this chapter, marks the coming on-line of the brain's left hemisphere).

Yet neither 'real' memories nor adult-supplied photographs and anecdotes give us much sense of how, as children of two or three, we actually *experienced* what T. S. Eliot called our 'first world'.[3] Again, we can turn to artistic creativity to provide a guide, and this time, we do not have to be as tentative as we were when discussing the traces that birth might leave on memory. Musicians, artists and writers repeatedly inform us in their autobiographical writings of the powerful impact of their conscious memories of early childhood – usually impressions of the physical world. And those impressions survive, sometimes quite literally, into their later creative work, often being recycled again and again throughout their lives.

It was not images but *sounds* – birdsong and bugles – that Gustav Mahler remembered from his 'first world'. Born in 1860, the Austrian composer commenced his first symphony, written at the age of 25, with an extended passage based directly on his earliest auditory memories. When he was five months old his family had moved to a town where they lived near a barracks; military bands would march past his house, and every morning the little boy would awake to the mingled sounds of birds in the nearby trees and bugle-calls summoning the troops to early parade. Here we are not, as in Wagner's *Rheingold* music, dealing with deeply buried *body* memories of whose influence the composer was probably unaware. Mahler knew where his musical images came from. But there is a freshness, an innocence about the opening of his Symphony No. 1, a sense of suspended time evoked by a sustained note in the strings against which the flutes and piccolos chirrup, which suggests that Mahler has imported directly into his composition the sunlit eternity of sense impressions in early childhood.[4]

Writing almost 90 years earlier, William Wordsworth had famously suggested the same sunlit eternity in words:

> There was a time
> When valley, rock and stream,
> The earth and every common sight,
> To me did seem
> Apparel'd in celestial light
> The glory and the mystery of a dream.[5]

Bathed in Wordsworth's 'celestial light', the world of early childhood is one in which even simple, everyday things are special and important, for we perceive them with senses not yet dulled, with minds still open. The same new minted quality can be revived when older adults require cataract surgery, and prosthetic lenses are inserted in their eyes. Suddenly, the world they see seems fresh, vivid, full of depth and detail – they are re-experiencing the sharp perception all of us once experienced as children. But surgery is not the only way to experience the 'vision splendid'. It can also occur (temporarily) when we fall in love, suffer from sleep deprivation or are under the influence of hallucinogenic drugs. The fact that all three of these states refresh our vision of the everyday world strongly suggests that they are re-creating a chemical environment in the brain similar to that which occurs naturally in early childhood.

A certain genre of 'supermarket art' offers us giant landscapes in which luminous waves break spectacularly on rocky shores, or primeval trees tower over glowing forest pools. Hackneyed and predictable, these pictures sell so well precisely because they re-create the eye of early childhood. Their vision apes that of nineteenth-century artists like Samuel Palmer (in Britain) or Caspar David Friedrich (in Germany). American artist Andrew Wyeth, who died in 2009, offered a somewhat similar vision. When we were two years old we did not need to visit exotic wilderness landscapes or gaze at examples of 'magic realism' because our own homes and gardens had the same sense of being lit from within by some special significance. The gate was 'our first gate'. The world outside the gate, or the back door, was 'our first world'. Our homes and gardens possessed that significance because we ourselves possessed it. For most of us, self-doubt had not yet become part of our experience. We knew we were important and special. *We perceived the world as we ourselves felt.* Of course objects and people seemed bigger then, because we were smaller (a process memorably evoked by Graham Greene in his haunting short story 'Under the Garden').[6] We registered their hugeness, their luminosity, recording not only sights, but sounds, smells, tastes and tactile sensations with equal vividness. And then 'forgot' them.

And so, later in life, we will walk into a particular house, and it will possess a mysterious allure: something about it seems 'right' for us. And surprisingly often (as those who sell houses are well aware) we will agree to purchase a home for no better reason than this. While I was growing up, I took little interest in houses. Yet, in my thirties, as I developed an interest in domestic architecture simultaneously with exploring the past of my own family, I came to realise that the houses which appealed to me most fell into a common pattern. They belonged to the era of Australian architecture (dating from around 1910) called 'Federation', which featured exposed wooden floor boards, tiled porches, leadlight windows and (often) combined brickwork and stucco outside. I felt as if I *belonged* when in such homes. Then, in my forties, I went back to see the house in Lindfield where my parents and I had lived when I was between two and four years of age – the house of my 'sitting in the porch' memory. As soon as I saw it, I knew where the roots of my mysterious attraction to Federation homes lay, for it was one of them: stucco, tiled porch, leadlight and all. And I knew why, as a graduate student, I had wanted to study the work of William Morris – his 'arts and crafts movement' was ultimately responsible for the kind of aesthetic that lay behind Federation homes.

So it is that in adulthood, many of us will unconsciously seek to re-create, in the living spaces we choose, some key aspects of the first living space we can remember. Of course this need not be in a complete, literal way as in my personal example. All that is needed for a buried memory to be activated is a certain arrangement of rooms, the smell of a certain floor polish or fabric, a combination of colours, a particular grouping of shrubs in a garden. Most adults will never be aware of the way their housing preferences have been determined in this way. In much the same way, when we come to buy presents for our children or grandchildren, we may be powerfully drawn to certain toys, and only later recall that we had once possessed such toys ourselves. Our strong sense of magic or specialness suggests that once again, the vision of early childhood has been re-awakened in us. Emotions can persist even when the real objects (and people) that originally evoked them can no longer be remembered.

The old brain and the new

When a baby is born, its initial behaviours – turning away from something or turning towards it, crying (to communicate pain, discomfort or hunger), the 'grasping' and 'rooting' reflexes that help the baby to find and attach itself to the breast that will nourish it – reflect those of most mammal babies, for a baby's brain contains within it the same neural structures that all mammals have. Indeed, the deepest-buried layer of a human baby's brain duplicates the primitive brain of snakes and lizards. At the very base of our brains is a bulb of tissue called the brain stem or 'R-complex' ('R' standing for 'reptile'). This 'oldest brain' governs eating, sleeping and the emptying of bowel and bladder. Around and above this bulb we find the 'limbic system' or 'mammal brain' – organs like the amygdala, which registers threat and stores memories at a non-verbal level, and the hippocampus (which takes over higher memory functions as children begin to speak). The 'human' part of its brain, the cerebral cortex, is functioning too, but

in infancy, it is far from mature.[7] A baby's instinctive behaviours and its experiences are governed by the most primitive layers of its brain. Most significantly,
for our purposes, these experiences include *feelings*. Our ability to feel fear, anger,
sadness and joy is embedded *below* the more sophisticated parts of our brains,
and comes on stream long before we can reason and think in a mature way. We
know this because when (a very rare event) a baby is born without a cerebral
cortex, this 'encephalic' infant is perfectly capable of displaying fear, anger,
sadness and joy, even though it has no 'proper brain' at all.[8] Much of what goes
wrong with us humans is the result of the fact that, developmentally, we *feel*
before we can *think about* what we feel. As a child grows from babyhood to
school age, its capacity to think, reflect and plan increases rapidly, allowing it
to *inhibit* actions which its feelings invite it to perform. Yet it may not be until
half a lifetime later that its 'thinking brain' will be mature enough to be an
effective counterweight to its emotions – and not always then.

We believe that the earliest feelings to evolve were those which related
directly to survival: *fear* warns any creature that it is under threat; *rage* floods its
body with aggression, enabling it to defend itself against the threat. *Purposeful
excitement* is important for survival too – it is the state in which an animal hunts
for food (and, later, for a mate). Jaak Panksepp calls this latter feeling 'seeking'.
Rats exhibit it in the form of a special high-pitched chirruping which they emit
as they run about sniffing frantically for something edible. It seems likely that
'seeking' forms the primitive foundation for the state that we humans call
'elevation' – the state in which we are suffused with the sense of meaning and
purpose that drives us in quests that have nothing to do with survival: quests for
understanding, for adventure, for discovery.[9] The great eighteenth-century
navigator James Cook claimed quite early in his career that he intended to go,
not only 'farther than any man has ever been before me, but *as far as I think it is
possible for a man to go*.'[10] More mundanely, 'seeking' propels us to work hard and
to try our best at any task to which we put our hands – whether it be mothering
a child, solving a software problem or composing a song.

Fear, rage and purposeful excitement probably occur in reptiles: they certainly
do in mammals. Rats, dogs and monkeys feel the feelings – they experience
the alteration in brain chemicals – but they do not *know what they are feeling* in
quite the way that we humans do, because their brains do not consciously
separate them from their own experience in order to observe it. It is the left
hemisphere of the cerebral cortex that gives us that capacity, but the capacity is
not operational in the early months of life. Both hemispheres of the cortex are
there and functioning in a newborn baby, but the left has not yet matured
sufficiently to operate in the way it will later do. What does this mean? It means
that a human baby is in much the same situation as an animal. Its feelings are
simply *part of its experience*: it has no awareness of a 'me' which 'feels' that anger
or fear or excitement. So its feelings 'take it over', flooding it with intense
sensations that trigger crying, thrashing or some other behaviour. These feelings
are timeless: as long as they are being felt, they are forever. Gradually, a baby

will learn that feelings, however powerful, do come to an end, that they 'mean' something and are predictably associated with certain events. But the full learning of these things will take years. In the earliest months of our lives, we all experience an existence akin to that of a meerkat, a wolf or a lion: a here-and-now world in which whatever we are feeling right then and there dominates our experience, propelling us into the 'instinctive' actions that are necessary for our survival.

However, as we saw in our last chapter, in order to survive, a baby must bond with an attachment figure (usually its mother), and this mammalian arrangement ensures that the 'limbic brain' is also involved from the very beginning of our lives. That means that, alongside rage, fear and 'seeking', an infant soon begins to develop the feelings we regard as more distinctively 'human'. So far as we know, reptiles do not play. Baby mammals *enjoy* things: once capable of moving around freely, they chase their siblings, exchanging the roles of pursuer and pursued. Of course these games are a kind of 'practice' for later hunting activities, but they are also fun. Baby animals snuggle close to their mothers (*proximity seeking*), feel safe with her and appear bewildered when they lose sight of her (*separation anxiety*). If she is suddenly removed permanently, they are shocked (*panic/grief*).[11] Human babies do the same. These distinctively mammalian feelings only arise in relationships. They depend upon our attachment to another person. We humans are above all *social animals*: without connection with others, we fail to thrive. Adults who live alone or whose key relationships have broken down are far more vulnerable to illness, emotional disturbance and suicide than those who are connected with others in a satisfying way.

If the reptile and mammal brains drive much of our behaviour from the beginning of our lives, this is because the right hemisphere of a baby's cerebral cortex is more mature, at birth, than the left. For we now know that the right hemisphere is closely connected neuronally with the reptile and mammal layers that lie beneath it. Just as the mammal brain takes over and enhances the functions of the reptile brain, representing them in a more sophisticated way, so the right hemisphere of the cortex represents – 'speaks for' – the functions of both the reptile and mammal brains, which collectively I shall call the 'Old Brain'.[12] The right hemisphere works to ensure our *survival*: guided by sense impressions (for example, a glimpse of a sudden movement that might signal a threat), it registers fear, and produces mental pictures of scenarios in the past that have inspired similar anxiety.

Because it needs to scan its environment for potential threats, the right hemisphere takes in the world in 'wide shot', 'panning' back and forth. It deals with wholes not parts, *patterns* (objects in relationship) not components. It sees events and people *in context*, against a 'background', if you like. It is every bit as 'conscious' as the left hemisphere (to which we'll come shortly) but its conscious awareness is not distinct from the world in which it exists. Instead, it has the kind of selfhood we believe that animals have: taking in sense impressions, experiencing feelings, acting, but not observing these things as if from a vantage point 'outside' of them. And human babies, born with a functioning right hemisphere but a still-immature left hemisphere, experience their worlds in roughly the same way.[13]

Psychoanalytic developmentalist Daniel Stern in his award-winning *Diary of a Baby* made a brave attempt to convey how an infant, still dominated by its right hemisphere, might describe its world if it had words (which, of course, infants do not – the Latin word *infans* means 'without words' or 'without language'). Stern's baby, Joey, describes a 'storm' that sweeps over him. Part of the 'storm' is the sound of his own urgent crying, but the little boy does not know that the loud, frightening sound he hears is made by his own vocal chords. He does not realise that he is hungry. He is not separate from the 'storm'. The storm seems to last forever, and then, suddenly, it is gone, replaced by a feeling of warmth and comfort as milk reaches the little boy's stomach.[14] Thus, as psychoanalyst Otto Kernberg reasoned, the earliest patterns into which babies organise their experiences – as the left hemisphere gradually matures – would be *alternating feeling states*: discomfort/comfort; pain/relief; cold/warm; alone/connected (with a caregiver). Stern was a scholar, not a poet, but he relies heavily on metaphors like 'the hunger storm' to convey to us how Joey experiences his world. The right hemisphere 'thinks in pictures' (and in sequences of pictures: 'stories'). In an infant's right-hemisphere-dominated world, each new experience will automatically call up images of previous experiences that are similar: the right hemisphere 'thinks' by associating like with like.

In the world of the infant, everything seems equally significant, equally imbued with meaning and possibility. It requires no explanation – it just *is*. Much art, literature and music simulates this right-hemisphere-dominant world. Think of Paul Klee's 1925 painting 'Fischzauber' ('fish magic'): the boy is technically 'outside' the aquarium, looking into it through its glass walls, but he is also 'inside' among the gorgeously coloured fish. Each of these luminous creatures that hangs motionless against a velvet-dark background is as important as any other: there is no hierarchy, no organising perspective to 'rank' objects as more or less worthy of attention. The fish are not 'going anywhere', they just *are*. There is no 'past' and no 'future'. The fish do not 'mean anything'; their meaning lies in their existence.

I said earlier that the right hemisphere is more fully functioning from birth in the human infant, but the left hemisphere develops rapidly throughout infancy. What exactly does this mean? What does the left hemisphere add to the capabilities of the right? First and foremost, the left hemisphere, unlike the right, concerns itself with *parts rather than wholes*. Instead of the right hemisphere's 'big picture' view, the left 'zooms in' on details, separating them from their wider context in order to perceive and understand them better. Think of a young child fixing its gaze on an object, staring intently for some seconds, and then shifting to a different focus. It's clear that it finds this particular object of great (if temporary) interest. That is how the left hemisphere interacts with the world, selecting individual bits from the 'blooming, buzzing confusion'[15] that surrounds it, and trying to grasp each bit mentally. As the infant's muscles come more under its control, it will be able to reach out and *literally* grasp an object that is within its reach, manipulate it, squeeze it or, perhaps, bring the object to its mouth to taste it. These are the infant's ways of *understanding*. Swiss psychologist Jean Piaget called this the 'sensorimotor' stage of cognitive development, because 'thinking' is done through actions, and of course infants need to repeat such actions multiple times with the same object. To an untrained observer, an infant's endless putting of the same thing in its mouth may look 'dumb', but this baby is *learning*.

The left hemisphere *selects* things, *evaluates* them and then *uses* them – as our Paleolithic ancestors would scan a river bed for a flint that looked the right shape and size for a stone axe, pick it out from the rest, heft it and then (if it still seemed appropriate) begin to shape it into a tool that would assist them to perform useful tasks. It may seem a big leap, but *language* too is a 'tool' – something that permits us to select, differentiate, judge and operate upon particular aspects of our world – and so it makes sense that the left hemisphere would make *words* its own to a far greater extent than the right. Once language develops to maturity, over the pre-school years, a child will gradually start thinking in words as well as in pictures. And words permit some important things that the right hemisphere does not encompass, most important of all being the ability to *negate*. Without the assistance of the left, the right hemisphere cannot say 'no' or 'this is wrong'. It can only make a picture of something different from the preceding picture. Language also enables us to think *symbolically*, because the word 'stone' is not a stone – it is a symbol which we collectively agree 'stands in for' a stone – it enables us to talk about stones in general (instead of just that particular stone which is in front of us), much as the symbol 'x' does in an algebraic equation.

Once we talk (and think) symbolically, we are no longer embedded in the world, as animals are: we are distinct from it, separate, looking at it from a distance, *operating* upon it, not only with words, but with the multifarious array of other 'tools' and technologies we humans have amassed over our millennia of existence. It is the left hemisphere which organises our sense of time as 'linear' – 'time's arrow' (in the words of Stephen Jay Gould) rather than 'time's cycle' – the 'endless now' of the right hemisphere, which is also the cyclic time we find reflected in myths and legends.[16] Linear time gives us the idea of 'progress' and, of course, the idea of 'development' (change across time). Linear time also teaches us about 'before' and 'after', 'cause' and 'effect', 'inside' and 'outside' (distinctions that are irrelevant in Klee's picture of the boy and the fish). It is the still-immature left hemisphere which makes it possible for a 12-month-old toddler to notice that if she cries loudly, her mother will speak angrily to her, or turn away and leave her alone. Even at this early stage, the left hemisphere will help her to make predictions based on this observation, and hence produce 'avoidant attachment': 'If I show my feelings, Mummy won't be nice to me; so I won't, and then she will be nice all the time'.

I find it highly intriguing to talk as if the hemispheres were distinct entities with their own 'world views' – and to a degree it is true – but normally the two hemispheres do *not* operate separately and our knowledge of their 'specialisations' depends on experiments in which the connecting tissue that normally bonds them together is temporarily anaesthetised.[17] Instead, the two 'halves' of our cortex co-operate to offer us (even as babies) a fuller, more useful sense of the world than either hemisphere could offer us alone. As Iain McGilchrist makes clear in his important book *The Master and his Emissary*, it is the right hemisphere which directly 'takes in' the world around us via the senses: it 'sends' information based on what it perceives to the left hemisphere, which then 'zooms in' on particular aspects of that information, selecting, evaluating and organising, then 'sends' its findings back to the right hemisphere. All of this happens virtually instantaneously, but we know the sequence from research: first the right, then the left, and then back to the right. The right hemisphere evolved first, is somewhat larger than the left, it guards our existence and keeps us safe, and for that reason (says McGilchrist) remains the 'master'. Yet without the special capacities of the left hemisphere, we would not be human. For our observing self – the sense of 'me-ness' that we bring to all our experiences – is largely the product of the left hemisphere. Without it, we would be just another clever monkey. And one of the early signs of an 'observing self', aware of how others might see it, is that curious emotion we call 'shame'.

Shame and doubt

Shame is not one of the 'primary' feelings for which the old parts of our brain equip us. It comes on stream later than seeking, fear and rage, and unlike them, is not primarily geared to physical survival. Perhaps, indeed, it has to do with *social* survival, for shame occurs when a disapproving reaction from others interrupts or cuts across our feeling of excitement or joy, telling us that our feeling is, in their eyes, 'wrong' or 'bad'. Whether a child laughs loudly at the 'wrong' time and embarrasses its parent, touches its genitals in a way that society frowns upon or wets its pants on its first day at school – whatever the action might be, it is in origin *innocent*, but the negative reaction it draws from others leaves the infant's pride in itself compromised. The behavioural signs of shame are found in all cultures from a very early age – certainly from 18 months: the child's head drops forward, he avoids looking at the eyes of the other person and his face reddens. A shamed child seems, temporarily, to 'collapse inwards', as if in a sudden realisation of its own 'wrongness'. Few of us escape some experience of being shamed – if not by our parents, then by teachers or peers at school – but of course, how deeply shame affects us will depend on how sensitive a temperament we possess. As we have already seen, the 'thick-skinned' child, particularly if securely attached, will feel a temporary drop in self-esteem when shamed, but bounce back from it without lasting emotional damage. For the highly reactive, 'thin-boundaried' child, however, experiences of shame will be remembered for years afterwards, and into adulthood; later experiences of shame will build on earlier ones, reinforcing an inner sense of unworthiness, which is expressed physically in a stoop, a tendency to blush easily, a downcast gaze. Later-developing signs of shame include 'picking' at one's face or body, as if to say 'I've got to clean myself up — I'm dirty'. These bodily signs correspond with what cognitive psychologists term 'mistaken beliefs', such as 'everything I do turns to shit' or 'I don't deserve to be loved, I'm just a worthless person'.[18] Yet the results of shame are not all destructive. Early shame tends to direct a child's attention inwards, resulting not just in self-criticism, but in broader-based self-reflection. Highly sensitive children's self-awareness is strengthened by shame, and it gives them greater capacities for self-examination and self-insight than their brothers and sisters who have thicker boundaries. Many famous artists, writers and musicians remembered being shamed as children, but in their case the experience sharpened their perceptions of self and others, and drove them to create works that would outlast them.

A few parents, themselves the products of a brutal and confusing upbringing, may confuse shaking or hitting their baby with 'protecting it', but thankfully this is relatively rare.[19] Most parents sense instinctively that hurting their infant, dropping it or shaking it is wrong, and may well damage the child. Many of us even feel guilty when, in a temporary fit of exasperation or despair, we *imagine* doing such things, even though we would never actually carry out these disturbing fantasies. But it is harder for normal parents to recognise that *emotional damage* may be caused to their child by their loud, angry or violent conflicts, even when their behaviour is not directed at the infant itself. 'She can't understand what we're saying, so how can she be affected by it?' is the common argument. 'And anyway, it's not about her — it's between us!' Their children *are* affected. Our pets clearly respond to our distress (by trying to comfort us) and to our anger (by cringing, whining or running away). Infants, like animals, feel emotional 'storms' around them and respond much as pets do. They may not know what adults' words mean, but they are programmed from the older parts of their brains to respond with *fear* to the loud, shocking sounds and the angry, distressed feelings that accompany them. Frequent or prolonged fear produces increased secretion of the stress hormone, cortisol, in the infant's brain. A chronically stressed infant becomes *accustomed* to this level of cortisol, which helps it to cope with the adrenal 'rush' occasioned by fear. Much as with any drug of addiction, a very young child can become, as it were, 'addicted' to cortisol, can develop 'tolerance', and need to maintain its levels of cortisol in order to feel normal or comfortable.[20] Memories of fear are retained by the amygdala well before the child can speak.

Of course this does not mean that an infant will be traumatised or become addicted to cortisol simply as the result of *occasional* quarrels between its caregivers. The 'storms' need to be frequent (that is what 'chronic' stress means) for lasting damage to occur. But (and here we return to the notion of temperament) there is little doubt that highly reactive children will be more affected by even an occasional 'parent storm' than thicker-boundaried infants, who have been blessed with the capacity to take such distressing incidents in their stride. When people use the word 'trauma', they usually think of adults being shot at, raped, tortured, held captive or perhaps robbed of loved ones by a sudden violent accident. In the case of children, they will imagine things like severe beatings, starvation or lack of proper care (nappies unchanged for days on end). These are examples of 'big "T" trauma', as experts are now calling it. By contrast, small 't' trauma might be exposure to screaming or violent interactions between adults, or periods of time when the infant's mother is depressed and unavailable for hours on end. A high-reactive, thin-boundaried baby will register such things as traumatic. *Pain is relative to the stimulus threshold of the person who is subjected to it.* A baby has no way of knowing that its mother's depression, or its parents' anger, has nothing to do with itself: 'inside' and 'outside' are not yet firmly distinguished (remember Joey's 'hunger storm'?)

At 18 to 24 months, all children are going to be far more governed by their feelings than by their capacity for rational thought ('putting two and two together'). But in the case of the ambivalently attached child (Type C), the very strategy that it falls back upon in order to gain parental attention is likely to strengthen the right hemisphere rather than the left, to reinforce its age-appropriate tendency to rely on feelings (and global, intuitive perceptions) as its guide to survival. We know that neuronal connections are strengthened when they are used more frequently. An ambivalently attached child's left hemisphere will receive less reinforcement from repeated interactions with parents than its right hemisphere. Its behaviour will evoke emotional and impulsive reactions from its caregivers, rather than calm, thoughtful, empathic ones. The left hemisphere will still mature, of course, but its capacities will be less utilized, may even lie dormant as the child develops a slight right hemisphere dominance that may persist into adulthood. I say 'slight', because, although we talk loosely of 'right brain' people and 'left brain people', all of us use both hemispheres almost simultaneously, all the time. Any 'dominance' is slight – though real and potentially significant.

Similarly, Type A (avoidant) attachment might represent early-emerging left hemisphere maturation, reinforced by parental behaviour that is *consistent* and thus *cognitively* predictable to the child. Reversing the pattern of ambivalent attachment, the avoidantly attached child favours left hemisphere activities and strengthens left hemisphere neuronal pathways (logical reasoning, analysis, detachment from feelings) at the expense of right hemisphere ones. This child will often appear mature and well-functioning, 'adult' in its way of approaching things – but a continuing slight dominance of the left hemisphere may mean that its awareness of its own feelings will be restricted, and its ability to accurately perceive the feelings of others will also be limited. It will be deprived of the right hemisphere's global, intuitive perception of the world, and of the rich (if some-times misleading) information supplied by emotions, just as the ambivalent child will lack the ability to *check out* those feeling-based perceptions and intuitions by examining the evidence for them in a rational way. *Both* major types of insecure attachment develop through a continuous interaction between the maturing brain and the child's interpersonal environment, in which some potentials of the cortex are encouraged by caregivers' behaviour, while others are inhibited.

'Look, Mummy, you can't see me!'

Everyone knows how a child learns to walk, and to talk: in a long, slow process, with endless repetitions of the same behaviour, until suddenly a breakthrough occurs, and the child reaches a new level of skill. It is often a case of 'three steps forward, two steps back', as children grasp at some new competency, then regress to an earlier stage for a while. When they do reach the new level, they may for a time 'overdo' the behaviour they've just mastered ('going to extremes' is a predictable feature of several later developmental stages too, including adolescence and midlife).

It's easy for parents to grasp aspects of their child's development that are externally observable – they can *see* the child walking and *hear* it talking; moreover, parents can measure a child's progress against their own adult competence at both movement and language. They know roughly how walking and talking are done, and they are aware that they themselves once acquired each skill in much the same way as their children are now doing. It is far harder to appreciate that *selfhood, the sense of being an individual, may also be learned in 'fits and starts' and by 'going to extremes'*. It's harder to appreciate because, unlike walking and talking, the development of selfhood is largely an internal process. Hard to appreciate, too, because most of us do not readily measure our own selfhood against our children's, at least, not consciously. We excitedly photograph our child's first step, proudly report how many new words he or she learned this week. But we cannot photograph our child's 'self'. To document its development means paying attention to patterns of behaviour that, at first, seem unrelated to what is going on *inside* the child.

The person who first drew our attention to this was the Hungarian-born pediatrician and psychoanalyst Margaret Mahler (no relation to Gustav Mahler the composer) who, after the Nazi shadow fell on Vienna, made her new home in New York in 1938. Mahler offered a very detailed description of the way in which toddlers gradually develop the ability to be physically distant from their caregiver ('separation'), while simultaneously developing a *psychological* sense of separate selfhood, which she termed 'individuation'. The ability to crawl, and then walk, enables children to explore their environment under their own steam. It also enables them to exercise their will in a far more decisive way than was possible when they depended entirely on a caregiver to pick them up and place them in a new spot. But walking can also make them *unsafe*, by taking them away from mother – hitherto the source of an infant's physical and emotional security. And so the toddler experiments. He moves away from mother, then rushes back to her side. He moves a bit further afield, looks round to reassure himself. He becomes used to being in another room, where mother is out of sight. 'Look,

Mummy, you can't see me!' he crows, meaning, quite often, 'I can't see *you!* (but I know you're there!)'. His triumphant remark is also a very early step towards the ability to imagine the world as someone else might see it. Cognitive psychologists refer to this, in its developed form, as 'theory of mind' – the realisation that others may not only *see* things differently, but also have thoughts and feelings that are completely separate from our own.[21]

Piaget described young children as 'egocentric'. He did not mean 'selfish', because to be selfish you have to be aware of others' needs and knowingly ignore them in favour of your own. Rather, he meant that infants and pre-school children tend to assume that everything that happens around them happens with reference to themselves: all of them are at the centre of their own 'universe'. A very young child assumes that 'if it happens to me, it must be about me. I must have somehow made it happen' (this is sometimes referred to as 'infantile omnipotence'). Today, we can understand this in terms of the early dominance of the right hemisphere, with its 'embodied self'. It is only as the left hemisphere of the cortex matures that young children *begin* to realise that the world has an existence quite separate from their own, that the sun does *not* go down 'so we can go to bed' (as Piaget's own child once told him).[22] But aspects of early egocentricity persist for years. Five- and six-years-olds often assume, for example, that if their parents separate, then it must be their own fault ('Daddy's gone away because I was bad'). Even when parents lovingly explain that this was not the case, the child is not convinced. The child genuinely believes that its own feelings and actions might 'cause' its parents to do dramatic things like leaving home – its left hemisphere has developed far enough to enable it to think in terms of cause and effect but its 'theory of mind' is still rudimentary. To imagine Mummy or Daddy's thoughts and feelings, it has to think in terms of its own, and so 'Daddy went away because I was bad' is not dissimilar to 'the sun goes down so we can go to sleep'.

Every one of us retains vestiges of this 'right hemisphere dominance' well into adult life. Coleridge, Lamartine and Hölderlin, the romantic poets of the period 1790 to 1820, wrote as if the natural world automatically resonated in sympathy with their own emotions – which, we can guess, is the way a baby feels. Adults subjected to extreme stress or trauma default to the same kind of egocentric thinking. Desperate to answer the question 'Why did this happen to me?' the accident victim, or the parent whose child has tragically died, searches for 'something I must have done' (or alternatively, demands that 'someone's got to pay!'). In such distress, we can all revert to three-year-old thinking, and it forms part of many emotional disturbances, including depression ('I must be a bad person because bad things are happening to me') and paranoia, where our own 'badness' gets comfortingly located in others ('I am a good person but evil forces are out to get me').

Piaget also noticed that a five-month-old child would lose interest in a ball as soon as it was removed from its sight, concluding from this behaviour that the ball had 'ceased to exist' as far as the child was concerned. Yet by three years old, the same child is clearly different. When the ball is taken away and hidden behind a chair, he heads purposefully for that same chair. When Mummy gets in the car and disappears for some time, he will start to become distressed if more time passes than usual before Mummy reappears, and will ask when she is coming back. The three-year-old can *remember* Mummy just as an adult can and, more to the point, he knows that she still exists even though she is not in his presence. And just as he knows that *she* exists, separate and distinct from him even though not concretely visible to him, *so he knows that he exists as a separate, distinct individual too*. Our awareness of ourselves develops simultaneously with our awareness of others, and each depends upon the other. Without the right kind of social interaction in infancy and early childhood, both our own selfhood, and our knowledge of others' selfhood, fails to evolve fully. The evolution of a child's self is choreographed intricately with the selves of those around it.

The inside and the outside

Silently, invisibly, a 'self' has grown during the period between 12 and 36 months. A four-year-old knows she is an individual, although typically, she can only answer the question 'Who are you?' by telling you her name, and that she is a girl. Five-year-olds can typically answer the question 'What are you going to be when you grow up?' Handsome, flaxen-haired 'Georgie' Patton was already convinced that he would be a soldier; shy, intense little Gustav Mahler said that he would be 'a martyr' (not surprising in a boy who was already achingly familiar with death); Claus von Stauffenberg, who was shot in 1944 for his part in the conspiracy to assassinate Hitler, thought that he would be 'a hero'. Most children answer the question less dramatically, and many identify future roles that are inappropriate or unlikely; yet the fact that they can answer at all shows that they are able to project their individuality into an unknown future: they can conceive of a 'life story' for themselves. The capacity to tell a story develops in parallel with the sense of possessing a separate self. Most five-year-olds can tell a coherent anecdote about something that happened to them, or to someone else ('episodic memory'). If they can't, this probably points to trauma (or to 'disorganised attachment', which may amount to much the same thing).[23]

Just as Margaret Mahler looked at the way children handled physical distance from their mothers in the process of learning to be autonomous 'selves', so we can look at the way in which a child responds to stories, and see evidence of evolving selfhood. One 18-month-old girl was briefly upset when she first heard the story of Little Red Riding Hood *because the wolf was killed*. The fact that the story ended happily for Red Riding Hood did not, as far as she was concerned, cancel out the wolf's death. There were many similar examples, where a happy ending failed to eliminate the distress caused to her by incidents along the way, even if those incidents happened to the story's villains, not its heroes! In these examples, the girl was not able to relate the part to the whole – as if each incident in the story were a miniature 'story' in itself. Perhaps, too, she did not 'identify' solely with Red Riding Hood as the story intends, but with the wolf as well. Such reactions are completely normal for children at that age.

By four, however, the same girl showed a completely different reaction, 'siding' with the heroine (or victim) rather than being seduced into sympathy for an evil-doer, and obviously understanding earlier incidents in the light of the story's ending. At 18 months, the girl had reacted to stories and pictures in unconnected 'bits' because, as it were, she experienced *herself* 'in bits'. Sometime around three-and-a-half years of age, she began experiencing her stories and pictures as 'wholes' because by then, she was a unified, indivisible 'self', capable of recognising and identifying with the 'self' of the story's heroine. At two or two-and-a-half, she would ask at the end of a story, 'and what happened then?' as if the story's closing words failed to satisfy her. To a child at this age, the right hemisphere's 'endless time' still prevails over the left hemisphere's linear time: 'conclusions' were not real to her. When she was four, she knew what the end of a story actually meant and, similarly, she was beginning to understand that human lives, too, come to an end eventually – though of course the full understanding of death takes many more years to develop in any child.[24]

The underlying psychoanalytic principle is that *what an individual does on the outside mirrors what is happening for that individual on the inside.* What we 'act out' in the world speaks volumes about the dramas that are being performed on the inner stage of our feelings and thoughts – as play therapists recognise. And throughout the human lifespan the same relationship between inside and outside prevails. The pattern of an individual's behaviour over time always says something about his or her inner life, although it may take intimate knowledge of the individual to perceive the connections. The language of actions speaks more truthfully than the language of words. Yet, as mature, language-using beings, we constantly fall into the trap of paying more attention to words than to behaviour. This is where the unaided left hemisphere can lead us astray: words can lie and conceal; repeated actions – the 'pattern' of which we may not recognise consciously – do not.

Psychoanalytic developmentalists have always understood that human beings do not simply learn *from* their parents: they *learn their parents.* Just as babies suck from their mother's breast, and later attempt to swallow any object of interest that comes within their grasp, so they 'swallow' entire patterns of behaviour, somehow taking inside themselves not just individual behaviours, but whole interactive sequences, along with the feelings with which they are associated. They are far too young to know what they are doing: it simply happens. This 'swallowing whole' again reflects the way that the right hemisphere perceives the world – seeing things in context, and not separating out the 'important bits' from the 'unimportant bits'. It is as if young children are programmed to save to their mental 'hard disk' not just attention-grabbing, dramatic bits of their caregivers' behaviour, but the context of that behaviour; not just Daddy's frightening clenched fists and loud, tense voice, but how he is standing, who else is in the room, even the temperature, or the smell of the food cooking on the stove.

When parents are saved ('internalised') in this way, things get complicated. Real parents change from moment to moment and, as the child matures, it comes to appreciate that they are people with needs and feelings of their own, human beings who are neither all good nor all bad. But 'saved' parents are likely to date from very early in a child's life, and so will comprise only those aspects of the real parents that the child could then understand and grasp. To a two-year-old, her parents are BIG and their emotions are HUGE. As we've seen, she does not properly understand that they are people distinct from her, and so she relates their loving or frightening actions mainly to herself. Just as the 18-month-old girl in our earlier example could grasp only 'bits' of stories at a time, so a two-year-old probably only grasps *bits* of her parents, and they will be the parents' *external appearance and actions*, not their internal feelings or motivations. The template she saves will contain a great deal of information, but it will be information interpreted and distorted by her own incomplete understanding and as-yet partial selfhood.

And so, at times of anger or panic in our adult lives, we all hear our own mouths utter words that we did not know we possessed, in a tone of voice that is not ours, while our bodies produce involuntarily actions that take us by surprise – flailing arms, stamping feet – even rocking, or hitting ourselves. No movie film exists to show us our own parents in their moments of anger or fear, and so it can never be decisively proved that we are doing what they did – but it seems plausible that we are. Like an animal swallowed whole by a boa constrictor, that bundle of actions and feelings bulges 'undigested' inside us, until the moment years later when something in our own marriage or parenting triggers our right hemisphere into *enacting* in the present a drama that once happened in our past – 'coughing it up', as it were, still alive. As adults we are shocked when this happens. 'But I *hated* it when my parents did that! Why would I ever want to *copy* it?' Whether we hated or loved a particular chunk of parental behaviour has nothing to do with whether we internalised it, for we internalise whatever crosses our personal threshold for emotional stimulus. The more dramatic the chunk of behaviour, the more likely many of us are to swallow it whole; and of course, if we are temperamentally thin boundaried, then almost everything crosses our threshold, and we will reproduce our parents' actions and moods from 20 or 30 years ago with uncanny power and precision. Once again, it is not a matter of morality, of goodness or badness. We do not *decide* to do it. We just do it. So we ought not be surprised when the 50-year-old leader of a political party explodes into a 'black rage' after an electoral reverse, stamps on the floor and screams at his loyal minders and assistants, blaming them for the 'failure' he now experiences. Under the overwhelming stress of seeing his ambitions crumble, he becomes, once again, a shamed toddler in an adult body, and his actions, in all probability, re-enact long-forgotten memories of what he saw his father (or mother) do, many years ago.

Those individuals whom therapists call 'narcissistic' never achieved closure on separation–individuation: for them, the curtain has not yet come down on that drama, and for many it has not even progressed beyond its first act. Where the average four- or five-year-old has already achieved sufficient separate selfhood to begin moderating her egocentricity, these individuals preserve into adulthood an inflated sense of their own importance. External objects, and *even other people*, are still experienced as *part of them*. They act as if others can be manipulated without consideration for their feelings and needs, just as a baby (quite rightly) expects to be fed and cared for without any awareness that its caregivers may be tired or ill. Yet when others criticise them, even mildly, such individuals react with rage, as if the cold water of disapproval were sufficient to dissolve them into nothing, like the Wicked Witch of the West. It is, I believe, *shame* that overwhelms them at such moments, shame that they never learned to tolerate as a child, and which they now keep at a distance through blaming attacks on others. Most political leaders have a strong component of narcissism. Many captains of business and industry exhibit the same grandiosity and childish egocentricity. Many of those who rise to the top in sober professions like medicine, law or even academia are just as narcissistic, though they may have learned to conceal their naked ambition behind apparent self-deprecation.

It is hard to believe that narcissists' outward appearance of success and confidence conceals an inner hollowness, that the balloon of their inflated selfhood is just a little bit of limp plastic stretched around empty air. Yet their very egocentricity makes it possible for them to lay bare their primitive emotional worlds without real awareness of how their confessions might strike others. In early diaries and letters to his father, the youthful Georgie Patton left us a repetitive portrait of his grandiose dreams of glory and his equally massive self-doubt. There could be no clearer picture of the inner world of the narcissist. How did Georgie come to be this way? As we saw in the last chapter, his temperamental sensitivity rendered him vulnerable to hurt and failure, but that alone did not predict that he would be a narcissist. Both his parents poured love and praise upon him, while also letting him know that his family expected great things from him. His especial protector was his 'Aunt Nannie', who refused to let him be punished for any misdemeanour – and read aloud to him books about Alexander the Great and Napoleon. So Georgie's doting family encouraged grand ambitions in their son, *while also shielding him from a realistic experience of failure*. He grew up without any objective standard against which to evaluate his self-doubt. He continued to expect others to support his fragile ego, salve his wounded pride and forgive his mistakes. His father played that role throughout his adolescence; then his wife Beatrice played it till the day he died.[25]

Sons and lovers

Sigmund Freud was much preoccupied with his childhood relationship with his mother. He had been her special son, and she favoured him blatantly over his younger siblings. Far younger than his father, Freud's mother was only 23 when she gave birth to him, and so his early childhood memories of her were of youth and beauty. He was nearly four when he saw her naked once, in the family sleeping compartment on an overnight train journey, and that image stayed in his mind forever afterwards. It is not really surprising, then, that a middle-aged Freud might propose the theory that all sons feel for their mothers an attraction that is partly erotic, and therefore experience a corresponding anger against a father who seems a 'rival' for their mother's affections. (Freud called his theory the 'Oedipus complex' because in the Greek myth, Oedipus unwittingly kills his father and beds his mother.) Conversely, Freud decided, a girl would feel a similar semi-erotic bond with her father, and resent the mother who shares her bed with him and bears him children (the 'Electra complex'). According to Freud, these dynamics flourish between the ages of three and five. The child's conflict is resolved by a kind of 'giving up'. The little boy abandons his hope of possessing his mother, and instead decides that growing up to be a man like his father will enable him, some day, to have a woman of his own. The little girl resigns herself to not being able to monopolise Daddy, and models herself on her mother so that she can one day have a man who will be hers.

Of all Freud's controversial theories, none has provoked more hostility or derision than this one. Feelings of loyalty and respect towards our parents make it almost impossible for many of us to admit to such feelings, and the inaccessibility of our earliest memories makes it impossible for us to verify them. In today's climate of community outrage about child sexual abuse, any theory that appears to suggest that incestuous attractions are in any way natural can hardly command widespread approval. Yet we do not have to agree with every aspect of Freud's theory to acknowledge that he seemed to have grasped an uncomfortable truth. Typically, mothers *do* bond strongly with their first sons, just as the stereotype would predict. Typically, fathers do the same with their eldest daughters. Of course there are exceptions, but it happens far too often to be merely coincidental. It is not for nothing that our language speaks of a 'Mummy's boy' or a 'Daddy's girl': they correspond to an observable reality. 'My best gal' was how Elvis Presley referred to his mother.[26] What Freud was really getting at was that parent–child alliances are likely to be ignited by what is, at base, a biologically based sexual attraction – of course he did not mean that five-year-olds desired intercourse with their opposite sex parent in an adult, genital way. What he meant was that they wanted to 'have', to 'possess' them, exclusively. Little Elvis Presley actually *occupied* the pillow that should have been his father's until he was 12, a behaviour that psychologists now quaintly describe as 'co-sleeping'. Our parents – unless they are particularly frightening and abusive, and sadly, sometimes even then – are our first love objects. Though we may forget how beautiful, how exciting, they once seemed in our eyes, the memories remain buried there for 15 or 20 years until, as adulthood commences, they influence us once again, 'across a crowded room', an influence all the more powerful for being totally out of our awareness.

Of course many adults assert that they love their parents equally, and that is their experience. But the complexities of child–parent feelings are not so easily swept aside. Children, after all, see their parents with the very partial, self-related vision which we talked about earlier. A child may indeed *love* both her parents, but she often feels instinctively more *in sympathy* with one than with the other. Jill Ker knew that both her parents loved her, yet she could not entirely forget being told that her mother had not originally wanted another baby. There was always a reserve there, although Jill does not tell us precisely whether it came before, or after, the knowledge that she had initially been unwanted:

> Her voice was cheerful, positive and relaxed as she hugged me warmly. I recall the comfort and security of being sung to sleep and also some tentative efforts to struggle out of the warm embrace . . . The tweed coat my mother was wearing as she cradled me scratched and prickled, so that mixed in with the security was a sense of being ill at ease.[27]

It was her father whom she instinctively turned to, modelling her interests on his, talking with him as adult to adult.

Freud's 'Oedipal' dynamics emerge more powerfully, and more destructively, in families where the parents are already in open or covert conflict. Little Gustav Mahler became his sick mother's ally against a violent father (who nevertheless admired and nurtured Gustav's musical talent). Children's author Enid Blyton was repeatedly told by her father that he alone had saved her from death when she had been seriously ill as an infant. He had held her in his arms all night long, willing her to live, he said, and by morning, the crisis was over. No doubt this story reinforced the strong hero-worship the little Enid already felt for him, reinforced her sense of specialness, and reinforced, too, the instinctive wariness she felt towards her less gratifying, more critical mother.[28]

But how would parent–child alliances run in a family where there are several offspring of the same sex? In such families, the siblings still bond differentially with one parent or the other but now, of necessity, fewer of the alliances will be cross-gender. If an elder daughter bonds with her father, then a younger daughter may well bond with her mother. If an elder son is closely allied with the mother, then his next brother will tend to bond with the father, and the third brother with the mother again. That was the pattern of my father's family of origin, where the first and third brothers were allied with the mother, and the middle brother with the father. This suggests that Freud was only partly right: the bonding between parent and child is not only about quasi-sexual attraction, but also about *being different from one's siblings*, 'emigrating' to a space that is not already taken. Both/and is usually a truer explanation than either/or.[29] I should add that the view just presented is supported by clinical and anecdotal evidence rather than by 'hard' data. The same goes for the whole question of the effects of birth order on personality, where recent research has failed to support the widely accepted view that eldests are 'bossy', middle children feel overlooked and youngests are irresponsible 'free spirits'. To be more precise, studies have found that birth order positions do correlate with personality types – but only minimally.[30] This may, of course, be due to the inherent difficulties of self-report questionnaires: how many eldests would be prepared to describe themselves as bossy, how many middle children would admit to feeling 'unsure of who they are', and so on? *Perceived birth order* ('functional birth order' in the family therapy literature) may be more influential on a child's later behaviour than *actual* birth order – hence a child who is the oldest in the 'younger half' of a large family may feel like an eldest more than she feels like a middle – especially if there is a considerable gap between her and her next-oldest sibling.

Siblings and spaces

Not only do siblings differ genetically, their environment is also different – different in that the parents of each new sibling are older, and altered to some degree by the experience of having parented their preceding children, as well as by whatever else has happened to them since the earlier births. In that sense, a younger child does *not* have exactly the same parents as her older brother or sister. In a large family, with children spaced out over many years, such differences can be marked: a 45-year-old father cannot possibly be the person he was at 25, though of course there will be enduring characteristics (probably temperamental in origin) that have not changed. A younger child's environment also differs *as a result of the presence of older siblings.* To be born into a family where one is the first, or only, child is to learn language and behaviour direct from parents. To learn to speak and behave from older siblings as well as from parents is to access much more diverse models, and often, to feel permission to be more 'childlike'. To have many older siblings is clearly different from having only one; to be in the middle, sandwiched between both older and younger siblings, is also different.

But, most of all, younger children are influenced by the fact that their older siblings have already established personalities, with clear traits, recognised and commented upon by parents; they have talents and abilities in certain directions, as a result of their temperamental inheritance; and they probably also have existing alliances with parents. I've proposed that where an older child is bonded more strongly with one parent, the next in line will more likely bond strongly with the other. In a very similar way, younger siblings will tend to steer clear of developing traits that are already strongly displayed by an older sibling, and instead will favour traits that are less obviously represented in existing family members. This process is not a conscious one, at least, not at the beginning.

In his magisterial study *Born to Rebel*, Frank Sulloway argues that younger siblings may be *biologically* driven to compete for parental attention, and to establish themselves as being decisively different is one way of claiming such attention.[31] Given that siblings already differ genetically, and that their individual temperaments will offer each considerable scope for variation even when they share traits with others, this seems like another instance of environment confirming heredity instead of contradicting it. Siblings will unconsciously favour the characteristics in their own nature that will render them different and special: after all, who wants to be a clone of an older brother or sister? Often, these same characteristics will appeal to the parent with whom you find yourself in alliance, so that being different from a sibling may also bring you closer to 'your' parent. Sibling differentiation extends beyond temperamental qualities and talents, however. Time and again, you will find that if an elder sibling is already established as 'good', then a younger sibling will tend to be 'bad' – whatever those things might mean in a particular family.

Left as the elder two of four by the sudden death of their two older sisters, Charlotte and Branwell Brontë fell into such a predictable opposition. Charlotte, originally the third daughter, now became the 'responsible eldest', trying hard (mostly) to do her duty, and displaying a fierce loyalty to her father's conservative politics. In the imaginary world the Brontë children jointly created in their tiny, handwritten 'books' and 'newspapers', Charlotte's heroes were the 'iron' Duke of Wellington and his two sons. But Branwell forged a very different fictional hero. Long before he left home and began to slide downhill into dissipation, he invented the character of 'Alexander Rogue', also known as 'Badman' – a drinker, a plotter and a rebel. It was as if he *knew* who he was to become in adult life.[32]

While the principle of sibling differentiation ought to, and often does, imply that each sibling will develop its individuality to the maximum, Sulloway also argues for a more general factor that separates all first-borns from all later-borns – regardless of the latters' precise birth order position. Later-borns, he says, have *more incentive to embrace change* than first-borns. His close study of scientific innovators across hundreds of years seems to lend strong support to this idea. First-borns do tend towards conservatism, rule-policing and exercising power and control (in business and politics, as well as in the realm of knowledge and ideas). It is later-borns who, for good biological reasons, are more likely to develop new ideas, create, break rules and boundaries, and vote for change – although of course, simply being born later does not necessarily make one a radical in any profound sense, just as being born first does not automatically make one a conservative.

In young adulthood many people would have described me (the eldest of three) as 'born to rebel', a classic 'radical youngest'; yet as a child, many of my fantasies revolved around the exercise of power, military or political, and my choice of two four-star generals among the case studies for this book, along-side a swag of musicians, writers and artists, is proof that that preoccupation continued. As I grew closer to the age of the parents I remembered from middle childhood, I came increasingly to see myself as I saw them then. In my own eyes, I was a conservative, dismayed by the dissolution of the values and traditions that had formed my parents and through which they, in turn, formed me.

Now we are five

The left hemisphere of the cerebral cortex continues to mature rapidly during the years between two and five. What does this mean, exactly? In terms of language, most five- and six-year-olds can speak fluently, although some may be unable to articulate their words clearly. They communicate effectively. Moreover, they are starting to *think* in words. Talking about something helps a five- or six-year-old to understand it: putting a puzzling, painful or interesting experience into words enables the child to work out what she thinks about it. Adults have used language in this way for so long that it seems second nature to them – but it is a revolutionary discovery for a young child, whose 'thinking' has previously been in the instinctive, holistic, feeling-governed mode of the right hemisphere (Freud's 'primary process'). The balance between *feeling* and *thinking* ('affect' and 'cognition', in the language of science) has shifted in favour of the latter.

In terms of *time*, a five-year-old has moved well beyond the 'endless present' of the infant, and can distinguish past, present and future. He can not only remember past occurrences, but tell a coherent story of something that happened yesterday, or last Christmas ('episodic memory'). He has some idea of how time passes, and how long it will be until *next* Christmas, or until 'I go to big school'. He can anticipate future events on the basis of past experiences, and imagine futures for himself – albeit in a rudimentary way that has more to do with actions and appearances ('outside') than personality or aptitudes ('inside').

In terms of reasoning, the five- or six-year-old has begun to think in much the same way as adults do – she is starting to analyse the relationship between individual bits of experience, to see events as connected by cause and effect. As long as the child is dealing with things that are concrete and familiar (food, household objects, toys, animals) she can think logically about them ('operate' on them mentally, as opposed to manipulating them with her mouth or hands). 'What do you think the dog will do if you take its food outside?' 'The dog might go outside too!' 'Why would it do that?' 'Because it knows the food's outside, not in here anymore!' That example shows logical predictions based on the child's existing knowledge of how dogs behave, and how one change may lead to another, logically linked to the first.

Significantly, a child nearing school age can *lie* ('Johnny, did you make that mess?' 'No, it wasn't me!'). What psychologists call 'falsifying cognition' typically becomes possible around the age of four. But children have learned to lie with their facial expressions or bodies ('falsifying affect') much earlier – in the second half of the second year of life. For example, avoidantly attached children fake a smile when they are actually distressed or angry, in order to keep a critical parent 'on side'. It may seem a little bizarre to see lying as a 'development', but it is – for it points to the child's growing capacity to *inhibit* its natural responses in response to a perceived threat. The ability to inhibit behaviour will continue to develop in response to the maturation of the frontal lobes of both the right and the left hemispheres of the cortex – an ability that will continue to develop for many years to come. In our early ability to lie, we can see an important example of human complexity. We can feel something but pretend that we do not feel it; we can know something, but use our words to deny that we know it; indeed we can even convince ourselves, along with others, of our falsified thoughts and feelings – as was fascinatingly demonstrated in the TV series *Lie to Me*, based on the real-life research of psychologist Paul Ekman. We know that 'the body does not lie' – but so dominated are we by our ability to use language that we override our half-unconscious perception of others' body cues in favour of believing what they *say*.

Jean Piaget's research investigated the gradual process by which children came to be able to reason 'scientifically', as adults (some adults, anyway!) do. Though he did not think in terms of the differential functions of the two cerebral hemispheres, it was essentially left hemisphere maturation that he was concerned with. Piaget described a key transition period which he called the 'Five-to-Seven Shift', during which the child increasingly became capable of mental 'operations' (thought processes), and, bit by bit, shed the animistic, pictorial 'thinking' which we have seen to be characteristic of a dominant right hemisphere. Piaget's shift occurs during the time that most children complete their first two or three years of school. On the one hand, it prepares them for the kinds of activities school will demand of them; on the other, school activities will support and enhance the 'shift' within the individual child. By seven, most children basically think in much the same way as we do.

Yet even clever seven-year-olds are very limited in their ability to articulate their inner world in language. 'What was it like when that boy called you names?' 'I ran away'. 'How do you feel when you hear Mummy and Daddy shouting at each other?' 'I go and hide under my doona'. These children are reporting their actions, not articulating their feelings. It will be years yet before the average school-aged child is able to answer more fully, and with greater insight into its own feelings and behaviours. This is why play therapy evolved, for as we've repeatedly seen, the ways of thinking typical of infancy do not completely go away. Even children beginning elementary school are more easily able to *show* us what they think and feel in their play with dolls and toys, in the pictures they draw, than they are to *tell* us about those thoughts and feelings. When left to play with a wide range of different materials, and without instructions as to *how* to play with them, children will, in the presence of an interested but non-controlling adult therapist, tell us the 'true story' of their inner world. In sand-tray work, children will *automatically* select figures, creatures and objects to represent their family members, or their schoolmates, so that an angry Dad becomes a fire-breathing dragon, or a friendly looking dog becomes a supportive older sister. Their play with such figures – endless, repetitive dramas full of threat and safety, fear and protection, aggression and conciliation – re-creates the right hemisphere world of early childhood, a world in which words are of only secondary importance, for the real message is embodied in characters and actions. These enacted 'stories' communicate the child's inner life in an emotional depth that no set of questions asked by a researcher, therapist or parent could ever elicit. If the child has endured major trauma (such as sexual abuse), that trauma will be played out in symbolic form, over and over again. It is almost unknown for children to 'lie' in play therapy, though their play may contain defences against their own awareness of painful or distressing experiences.[33]

By the time the 'five to seven shift' is complete, a child will be displaying most of the elements of its fully developed *personality*, a personality formed around its temperamental traits, but substantially modified by its attachment style, its gender, the 'modelling' provided by its parents, its birth-order position, and the values, attitudes and practices of its social atom (usually, its birth family), which in turn reflect the values and practices of its social class, ethnic group and culture. In the last chapter, I deliberately emphasised the genetic basis of personality, because (at least until recently) this has often been downplayed or ignored by experts, and most of all by therapists. But I hope I have also indicated how important environmental influences are, in both *reinforcing* some of a child's genetic potentials, and in *inhibiting* or modifying others. Margaret Roberts (as she then was) did not have to end up as Prime Minister of Great Britain: both her birth order (younger of two girls) and her gender could have lessened her chances of that. But Margaret was almost certainly a thick-boundaried individual. Her autobiography contains hardly a word of self-doubt or self-questioning. She *knew* she was right. Her family environment had reinforced her genetic qualities, encouraged her high self-esteem, and smoothed her 'path to power'.[34] When her grasp on it slipped, as we'll see later in this book, her lifelong belief in herself began to falter.

Notes

1 See Jerry Mander, *Four Arguments for the Elimination of Television*, NY, Morrow, 1978: 141–142. Mander was a former adman, and his book is a polemic rather than a scientifically supported argument; nevertheless, he makes many telling points and his book, now largely forgotten, remains worth reading.
2 'Field memories' versus 'Observer memories': see Daniel L. Schacter, *Searching for Memory: The Brain, the Mind and the Past*, NY, Basic Books, 1996: 21–22.
3 T. S. Eliot, *Collected Poems 1909–1962*, London, Faber, 1962: 189–190.
4 All details of Gustav Mahler's 'first world' from Henri-Louis de la Grange, *Mahler* (Vol I), NY, Doubleday, 1973.
5 William Wordsworth, 'Ode: Intimations of Immortality from Recollections of Early Childhood', first published in 1807, but written between 1802 and 1804, when Wordsworth was in his early thirties: lines 1–5.
6 'Under the Garden': see Graham Greene, *A Sense of Reality*, Harmondsworth, Penguin, 1968: 9–64. [First published in 1963.]
7 See Paul D. MacLean, *The Triune Brain in Evolution, Role in Paleocerebral Functions*, NY, Plenum, 1990. MacLean's 'triune brain' (three brains in one) concept has since been challenged, and it should be remembered that all three 'brains' are densely interconnected, with great duplication of functions.
8 See Jaak Panksepp and Lucy Biven, *The Archaeology of Mind: Neuroevolutionary Origins of Human Emotions*, NY, Norton, 2012: 491.
9 See Panksepp and Biven, 2012, op. cit.: 95–144.
10 Cook made this claim following his early Newfoundland expedition, and long before he explored the Pacific in his great voyages of exploration.
11 'Proximity seeking' and 'separation anxiety' are John Bowlby's terms; 'panic/grief' is Panksepp's (see Panksepp and Biven, 2012, op. cit.: 311–350).
12 In using the name 'Old Brain' I follow a number of others including Paul D. MacLean, 'Man and his Animal Brains', *Modern Medicine*, 3 February 1964; and most recently,

Bessel van der Kolk, *The Body Keeps the Score: Mind, Brain and Body in the Transformation of Trauma*, London, Allen Lane, 2014.

13 All details of the specialised functions of the right and left hemispheres of the cerebral cortex are from Iain McGilchrist, *The Master and his Emissary: The Divided Brain and the Making of the Western World*, London/New Haven, Yale University Press, 2009: 32–93.

14 See Daniel N. Stern, *Diary of a Baby*, NY, Basic Books, 1990: 31–43.

15 'Blooming, buzzing confusion': a term first employed by William James in *The Principles of Psychology*, Cambridge, MA, Harvard University Press, 1981: 462 and much quoted since. [*Principles* was originally published in 1890.]

16 The distinction between linear time and 'cyclic' time was introduced by John Bleibtreu in *The Parable of the Beast*, London, Paladin, 1970: 38–83 [first published in 1968]; it is continued in Stephen Jay Gould's *Time's Arrow, Time's Cycle: Myth and Metaphor in the Discovery of Geological Time*, Cambridge, MA, Harvard University Press, 1987.

17 'Temporarily anaesthetised': this refers to the so-called 'split brain experiments' which commenced in the 1970s. See McGilchrist, 2009, op. cit.

18 See Donald Nathanson's *Shame and Pride: Affect, Sex and the Birth of the Self*, NY, Norton, 1992. In this lucidly written book, Nathanson makes much use of Silvan Tomkins' pioneering studies of emotions (published in the three volumes of *Affect/Imagery/Consciousness*, NY, Springer, 1962; 1963; 1991).

19 This is the controversial but persuasive argument put forward by Patricia McKinsey Crittenden in *Raising Parents: Attachment, Parenting and Child Safety*, London, Routledge, 2008.

20 For an up to date summary of our current knowledge of how early stress and trauma affect the growing brain, see Bessel van der Kolk, *The Body Keeps the Score: Mind, Brain and Body in the Transformation of Trauma*, London, Allen Lane, 2014: 51–104.

21 Margaret Mahler's best-known work is probably *The Psychological Birth of the Human Infant: Symbiosis and Individuation* (with Fred Pine and Anni Bergman), London, Karnac, 1985. [First published in 1975].

22 Jean Piaget, *The Child's Conception of the World*, trans. Joan and Andrew Tomlinson, London, Paladin, 1973: 236ff. [First published in 1926.]

23 See Endel Tulving, 'Episodic and Semantic Memory' in E. Tulving and W. Donaldson (Eds), *Organization of Memory*, NY, Academic Press, 1972: 381–403. The inability to tell a coherent story of one's childhood experience is considered to be an indicator of possible trauma and/or disrupted attachment in the assessment procedure for the Adult Attachment Interview (developed by Carol George, Nancy Kaplan and Mary Main in 1984).

24 See Maureen Crago, unpublished record 24 May 1975: MS p. 134; Maureen and Hugh Crago, *Prelude to Literacy: A Preschool Child's Encounter with Picture and Story*, Southern Illinois University Press, 1983: 234–239.

25 See Carlo D'Este, *A Genius for War: A Life of General George S. Patton*, NY, HarperCollins, 1995.

26 Details of Elvis Presley's life and personality from Peter Whitmer's *The Inner Elvis: A Psychological Biography of Elvis Aaron Presley*, NY, Hyperion, 1996. See also the more recent authoritative two volume biography of Presley by Peter Guralnik, *Last Train to Memphis: The Rise of Elvis Presley*, Boston, Little, Brown, 1994, and *Careless Love: The Unmaking of Elvis Presley*, Boston, Back Bay Books, 1999.

27 See *The Road from Coorain: A Memoir*, Sydney, William Heinemann, 1989: 20.

28 See Barbara Stoney, *Enid Blyton: The Biography*, 2nd Edn, London, Hodder & Stoughton, 1992.

29 Freud's early associate, Alfred Adler, was the first to formulate a theory of the effect of birth order on later personality. More recently, Walter Toman's *Family Constellation: Its Effects on Personality and Social Behaviour*, 4th Edn, NY, Springer, 1961, has elaborated considerably upon that basis.

30 See for example Rodica Iona Damian and Brent W. Roberts, 'The Associations of Birth Order with Personality and Intelligence in a Representative Sample of US High School Students', *Journal of Research in Personality*, 58 (2015): 96–105; Julia M. Rohrer, Boris Egloff and Stefan C. Schmukle, 'Examining the Effects of Birth Order on Personality', *Proceedings of the National Academy of Science of the United States of America*, 25 September 2015, www.pnas.org (accessed 31 October 2015).
31 Frank Sulloway, *Born to Rebel: Birth Order, Family Dynamics and Creative Lives*, Boston, Little, Brown, 1996.
32 All details of the Brontë siblings from Juliet Barker, *The Brontës*, London, Weidenfeld and Nicholson, 1994.
33 Play therapy was used by child psychoanalyst Melanie Klein in 1955: see 'The Psycho-Analytic Play Technique: Its History and Significance' in *Envy and Gratitude and Other Works, 1946–1963*, London, Vintage, 1997; the classic text is Virginia Axline's *Dibs: In Search of Self*, NY, Ballantine, 1964.
34 Margaret Thatcher, *The Path to Power*, London, HarperCollins, 1995.

4

WIDENING HORIZONS

Pre-school to high school

Nourishment and selfhood

By the age of four or five, children have long since outgrown their infant diet and are tackling a wide range of foods. Yet already, many of them are addicted – to sugar and salt. Like drugs of addiction proper, both these innocuous substances alter behaviour, if only mildly. A bag of highly salted crisps elevates blood pressure, lowers levels of 'good cholesterol' and creates a thirst that is typically quenched with a sugared soft drink. Large quantities of sugar, in turn, make children restless, over-energised, and (as the sugar high wears off) prone to emotional over-reactions.[1] The institutionalisation of sugar and salt in our diet for the past several hundred years thus has a side-effect of which most of us are completely unaware: it intensifies the restlessness and quick shifts of mood that are typical of many children on the threshold of school, and prolongs them beyond the point at which they would otherwise decline. The almost universal association between children and sweets lays a foundation not only for later problems with obesity, tooth decay (for those who don't grow up with fluoridated water) and type 2 diabetes, but also for the widespread use of sugar-laden foods as emotional comforters. When adults want children to be quiet or compliant, they tend to offer sweets. Intense, immediate gratification is what sugar provides, a sort of substitute for the breast to which the same child once turned for comfort and nourishment – except that babies have to *work* at the breast, whereas ingesting sugar requires no effort. Our very words betray us: it is not coincidental that 'sugar' and 'honey' are lovers' endearments. Yet sugar offers pleasure without nourishment: thus is laid the foundation for caffeine, nicotine, alcohol – and for some, marijuana, cocaine, heroin and crystal meth.

Already, the ways in which four- and five-year-olds interact with food and drink are starting to fall into individual patterns. Once again, what the child does to the external world reveals something of what is happening inside. Children who temperamentally embrace new experiences will have positive expectations of new foods and readily try them; fearful, easily overwhelmed children will hang back, and a single negative experience of a particular food may result in their unwillingness ever to try it again. Children who will later struggle with eating disorders may be eating enough at six, but already, they are narrowing their options down to a small range of preferred foods. Children whose sense of selfhood is compromised or uncertain are consistently leaving food on their plate or drink in their glass, almost like an external sign of the incompleteness they feel within.[2]

Alliances with parents can be expressed through food preferences, and so can a child's differentiation of itself from its siblings. As an eldest child, I began drinking tea very early, not because I particularly liked it at first, but because I saw it as desirably 'grown up'. It made me part of my parents' world. Of that much I was fully conscious at the age of six, but I was unconscious of the way that tea drinking allied me with my mother (since at the time my father generally favoured coffee). Neither my brother nor my sister followed me in embracing tea, either then or later. They have always simply said that they 'didn't like' tea or coffee, but was this also their way of being different from me – and from *both* our parents? In my case, my early devotion to tea drinking eventuated in a lifelong caffeine addiction. Even now, in my late sixties, I need my 'maintenance dose' of two coffees a day.

Yet by the time they are ready to go to school, children have already absorbed far more from their families than simply their food and drink preferences. On top of inaccessible memories of the lost time before language, on top of emotional templates stored from infancy, children have also been influenced, again without fully realising it, by the *overt* values of their families and immediate communities. These values can substantially modify their temperamental inheritance. How might my grandfather Albert's genetic restlessness (hyperactivity?) have developed had he not been raised in a family where hard work and responsibility was expected of everyone? Would the three Brontë girls have expressed their intense emotional lives in writing had their father not been a man who himself had dabbled in verse and story-writing, as well as being a frequent writer to newspapers?[3] Would Margaret Roberts have fallen so easily into a political career had she not served an apprenticeship in local politics while still a schoolgirl, because her father was Mayor?[4]

Families both teach and model. As every parent knows, teaching in the absence of direct parental example is fruitless ('Do what I say, not what I do!') but parents who 'practise what they preach' are a powerful influence on a child – particularly one already allied with that parent. We do not learn *from* them; we learn *them* – we hear the words they say, but we also internalise the ways they act. Attitudes to duty and pleasure, to spirituality and sexuality, to sickness and health, to maleness and femaleness – all these things are going to affect children strongly, in ways that they will not be fully aware of until they raise children of their own. Whether a sensitive child grows up believing that his suffering is 'a cross to bear' or grows up angrily railing at a world that has mistreated him may make the difference between a future as a dutiful churchgoer and a career as a criminal or a terrorist. None of these things will change a child's temperament, but they can make a dramatic difference to the way in which it is channelled.

'Shades of the prison house begin to close . . .'

If birth is the first migration then, for many children, beginning school is the second. Once again, a familiar, unquestioned world must be left, and a wider, more alien, less reliable world must be encountered and mastered. Once again, the transition is not voluntary. As muscular contractions push a baby from the womb, as parent birds force a fledgling to flex its wings, so the bus or the family car takes the child to her first day at school.

However, going to school is far from being a simple repetition of birth. First, the new world of school does not replace and blot out the old one; rather, both school and home will be part of the child's experience for the next ten or 12 years. Both worlds can be experienced together, contrasted daily. Humans learn best and most powerfully from repeated experiences of comparison, something Gregory Bateson called 'news of difference'.[5] They learn how the rules differ when you are with different people, they learn about their own personality by observing how two different sets of people respond to that personality ('My parents are proud of me, but the other kids think I'm stuck up'), they learn about their limits and potentials by testing themselves in two different environments – and some of them, at least, may begin to learn how different cultural groups see the world in very different ways.

Second, the transition from home to school is a *conscious* landmark. When children attend school for the first time they know what is happening to them, even though they cannot know fully what to expect. They can remember what parents or older siblings have told them – and feel pleasantly surprised (or shocked) if those predictions fail to come true. They can form mental images to help them anticipate change, and to cope with the temporary loss of their familiar caregivers. They can be *knowingly* excited, or *knowingly* afraid – though they may not be able to articulate those feelings particularly well. Whether a child looks forward to school as an adventure or shrinks in anticipation of threat and loss will depend a great deal on her temperament, and on how well her family has been able to anticipate its requirements. Many adults remember their first day at school more vividly and reliably than almost anything else in their first five or six years. For those who are temperamentally shy, the first day at school may even set a pattern for all later social encounters. Adult after adult recalls how she cried miserably at the school gate, or wet her pants when faced with the strangeness of the new place and its thronging, noisy, apparently confident inhabitants. At the time, these children probably experienced their personal shames and fears as unique. Only much later would they come to realise that many others had felt similarly. Some thin-boundaried adults never learn to see themselves in the wider perspective: their childhood hurts, great or small, real or imagined, dominate their entire lives. Most of us grow past them, but they remain, nonetheless, lodged deep in our memories, to be reactivated much later, usually at times of crisis and vulnerability.

The starkness of the transition from home to school, as it used to be experienced by six-year-olds, has been softened considerably for today's children. The advent of pre-schooling means that children can be introduced gradually to some of the features of school a year or two before their formal education begins. The old day of reckoning, on which a child approached the frowning gates of the 'big school' with trepidation, is either no longer with us, or is deferred until the later transition to high school. Yet it remains a landmark for many children even now.

Western societies have successfully brainwashed their citizens into believing that schooling exists mainly to prepare children for higher education or the workforce. School was traditionally the place where a child learned how to read and write, master arithmetic, and gained some basic knowledge of its own society – its geography, history and governance. Yet the *lasting* effects of schooling, even then, had less to do with the acquisition of particular skills and knowledge than with accustoming the young of our society to what they would spend most of their adult lives doing. Schooling occupied the bulk of children's daylight hours; those same hours, plus or minus a few, would later be occupied by paid work. School, where children learned to do what they are told, and to busy themselves for long periods of time on activities which were not of their choice, was practice for the tedium of work. School, like adult life, contains hierarchies, systems of laws ('rules') and competitiveness – some imposed by teachers and some generated by children themselves. But from the point of view of family and individual development, school provided a bridge between home and world, where children could gradually learn to cope with individuals very different from themselves, to master a complex system of expectations, to stay (more or less) within rules and boundaries. In this environment they could practise forming attachments outside their families, and were able to test out their talents and motivations against a range of possible futures: school was more about *social learning* than academic knowledge or work-related skills.

Since the computer began its drive to dominate the world, digital technologies have reduced the need for what were once called the 'three Rs' to a point where store clerks/sales assistants rely on a calculator to add and subtract, and university students no longer know how to construct a lucid, grammatically correct sentence. What happens at school depends more and more on interaction with screens, on searching for information (increasingly pictorial) via the Internet, and on spelling that is automatically 'corrected' by word-processing software so that (in theory, at least) it emerges faultless. Yet, despite massive changes in the curriculum and in learning methods, social learning continues to be what children take away with them from school, rather than skills or knowledge.

Curiously, some of the things that children most resent in their schooling will later seem like old, familiar clothing. The rituals of assemblies, flag ceremonies, prize nights and school sports carnivals do not deeply engage many children. Few of us listened intently to the words of dubious wisdom that our principals, teachers and visiting dignitaries offered us, few of us thought deeply about the oaths, promises and prayers we were required to voice. Yet these things seemed somehow to sink in and, many years later, when we are 50- or 60-year-old adults, we will offer similar sentiments, in much the same sententious tones, to our grandchildren – or even to a new generation of school children, when we ourselves have become 'visiting dignitaries'. Those who insist on such public rituals for children between six and 12 are smarter than we once thought. The rituals we ignored at the time, then rejected openly in late adolescence and early adulthood, will experience a late, faint resurrection when our youthful faith in our ability to remake the future is starting to fail, and what is familiar seems suddenly comfortable and reassuring. What is taken inside us at the stage of middle childhood is the *outward show* of society's order: rules, norms, conventional wisdom, respect for authority. It has little to do with individually discovered political or religious convictions, which must normally wait for adolescence, but a great deal to do with knowing how to behave and what to say.

The cradle of pathology?

We have already seen how the temperamentally thin-boundaried child may face big challenges in the transition from home to school. Yet arguably an even greater hurdle faces children whose temperament predisposes them to a very high level of physical activity. They are usually boys, a fact that demonstrates once again how environment tends to enhance (rather than diminish) biological differences. The faster-maturing brains of girls enable them, on average, to 'sit still' and concentrate earlier than boys of the same age; but by the same token, parents typically *expect* boys to be energetic and active, excusing even excessive restlessness with 'boys will be boys', while most girls are socialised much earlier into stillness and compliance. Hence many restless or 'hyperactive' children are often identified as problems only when they commence school. Even pre-school, with its less exacting requirements and greater freedom to roam, can provoke harried teachers to complain that such children are 'uncontrollable'.

I vividly remember my younger daughter's pre-school, where the resident problem child was a handsome four-year-old named Trenton. Trenton wandered around the room while the others sat (relatively) still on the mat at story time. He ignored requests to sit down, interfered with his classmates when they were trying to paint, and eventually scored his greatest triumph: flushing the preschool's pet goldfish down the toilet. None of this behaviour seemed aggressively motivated or deliberately disruptive, but it certainly created problems for the smooth running of the pre-school. As always happens, the other children watched what he was doing rather than listening to their teacher, and formed a shocked or admiring audience for the drama of the goldfish.

What went wrong for Trenton? His extremely high activity level (a temperamental factor, probably exacerbated by sugary foods and drinks) was part of the problem, because his new social environment could not easily cope with a free-range boy. However, Trenton was also a temperamentally confident, sociable child, something that was potentially both good and bad for him. He found it easy to win little friends and gain adult trust, so he would be given second chance after second chance; his behaviour seemed daring, inventive, even glamorous, in part because he was charming, in part because he was good looking. So Trenton's lack of impulse control, his short attention span (another trait with temperamental foundations) and his failure to respect the needs of others could, for a time, be downplayed or excused. He elicited from adults (and ultimately from other children) either negative, judgemental responses, or uncritical adoration – but not the balance of caring and firmness that he most needed. Trenton's mother always described him, half-loving, half-exasperated, as 'a strong-willed little spunk' (an inappropriately sexualised term for a small boy, of course – what would Freud have said!). But as soon as he reached pre-school, she began receiving worried reports from the staff about her son's 'attention-seeking behaviour' or even his 'aggression'. Why? Because the pre-school environment required a much more exacting set of limits than she had imposed on him. Because Trenton, for all his appearance of *sang-froid*, almost certainly experienced 'stimulus overload' at pre-school. This new world, with its alien rules, its alternation of activity and enforced stillness, and its mass of other children, probably felt to Trenton like an aggressive, confusing intrusion: so he wandered around intruding aggressively on others. *Without consciously intending it, he made them feel what he felt within himself* – something Melanie Klein called 'projective identification'. His behaviour on the 'outside' showed us what he felt on the 'inside', even though he could not express that in words.

Recently a new (unofficial) diagnostic category has emerged, pinpointing many of the same symptoms as ADD/ADHD. Where ADHD focuses on the child's difficulty in staying still and concentrating, 'Sensory Processing Disorder' focuses on the stimulus overwhelm that may underpin those concentration difficulties. Stimulus overload, we remember, is what Kagan's 'high-reactive' child typically experiences in environments that fail to bother low-reactive children. A child like Trenton does not *look* like Kagan's high-reactive or inhibited type – he is not obviously sensitive or fearful; indeed, he seems confident and happy. Yet it is possible, as we noted above, that his chaotic behaviour reflects his genetically based difficulty in regulating himself in an overstimulated environment. Not all thin-boundaried children are shy, introverted or obviously anxious. Their outward appearance of social confidence may conceal their inner level of anxiety. And, as I pointed out above, good looks (both in a child and in an adult) can blind many of us to their inner turmoil. Who, other than her intimates, would have guessed that Marilyn Monroe was desperately unhappy, and (despite her reputation as a siren) did not enjoy sex very much?

Yet it would be a grave mistake to assume – as so many teachers do – that Trenton's problems were caused solely by his single-parent family status, or by his mother's 'failure to set limits'. This is precisely the kind of either/or thinking which makes problems worse. Because Trenton's hyperactivity and difficulty in sustaining attention were partly rooted in his temperament, they cannot possibly be explained solely by reference to his parents' marital status or even his mother's parenting. A child with such a temperament would pose a challenge for most parents. In an intact family, one adult is typically more indulgent of the child's demanding, intrusive or inattentive behaviour, the other harsher and less inclined to excuse it. When one biological parent is absent through divorce or death, the dynamic shifts: in the case of Trenton, the 'split' occurred between his pre-school and his mother. The punitive attitude of the one then drives the other into a closer protective alliance with the child, and so the pattern continues and intensifies. This type of evolving dance occurs around many different types of childhood problems, of which hyperactivity is only one.[6]

Just as potential problems in childhood are inadvertently maintained by adult attempts to solve them in contradictory ways, so the solution to many of these same problems lies in an abandonment of the power struggle and the achievement of balance. Children like Trenton need *both* love *and* firmness; *both* understanding *and* reasonable limit-setting. This is considerably harder to achieve in practice than it is to prescribe; but it is do-able. Moreover, children like Trenton need *consistency* from the adults surrounding them. Whether it is one parent against the other in an intact family, a custodial parent struggling against a former spouse, or a sole parent against a school system, the result is bad for the child. Only when both parties can talk to each other honestly and agree to take the same line, for the child's good, are things likely to improve. Otherwise, as every parent knows, Trenton and his ilk will rapidly learn that they can exploit the gap between one parent and the other, or between home and school, to their own advantage.

The case of Trenton is just one example of how problems tend to be diagnosed shortly before, or shortly after, the big transitional points in the lifespan. It is not that the problems were not foreshadowed by earlier patches of difficulty. But when a human being is expected to make a big leap into a new stage of life, attended by anxieties, expectations and challenges, potential problems emerge into clearer focus. When the new stage brings us into contact with new people, and wider horizons, there are different people around to notice our behaviour, and to react with fresh alarm or concern to the things that others have learned to adapt to and even condone. The same thing will happen again as children begin high school – and as they leave it.

The body triumphant

I watch a group of Maori children stride along the seafront in a New Zealand city, on their way to the beach. The older boys are teenagers, heavily built, anticipating the massive physique they will later develop; the two youngest boys, still small and skinny, look to be around six and seven respectively. They swing along, their surplus energy palpable in almost every movement. Each footstep is exaggerated, their legs flung forward, arms swinging boldly; the youngest pauses at each metal post along the pavement, and exhibitionistically kicks it so that the metal rings loudly. Are they already displaying the physical self-confidence and the proud defiance that their ancestors needed for constant battle?

We see in others what is true, but disowned, in ourselves (Freud called it 'projection'), and as a culture, we see in other cultures the disowned or unconscious features of our own. How much of these boys' behaviour is typically Maori, how much would equally be displayed by young children from middle-class homes in my own European-derived culture? Quite a lot, in fact. The exaggerated movements, and the physical 'overkill', are visible in any group of seven-year-old boys in the streets of the small town where I live. Most pre-school children are extremely active, and this continues into the earlier years of school. As any school teacher will tell you, most six- and seven-year-olds are easily distracted, cannot concentrate for long (unless it is on something that is of extreme interest to them personally) and have a seemingly boundless need to move their bodies. Forced to sit quietly in a classroom, they tap their feet, fiddle with their fingers and push objects back and forth on their desks. Their eyes wander constantly around the room, observing one another, noticing what is going on outside the windows – the 'wide shot' vision typical of the brain's right hemisphere. Released into the playground at break, they almost *explode* out of the school door, tumbling over one another in their haste to be physically free, shouting, yelling, screaming and pushing.

Several things are going on in these small, galvanic bodies. In part, they are so restless because their still-maturing brains do not yet permit them to be anything else. Myelination, the process by which the neurons are sheathed with fatty tissue, has been proceeding gradually for years. It will continue to proceed rapidly into mid-adolescence, and more slowly thereafter into middle age. The fatty coating of the neurons permits greater concentration, so that a child can focus mental as well as physical energy on a single spot for longer. Myelination of the frontal lobes of the cerebral cortex increasingly enables children to inhibit their impulses instead of acting on them immediately. As we noted above, myelination proceeds faster in girls than in boys, a difference that enhances the ability of girls to 'sit still', and generally to conform to the requirements of public settings like schools. Perhaps we would do better to send boys to school one or two years later?

Second, the restlessness of a child beginning school has a positive aspect: he is learning to use his body. By now, he has good control over his arms, legs, fingers and toes. Almost instinctively, he knows that he needs to exercise his limbs, to put his muscles through their paces. Children of this age are pre-occupied with *mastery*: being able to swing on their arms through the climbing structure/jungle gym, twirl one another ever faster on the roundabout, wiggle their ears, crack their finger joints, manipulate skateboards, create origami birds, shoot marbles accurately, skip at blinding speeds while chanting the approved playground rhymes or beat their own scores on 'shoot-em-down' computer games. Long before they are capable of playing adult sports in a mature manner, children create physical play of their own that embodies both rules and competition. In this way they practise for competencies they must later display as part of earning a living or in active recreational activities. When a three-year-old learns a new word, she may use it two dozen times the first day for the sheer joy of demonstrating her mastery. Similarly with children in the first few years of school: their bodies' new abilities demand display, as well as practice. On top of this natural exuberance and physical over-statement, diet plays its part too. Once again, nurture compounds nature, adds to it instead of subtracting from it.

Seeing is believing

In un-self-conscious play with others, or even on their own, elementary school children will imitate the mighty kicks of their heroes on the football field, the swoop of a fighter aircraft, the grace and balance of an Olympic gymnast on the bar, even the blatantly sexual self-display of the latest pop diva as she gyrates amidst her back-up dancers. Children's viewing of adult activities offers them endless models which they seem impelled to copy, overdoing the movements with a kind of deliberateness that is midway between self-mockery and serious imitation. Just as pre-schoolers 'play out' in their pretend games all sorts of inner fantasies about being grown up, and accompany their play with dialogue or solo chanting that describes what they are doing, so the play of older children still reveals much about their inner worlds, but usually, this time, without words.

What a child can see with her own eyes – the external appearance of people and things – dominates her understanding of the things she cannot see – the hidden feelings and motivations of her schoolmates or adults, the inner mechanisms of a car engine or a computer. Typically, children prior to puberty 'judge a book by its cover', and good looks are assumed to mean that their possessor is 'nice'. The popular girls are the pretty ones; they set the trends for the rest. No wonder that a handsome boy like Trenton is going to win so many friends at school – despite his annoying behaviour, others will follow where he leads. (Conversely, as many unattractive individuals have found to their cost, plainness or possession of some facial scar or birthmark almost automatically makes many children assume that you are an unpleasant and unreliable person.) This is why school-aged children are so ready to entertain fantasies about careers which their own modest talents are unlikely to support. Confusing the outside with the inside, they assume that being a rock star involves strutting with a microphone, that being an astronaut means wearing a space helmet or firing a laser gun. Their knowledge of their real capabilities is as limited as their reserves of hope are unbounded.

Similar principles show up in elementary school children's writing. Their characters are 'nice' or 'mean' and, as in fairy tales, the good characters are nearly always good looking; the evil ones are ugly. They produce narratives about *things happening*. Description and introspection play hardly any part at all.[7] Even when writing about adult life as they imagine it to be, they are confined to describing what they can see and hear. Here are three nine-year-old girls (they wrote the story jointly) describing how a young woman, Jo, consults a doctor because she has not been able to fall pregnant:

> In the morning
> Jo went to the doctor's
> He said
> I think if you tried harder
> You will have twins.
> What, do the − − harder?
> Yes, dear.
> Thank you doctor. Bye.[8]

In this excerpt we hear what the characters *say*, but we do not know what they think and feel (Jo's interpretation of the doctor's advice is equally 'outside-in': if you aren't conceiving a child, you should 'do the − harder'!). A century earlier, we can see in the work of the Brontë children the same 'flat' characterisation and reliance on clichés that would characterise the work of the average school child today: despite their wide reading and precociously adult vocabulary, we would never guess from Charlotte's and Emily's writing at ten and 11 years of age that either of them would, less than 20 years later, create some of the most memorable, psychologically convincing characters in English fiction.

That does not mean that school-aged children do not *have* thoughts and feelings and motives − of course they do − but simply that they do not reflect much on what is going on 'inside', unless circumstances force them to do so. Nor does it mean that children do not know that *others* have thoughts and feelings. They know it, but 'from the outside in'. Parents who are going through a painful crisis in their own lives often notice that their school-aged children, although sympathetic, do not seem to really understand. They don't. Full empathy is not possible until one has sufficient consciousness of one's own inner life to imagine that of another. 'Theory of mind' is still developing.

Us and them

Because the body is at the observable forefront of development for children beginning school, it is *physical* differences that children first learn to identify as markers of the boundary between 'us' and 'them'. Thrown together suddenly with a much larger group of age peers than most have ever experienced before, children rapidly extend their existing awareness of differences. A big nose or big ears, abnormal tallness or shortness, being a 'fatty' or a 'skinny', freckles, red hair or a different skin colour – all become the focus of attention for a short time, until children, mostly quite rapidly, adjust and accept a wide range of physical differences. Nicknames bestowed by peers can even be a source of pride, a badge of acceptance into the gang, into 'our group' or 'our class'. The temperamentally thin-boundaried child faces a further challenge at this time, and if his capacity to tolerate the critical limelight is small, then his own cringing, tears or angry defiance will prolong the unwelcome attention of others. Teasing seems an almost unavoidable feature of school-age interactions, partly because (as we saw above) elementary school children cannot fully understand what others might be feeling, and easily underestimate the hurt they may cause.

Faced with the necessity of relating to a larger group of often unfamiliar children under strange conditions, children not only notice differences, but put great energy into promoting *sameness*. Playground gangs and groups form almost immediately, in a pattern of behaviour that will continue, waxing and waning temporarily, for the next decade or more, eventually to be replaced by the sporting clubs, professional societies and cliques of adulthood. A group, however superficially based and short lived, offers the security of belonging. As once the child 'attached' to its mother, so now it seeks the safety and comfort that comes from attachment to 'my friends'. Children's collective play at this stage leans heavily on us-and-them groupings: in my schooldays, 'goodies' and 'baddies' were usually drawn from movies or comics. In the multicultural society that has succeeded the one I grew up in, social groups may be ethnically based: 'we' stick together and 'they' don't understand our ways. It is at this stage that rules become so important to children. Keeping 'our' rules makes you one of 'us': breaking them may mean that you are expelled from the group, and have to sit alone at lunch or recess, a fate that sensitive children feel keenly as a continuing humiliation.

In paying so much heed to rules, children are once again practising in fantasy, far ahead of time, for what will later absorb and preoccupy them as adults. In playing goodies and baddies, they are also practising for racial hatred, homophobia, gender oppression and war. And interestingly, those adults who feel such differences of skin colour or sexual preference most strongly often feel them in the same crude, physical way as seven-year-olds. A kind of instinctive biological shudder of revulsion, a 'visceral clutch', seems to govern their dealings with 'Them', which is precisely why such prejudices are so hard to shift even in intelligent adults.

Playground gangs are often the first attempts of children to create stable groups *outside* of their families, and though these groups often seem to coalesce as if by magic, there *is* some element of choice involved in them. Similarly, children's choices of 'best friends', however inadequately based, are their way of practising for the pairing and mate selection they will engage in as adolescents and adults.

Boundaries and secrets

Just as middle childhood is a time for rules, so it is also a time for secrets. Often the two go together, as when the difference between 'our' gang and 'yours' is defined by the hidden knowledge *we* possess, and *you* don't. Though boys and girls may play together amicably, children tend to create their own gender segregation at this stage, even in the absence of adult pressure to do so. Girls get together to talk 'girl things'; boys do 'boy things'. There is much giggling and playful disgust directed at the other sex. This is not really very different from the world of traditional tribal societies, where girls learned 'secret women's business' through association with other girls, and powerful taboos operated to prevent the communication of such secrets to the other sex. It is as if children at this age are absorbing the observable 'outside' of gender differences, 'how to *act like* a male or a female', long before they will need to cope with the more demanding task of integrating a fuller, deeper concept of what it means for them to be a woman, or a man.

Considering the importance of secrets and gangs in middle childhood, it comes as no surprise that Enid Blyton was, from 1940 to 1970, the most popular author with children at this stage of life in much of the English-speaking world – and well beyond (her 'Mallory Towers' books, about a British girls' boarding school, were best-sellers in postwar Germany,[9] and after her death in 1968, German-language sequels were written). Gangs and clubs, belonging, the exclusion of those who are 'different', children operating independently of adults and, above all, secrets and mysteries are the motifs of Blyton's *Secret Seven* and *Famous Five* series. Perhaps it should not surprise us, then, that Enid Blyton herself knew all about secrets.

When she was on the cusp of adolescence, Enid's beloved father secretly began an affair, and eventually left the family to live with his lover. Twelve-year-old Enid was devastated. Her mother insisted that she and her younger siblings pretend to neighbours and friends that their father was 'away on business'. The deception went on for years. When Enid discovered her vocation as a children's writer, she seemed to communicate most directly with children of primary school age – the age she herself had been prior to her father's 'betrayal' – creating for them fantasies of the kind she had consoled herself with in those dark years. She half believed in the secrets and adventures she created. When, for 30 years, children all over the world read Blyton's stories with absorbed enjoyment, they were not simply responding to her undemanding language and gratifying plots, they were also unconsciously recognising *a mind that functioned in much the same way as their own.*

Blyton's name is a byword among children's literature critics for bad writing and shameless pandering to her readers' tastes. The classic nineteenth-century novels of Charles Dickens, most of them since turned into television serials and movies, would seem at the opposite end of the literary spectrum from Blyton's. Yet there are some intriguing similarities: Dickens, too, is preoccupied with secrets; Dickens, too, offers stereotyped characters who are presented in terms of observable oddities like wooden legs, peculiar habits or idiosyncratic speech. For all the acuteness of his vision and the range and power of his writing, Dickens, like Blyton, saw the world 'from the outside in'. Both Blyton and Dickens lived their entire lives in denial of childhood trauma and, in some key ways, neither really developed emotionally beyond the level of a 12-year-old. When they wrote their stories, they wrote their *own* stories – over and over again.

It is partly because school-aged children are so aware of secrets that the trauma of repeated sexual abuse can so easily be perpetrated on them: 'our secret' is a manipulation that is often very successful in silencing the child even for many years. When 'our secret' is reinforced by powerful threats – 'Nobody will believe you', 'I will be put in jail if you tell anyone what we do together', the child's sense of complicity is doubled. Children understand secrets; they understand loyalty, well before they can fully understand another's feelings or motivations. Their ability to comprehend why an adult (even a parent or a sibling) would need to do this to them is very limited; but they may find themselves bound in a sticky web of warped loyalty, in which 'betraying' the abuser would leave them feeling somehow dirtied and diminished, even though the abuse itself dirties and diminishes them far more. But it is not simply the manipulations of the abuser that bind their silence: it is also their own parents' blindness to the child's signals that something is wrong, and (quite often) their parents' refusal to listen when the child finally attempts to disclose the secret. For such children, the secrets forced on them by abusive adults or older children will beget secrets in their own adult lives, and all too often, the painful cycle will continue – for while *keeping* secrets is something almost all children practise, deliberately *breaking* them, for a higher good, is not something for which most of us get any training at all.

And all of this is further complicated by the fact that our bodies, even the immature bodies of children, are biologically programmed to respond when touched sexually. 'If' (the child reasons) 'I felt some excitement or even pleasure, even though I knew it was wrong and I didn't want it to happen, then somehow the whole thing must have been my fault. I must be to blame.' Children *naturally* think this way, it is almost impossible for them not to: the egocentricity of early childhood is still operating, and their sense of guilt and responsibility will travel with them, in many cases, well into adulthood. As I write this, wide-ranging public enquiries into the sexual abuse of children by institutions have become common, and almost every week we witness the confronting sight of middle-aged or elderly adults weeping as they tell the enquiry about what happened to them 20, 30 or even 50 years before, at the hands of priests, ministers, members of religious orders and scout leaders – all of whom were supposed to 'protect' the children in their care, instead of callously exploiting them for their own gratification.

Culture and cool

In the affluent West, television has brought the global culture (American-accented English, commercial, self-centred) into almost every home. It has become a potent factor in influencing children's expectations even if their viewing is confined to the limited number of programmes designed specifically for them: it raises their consciousness of sex and desirability long before puberty, highlights emotions and relationships, probably alters their attention span, alters even their brain waves.[10] The advent of digital technology and the Internet, with its streaming video, means that television viewing can now be customised. In their own rooms, with their own smart phones, children and adolescents can increasingly view whatever they wish.

The wider world of schooling reinforces such influences. Children, desperate to belong and to be accepted, find that they must watch certain programmes, play certain computer games, visit certain Internet sites and become the possessors of certain products. These entertainments are not innocent. They are created by adults, and they tell children very specifically what their society values: sexual attractiveness (not emotional maturity), physical strength (not intellect or creativity), quick reflexes (not wisdom), violence (not peace-making), fame (not peace of mind).When they want to relax, most people, for most of their lives, will turn to grown-up versions of these same entertainments, embodying the same values – those of a society still at the warrior stage. Homer's Achilles – vainglorious, egocentric, living wholly in his physical strength and agility, viewing women solely as possessions – would feel perfectly at home with our entertainments. Action movies, in which scene after scene of violence, destruction and high-adrenaline chasing follow one another, are the adult cultural equivalent of 'hyperactive' behaviour in childhood. Implicitly, they both sanction it, and reinforce it. Fast-talking sitcoms with rapid-fire dialogue do the same. Western societies have created a culture that privileges speed, impulsivity, physical and verbal aggression, and the resolution of problems through acts of violence. It is fortunate that many children are able to engage with these 'entertainments' without lasting damage, and become relatively peaceful, law-abiding adults – but for the more vulnerable, the ones with thinner boundaries, this will not so often be the case. What they experience vicariously, via film, television and computer games, will impact on them more deeply. When worried adults create 'moral panics' around the potential impact of television, computer games and social media sites – in the 1950s such a panic was generated by comic books![11] – it seems to me that these controversies are simply another form of 'splitting' (one parent versus the other; parent versus the school). The television programmes, the games, or the porno sites *can* indeed impact on the vulnerable young person, but by attacking the external 'enemy', adults manage to avoid seeing the part that they – and their families – play in the process. It is those children who feel ignored or dismissed by their parents who are most likely to crave the comfort provided by apparently sympathetic peers on the Internet. It is children already full of confused, angry feelings (absorbed from the adults who share their living space) who are most likely to find momentary satisfaction in aggressive games and dramas full of mindless brutality. The girl who fills her room with cuddly soft toys well past the age when her peers have switched to posters of 'hot' young men; the boy who draws endless pictures of tanks and fighter planes, or sits for hours playing violent computer games − both are signalling more than just the mindless following of kid fashions: they are telling us about their inner life.

For most school-aged children, inner feelings, especially ones that are confused and inchoate, tend not to be expressed directly in words. Instead, they seem to take shape as external behaviours. Pre-school children do the same, of course, but they will often accompany their behaviour with amazingly self-revealing verbal commentary. 'I'm pushing the Daddy doll over, because he hits the Mummy doll, and I'd like to *kill* him!' says a four-year-old in the course of play therapy. An eight-year-old would be unlikely to be so explicit: the words have 'gone underground', while the emotions still get played out in behaviour.

But one 11-year-old boy, reticent and cool though he seemed initially, eventually talked very freely in counselling sessions, giving me a powerful key not only to his own thought processes but to the way in which many of us secretly think and feel. We were discussing his fear of the dark. Like most children with Obsessive Compulsive Disorder (OCD), he had many fears and felt compelled to 'do things' in order to keep these fears at bay (checking, hand-washing, avoiding cracks in the pavement, counting every second step). He found it very hard even to walk from one room to another after dark, unless there were lights on in all of the rooms. What made it worse, he said, was if he knew that only his father and his brothers were at home. 'What makes it different if your Mum's away from home?' I asked. 'Because then the circle's not fulled in', he replied. *Because the circle's not fulled in*: for this boy, his family was a sort of 'wholeness'. If the most important member of his family was away, even temporarily, this wholeness was breached.

Here was a boy, soon to be adolescent, who still felt at some level like an infant prior to full separation–individuation (even his use of 'fulled' instead of 'filled' suggests a much younger child). His family circle, and the circle of his own selfhood, were one and the same. Needless to say, this boy belonged to Kagan's high reactive type. He was fearful and shy, clinging to what he knew best (his family). He found stimulus (including the stimulus of his own anxieties) overwhelming, and resorted to rigid behaviours and rituals in order to cope with it, as if the normal preoccupation of the school-aged child with 'rules' and 'the right way to behave' had come to dominate his entire existence. Yet underneath it all were survival-level fears that his family, his protectors, might somehow be lost to him.[12] There is in all of us a great need for wholeness, for the 'circle to be filled in'. When that circle is broken, or incomplete, we ourselves falter.

Most children between seven and 12 do not feel as strongly connected with their families as this boy. Even though their relations with parents usually remain cordial and largely unconflicted, there is a certain remoteness in middle childhood that is not entirely the product of school. The pre-school years, when their whole lives were open to us, when they readily blurted out what was in their thoughts, have passed. Adolescence, when they will become aggressively, consciously private, is still to come, but something has changed. Not for nothing did Enid Blyton's stories feature children for whom parents were only important when a picnic tea needed to be provided. Freud described middle childhood as a time of 'latency'. He meant that the intense proto-sexual feelings that bonded parents and children in early childhood, and which both bound and separated them in adolescence, were temporarily 'on hold' between six and 12. These days, of course, our advertising, fashion industry and entertainment media have invited children to see themselves – and to be seen by adults – in sexualised ways, and those who have already been sexually abused are particularly vulnerable to such invitations. Yet despite changing times, there remains some accuracy in Freud's ideas about 'latency'. Although they will be affected by cultural invitations to see themselves, prematurely, as little adults, with 'boyfriends' and 'girlfriends', children between six and ten cannot be entirely wholehearted about it, because their bodies are not yet congruent with such behaviour. They will do it to belong, they will do it to be 'cool', but it will not go very deep until the onset of puberty.

Childhood's end

Approximately two years before the physical signs of puberty appear, children's bodies begin to produce the hormones that will trigger those changes. First girls, and then boys, begin to grow more rapidly and unevenly, tempers flare more readily, anxieties are sharper. Friendship groups that have stayed relatively stable, perhaps for some years, often break up, as the next big transition – to high school – looms. Of all human behaviours, this is one of the most puzzling, for it does not immediately make sense that at the very time we most need the security of friends, we seem to alienate them. This process will occur again, far more intensely, at the end of high school, but even here at the end of the elementary school years it can be upsetting. Girls, who typically value connectedness and relationships more than boys, are most affected. But why does it happen?

Human beings *know* when they are approaching a transition point. They *know*, even if not fully consciously, that things are going to change for them, maybe change profoundly. They are, at some level, afraid as well as excited. They know that some of their existing life is going to be lost or diminished. They anticipate the change, as if its effects, still in the future, ripple backwards to them in the present. It is not surprising that all of my youthful clients with OCD experienced the onset of their symptoms around the age of 11 – when they knew that they would soon be moving 'up' to high school. Knowing that an ending is coming, humans act out that ending in small ways that they can control. Knowing that a new beginning is coming, they practise clearing the ground for new beginnings. What we will later do in reality, we first experience in fantasy. That is how we are.

Notes

1 The effects of sugar and salt on children are firmly established in the scientific literature, and have generated campaigns to modify their ill effects. See for example 'Public Health Takes Aim at Sugar and Salt', Harvard School of Public Health, Fall 2009 (www.hsph. harvard.edu/news/magazine/sugar-and-salt; accessed 21 July 2015).

2 This observation is supported only by my own observations of troubled children, and questioning of their parents.

3 See Juliet Barker, *The Brontës*, London, Weidenfeld and Nicholson, 1994.

4 See Margaret Thatcher, *The Path to Power*, London, HarperCollins, 1995.

5 Bateson 'the difference that makes a difference': see Gregory Bateson, 'Form, Substance and Difference' in *Steps to an Ecology of Mind*, NY, Ballantyne Books, 1972: 448–466.

6 Matthew Smith's *Hyperactive: The Controversial History of ADHD*, London, Reaktion, 2012, supplies an often-neglected historical perspective on this type of child. It is well worth reading.

7 See Hugh Crago, *Entranced by Story: Brain, Tale and Teller from Infancy to Old Age*, NY/London, Routledge, 2014: 71–75.

8 See Carolyn Steedman, *The Tidy House: Little Girls Writing*, London, Virago, 1982: 53.

9 See Barbara Stoney, *Enid Blyton: The Biography*, 2nd Rev Edn, London, Hodder Headline, 1992: 159. [First edition published in 1974]; Sheila Ray, *The Blyton Phenomenon*, London, Deutsch, 1982.

10 Television watching induces low alpha waves in the brain rather than the beta waves typical when reading. Alpha waves generate a calm, quasi-meditative state which can be positive in its effects, but which can also promote passivity and suggestibility. Unsurprisingly, unhappy and dissatisfied individuals tend to watch more television than happy ones, and this includes child viewers also. See Peter Bongiorno, 'Your Unhappy Brain on Television' (www. psychologytoday.com/blog/innersource/201110/your-unhappy-brain-television; accessed 24 August 2015).

11 See Fredric Wertham, *Seduction of the Innocent: The Influence of Comic Books on Today's Youth*, NY, Rinehart & Co, 1954. On 'moral panics' see Stanley Cohen, *Folk Devils and Moral Panics: The Creation of the Mods and the Rockers*, London, MacGibbon & Kee, 1972.

12 See Hugh Crago, 'The Anxious Boys' Newsletter', *Australian and New Zealand Journal of Family Therapy*, 16, 1 (March, 1995): 29–37.

5

DISCOVERING SELF AND SEX

Adolescence

Back to the future

The year is 1998. A gaggle of teenagers enters the intercity train shortly after I do. They mass in the aisle, talking, laughing – and blocking the way for other incoming passengers. There is no malice in this, but they are doing what most teenagers do: taking up space, and intruding, deliberately or unconsciously, into the lives of the adults who coexist with them, but whom they treat almost as if they were invisible. When the group sits down, they sprawl, their long, gangly limbs propped illegally on the opposite seat, or stuck out into the aisle. All but two of them immediately plug into Walkmans, and the regular pulse of 'techno' resounds tinnily. A striking 16-year-old makes herself the centre of attention, talking loudly to compete with the noise she does not bother to remove from her ears unless the conversation of her friends becomes temporarily more important to her.

The girls have modishly bobbed hair – the fashion of their grandmothers' youth, only they do not know it. Two of the boys have soft, downy upper lips and alto voices, pitched midway between boy soprano and the depth they will soon have attained. Their faces are soft and padded with unlined flesh, yet each set of features hints at how it will look in 20 or 30 years' time. The coltish 16-year-old will still be handsome at 40 because of her elegant high cheekbones, although her body is unlikely to be as slim; the thickset, jocular lad of 16 with the shoulder-length hair will still bear that easygoing expression at 50, though it will probably be teamed with a paunch. It is a little harder to be sure in the case of the younger boys, the pitch of whose voices wavers uncertainly, although they, like all the others, talk with apparent confidence in that odd, clipped, mid-Atlantic accent affected by the well-bred young (have they, perhaps, learnt it from the currently popular American soaps, *Beverley Hills*

90210 and *Melrose Place*?). They address one another as 'dude'. The youngest-looking of the three boys, who appears to be only 14 or 15, is absorbed for most of the seven-hour journey in a solo role-playing game, entering details of his characters in pencil on a sheet of paper in front of him. He is the only one who never uses a Walkman, he interacts only rarely with the others and, when he does, he is less brashly self-assured than they. There is a softness and a vulnerability about him. Is he an academic in the making? A future artist or composer? Or will he, in just a few short years' time, develop schizophrenia? The complexity, intensity and set-apartness of role-playing games attracts not only the highly intelligent, but also the unworldly – and those whose grasp on reality is already faltering, though they do not yet know it.

Later the same day, I walk past a different group of adolescents, on the footpath of a busy suburban shopping street. Yelling loudly to one another, the boys, on rollerblades, weave in and out between pedestrians, giving no warning, and almost (but not quite) knocking them over; they jump their skateboards across kerbs and gutters, making nonsense of the neat dividing line between street and pavement that adults dutifully observe. On the road, they weave between cars just as they did between pedestrians, always seeming to court death, swerving in front of buses, while middle-aged drivers swear exasperatedly.

Fast-forward to 2015. On the streets, the rollerblades have disappeared, though some skateboards are still around. Whether they're indoors or outside, today's teenagers are plugged into handheld digital devices that make Walkmans look primitive. 'Smart phones' combine the functions of mobile telephones, miniature computers with Internet access and music libraries, permanently online and sending and receiving messages and information. The eyes of today's teenagers wander constantly to their screens, even when talking to people next to them: they are checking for new text messages, typing responses in the 'Newspeak' of SMS,[1] or checking their Facebook page to see if their virtual 'friends' have responded to their latest risqué selfie. Fashions in speech and dress have changed. Today's adolescents say 'like' every third or fourth word (as teenagers in my own generation said 'you know' constantly) and frequently exclaim 'Oh My God!' (shortened in text-talk to 'OMG'). Some of the girls have dyed their hair a vivid pink, purple or green, and both sexes sport facial piercings as well. Role-playing games are now the province of computers, their complexity and sophistication creating imaginary worlds that can monopolise attention for weeks and months at a stretch. *World of Warcraft* is more real than the real world, a 'second life' that trumps their first.[2] After all, even if you die, you can always come back as a different character. Being a Wizard didn't work? Try a Rogue!

What has happened? Has the nature of adolescence changed forever as a result of the massive technological shifts that have occurred in the 15 years since I wrote the first version of this book? I don't think so. The teenagers we've just been watching are still typical adolescents at base, despite the superficial differences. Just like their predecessors in the 1990s, they adopt whatever is new and 'cool' with lightning speed – and in doing so alert us to a fundamental characteristic of humanity as a whole: of all creatures, *homo sapiens* is the most readily co-opted by newness, the most powerfully influenced by what 'other people are doing', the most desperate to do whatever-it-is themselves.[3] From the evolutionary point of view, our devotion to the new and desirably different can be very useful. It makes us flexible, able to survive because we can adapt so rapidly to changed conditions. But it can also lead us into addictive behaviours that then come to dominate our lives and diminish the gratification and escape they originally promised. When the conditions to which we must adapt are self-created by our own 'technological imperative' (if the technology exists to do something, human beings seem driven to do it), we are no less quick to embrace the new and discard the old.

Today's teenagers not only rush to be like everyone else, they also seek affirmation in that sense of belonging. The words that they use, the styles that they adopt – all are geared to belonging. Just as the infant needs to attach to its caregivers in order to ensure its survival, adolescents need to attach to their peers, for their own *social* survival. Today's teenagers still want to have friends and share secrets with them, still practise for intimacy with desirable partners, still hope that *looking* 'cool' and *sounding* confident will conceal their inner self-doubts, anxieties or (in a few cases) self-loathing. Facebook and other social media facilitate these things without changing their fundamental nature. Kagan's 'uninhibited' adolescents[4] – thick-boundaried, sociable, easygoing – will negotiate their new relational world with reasonable aplomb, only temporarily cast down by setbacks ('OMG, Liz just unfriended me!'). They continue to indulge in risky behaviour because deep down they don't believe that anything bad is ever going to happen to them – the conviction of invulnerability that teenagers and young adults have always felt.

By contrast, inhibited or high reactive types – thin-boundaried, self-doubting, wary – will withdraw into the safer worlds of academic achievement or on-line gaming, be less quick to risk real-life encounters with potential friends and more devastated when they do not work out, brood more obsessively on their perceived deficits (my nose is too big, my hips are too wide, my boobs are too small, no one will ever want me). Internet sites where other anxious, self-hating kids tell their stories may model particular kinds of 'spoiled identity',[5] and may even encourage them in 'cutting', self-starvation or suicide attempts – but without the technological facilitation, many of these teenagers would sooner or later have discovered those options anyway. Today's adolescents are very different on the 'outside', but the 'inside' has probably changed very little.

Living on the borderline

In public, it really seems as if teenagers exist most intensely in the interstices of the adult world. Their behaviour seems to be aimed solely at one another, yet at another level they often seem to be 'performing' for the very adults they studiously affect to ignore. Suddenly, they will turn up the volume on their music, startling the adults sitting close by, then, as suddenly, turn it down again, pretending that the action was random and unmotivated. 'Mem–or–ies!' sings a girl loudly, as she and two companions swing through a commuter train compartment, giggling and staring at the boy in question in a way which positively invites other passengers to pay attention, yet simultaneously makes adults feel embarrassed if they begin to listen in. *Embarrassment* is something that teenagers frequently feel: indeed, they virtually specialise in it; and perhaps because of this, they also seem exquisitely skilled in *creating* embarrassment in older people around them. Embarrassment is effectively a mild form of shame, and by 'performing' it constantly on others, adolescents attempt to deny its potency. *What we feel within ourselves, we enact upon the world outside us.*

Of course, children of elementary school age also weave in and out of the adult world, going about their own business, but younger children do not possess the physical strength and mental agility to 'work the system' of adulthood in such a masterful, visible way as adolescents. School, parents and the government impose a variety of regulations on teenagers, and most of these rules teenagers contrive to evade, finesse or subvert. Mostly, they do so by staying just close enough to the boundaries of what is acceptable to avoid serious trouble. But there is a natural affinity between adolescents and criminals. Not, of course, because adolescents are 'naturally criminal' but because both teenagers and criminals are 'the dispossessed', denied (or perceiving that they are denied) status, power and material possessions. They therefore set out to *take* what life has denied them. And perhaps, too, because both teenagers and criminals live in a secret world, much of which is unknown to the adults around them. At the time I am writing this, there is a great deal of concern about vulnerable adolescents who are being recruited via social media by terrorist organisations. Time and again, when their 17-year-old ends up in Syria or Iraq, the bemused parents say, 'But we had no idea he/she was involved in all of that!' They didn't – but then, parents have always had a tendency not to see the signs of withdrawal that might signal a troubled kid, and teenagers have always found ways of avoiding parental scrutiny of their private preoccupations. How is a mere parent to know the difference between a teenager's temporary overvaluing of privacy and a gradual slide into pathological behaviour? Moreover, teenagers are readily co-opted into a 'cause' – especially those who, deep down, doubt themselves and question the worth of their own existence.

The adolescent challenge to the adult world is partly, though not entirely, a product of the arrangements post-industrial societies have made for their young. In many tribal societies there was a clearly marked boundary between childhood and adulthood. Children were left in no doubt whatsoever when they had left one behind and entered the other: initiation rituals were deliberately designed to simulate a new 'birth' into manhood or womanhood. On the other hand, however, children in such societies were mostly expected to work alongside of adults from an early age. The transition to adult work roles came gradually, with no sudden, unexpected demands; and while marriage might well be surrounded with strong rules and sanctions, sexual expression in the adolescent years was often viewed more permissively. Three or four hundred years ago – even two hundred – many Europeans experienced the transition from childhood to maturity in much the same way, with early participation in adult-level work, and socially sanctioned sexual experimentation short of marriage.[6]

By contrast, our contemporary social arrangements seem almost perversely designed to make the transition to adulthood more difficult than it need be. Compulsory education keeps young people at school not only for the years of rapid physical and mental growth in adolescence, but often well into their twenties as well. During much of this time, young peoples' earning capacities, social status and life choices are severely restricted. With adult minds and physical strength and agility equal to those of most adults, adolescents are nevertheless expected to exist for years in a twilight state of economic dependency. In recent years, rising unemployment has increased this period almost indefinitely, especially for society's most vulnerable young people. Their sexual drive is higher than it will ever be again, and yet early adolescents have been expected (at least in theory) to refrain from full sexual expression. No wonder our arrangements for adolescence have bred a subculture that delights in thumbing its nose at the adult world: *WTF!*

The weaving, risky skateboards; the loud, public farts and burps; the purposeful making public of what adults keep private; the sniggers and catcalls; the 'sharing' of one's naked body via 'sexting' – all are challenges to the thin but real barrier that excludes adolescents from the privileges of adulthood. The one commodity that teenagers possess in abundance, but which adults have only in ever-diminishing supply, is *youth*, and they exploit it shamelessly. They can stay up all night, drink themselves senseless, waste themselves with drugs, and still bounce back. In the long succession of derogatory words that over the past half century teenagers have applied to adults ('oldies', 'squares', 'fossils') there was none more eloquent than 'wrinklies'. Their own wrinkles will come soon enough, but right now adolescents are secure. For all the manifest angst that many teenagers suffer, and that drives a small minority to premature death, their youth is something that nobody can take away from them. And sometimes it seems that they do their best to age themselves prematurely, punishing their bodies to make up for the lack of the very wrinkles they laugh at in adults. As rock guitarist Pete Townshend memorably wrote in 1965, *'Hope I die before I get old!'* Only he didn't.[7]

Changes, changes

Several things happen simultaneously at puberty, and it is the pace and the extent of these changes that probably does more than anything else to produce the embarrassment and self-doubt of early adolescence. Since birth, children's physical maturation has alternated between rapid growth spurts and longer periods of more gradual development – middle childhood falls into the latter category. Children between five and 11 take pride in their growing height and physical capacities, but the changes come in small increments. As early as ten for girls and 11 for boys, there are signs that the relatively serene period of middle childhood may be coming to an end.[8] There is a growth 'spurt', and hormonal changes begin which will usher in the distinctive developments of puberty – the growth of breasts in girls, enlargement of the genitals in boys; the growth of pubic and underarm hair in both, and body and facial hair in boys. Young people cannot but be aware of what is happening to their bodies, for there are observable changes happening almost weekly. Moreover, this growth is uneven. Genetic blueprints ensure that the average adolescent boy's limbs will grow to near-adult proportions before his trunk does, that his height will soar before his body mass catches up with it. The balance between muscle and fat changes dramatically in just a few years. No wonder teenagers feel a little unsure, out of balance with themselves and the world around them! No wonder they make a virtue of necessity, and sprawl so exaggeratedly into the space of others, for they are no longer so sure of where their own body space ends and begins. No wonder pubescent girls feel alarmed when they begin to develop the fatty tissue that rounds their breasts and thighs, for they *are* 'fat' – by comparison with how they were only a year or two earlier.

Hormonal surges before and during puberty are also largely responsible for the fact that young people begin to experience *feelings* more powerfully. A friend writes to me about his newly teenage daughter, Fiona: 'Everything seems particularly fraught and minutely significant. Ordinary events and interactions are blown into major encounters and dramas. Minor misunderstandings can transform a normal peer or teacher into a "complete bitch" in an instant'.

For an adolescent like Fiona, such intensity is partly real and partly theatrical. She knows (from watching the 'right' television shows and from her connections on social media) that this is how she is *expected* to act, and so she is eager to demonstrate that she can perform the role of teenager with skill. Yet, at the same time, she really *does* feel more strongly, and it is invisible hormonal changes that are responsible for that. In the last chapter, we noticed the way that younger children seem to 'overdose' on sheer physical activity. A few years older, Fiona is starting to *notice* and *articulate* her own emotions in a more self-conscious way, but first she must 'overdose on her own emotions'. In a very similar way, many teenagers will experience their sexual feelings as intense, overwhelming, triggered by almost any object of potential desire, regardless of whether that person is an appropriate (or attainable) sexual partner for them. The embarrassing automatic erections of teenage boys fall into this category.

With the coming of puberty, sexual sensations intensify as the teenager's body begins to form itself into that of a sexually mature adult. As breasts bud and nipples grow in size and sensitivity, as hair sprouts in new and private places, a young person cannot but be constantly reminded of what is happening. This is very different from the mere growth of arms and legs, the mere gain of height and weight. This is *change* – the beginning of another migration, a journey into adulthood. The teenager's body startlingly asserts its independence, thrusting its new curves and bulges out through the slim, predictable shape of the ten- or 11-year-old. And then, the first menstrual period and the first ejaculation tell girls and boys unmistakably that they have crossed a threshold from which there is no return. Though it may be years yet before they experience sexual intercourse, or even engage in sexual play, they *feel* their bodies' potential, and their consciousness changes along with that. Between ten and 13, said his former classmate, the young Elvis Presley 'talked about girls and what to do to get girls. But I don't know if any of it actually happened'.[9]

Being humans, we do not simply experience our physical changes, as other animals do. We *interpret* them. And the meanings we make may be pleasing or painful, reassuring or doubt-inducing. To know sexuality is to know power – not just new sources of pleasurable sensation within one's own body, but power over others through sexual attractiveness and, ultimately, the awesome power to bring a new being into the world. Equally, to know sexuality may be to know fear: fear of the pleasurable sensations themselves, which may seem overwhelming; fear of others' desire for us (*'I'm a king bee, honey, buzzin' roun' yo' hive'*),[10] which we may feel quite unprepared to handle; fear of our reproductive capacity itself. When the pubescent adolescent compares her new breasts to those of other girls she may feel pride, but she may also feel shame. Talk to young women, far enough away from the agonies of puberty to be honest, and they will tell you again and again that whether they got their periods earlier than the rest, or later than the rest, they saw it more as a cause for worry than for comfort: only those who seemed totally 'average' escaped that anxiety. No wonder teenagers are so obsessed with being like everyone else, for their bodies force upon them an intense awareness of difference, which they readily turn into a source of embarrassment or self-criticism.

As if all of these changes were not enough, the adolescent experiences massive developments in cognitive maturity. The myelination of the neurons, which has been proceeding ever since infancy, now enters another period of rapid development, and yet more of the left hemisphere's unique capacities come into their own. By the age of 17 or 18 (but allowing for the possibility that some will get there a year or two earlier, and some will take a bit longer), these developments mean that we can (or most of us can, at least part of the time) use symbols to think beyond the concrete (the algebraic 'x' replaces the additions and subtractions of arithmetic), make valid generalisations and abstractions from concrete evidence. For Piaget (a scientist himself), cognitive development meant the ability to master the 'formal operations' required by mathematics, science and logic. Yet few of us become mathematicians or logicians, so what exactly do 'formal operations' mean for people generally? Nine-year-olds, when asked to explain the *theme* of a story like 'Cinderella', or to state the *meaning* of a fable like 'The Fox and the Grapes', will typically *tell the story again*, or possibly *tell you about the main character in the story*. Asked why she liked the fairy tale 'Cinderella', one girl replied, 'Cinderella is a girl who has very interesting adventures'.[11] When you explain to nine-year-olds what a 'theme' or a 'meaning' is, and give them an example, some may be able to grasp the concept, and explain, 'Cinderella's sisters are mean to her, but in the end, she gets to marry the Prince, not them'. One or two might even say something like, 'Cinderella makes you feel like dreams can come true, even if people are nasty to you'. However, *most* nine-year-olds will simply continue to retell the story, or talk about the people in it. *Shortening* a favourite story may be the closest they will be able to come to 'abstracting' a statement of the ideas that it embodies.[12] The right hemisphere of the cerebral cortex 'thinks' in stories, but when we ask children to extract a meaning or a moral from a story, we are requiring that their *left* hemisphere be capable of standing back from that story and translating its events and characters into the abstract language of analysis – something that most children cannot begin to do before the left hemisphere maturation that occurs in adolescence.

Given some prompting, *most* 16-year-olds will be able to see how the specific, individual actions and characters that make up a story form a pattern, a pattern with a meaning. They can see that William Golding's *Lord of the Flies* is not just an exciting and frightening story about a group of schoolboys alone on a tropical island, but also a 'fable' about how human beings inevitably fall into barbarism once the rules of civilised society are removed. That statement is never made by Golding at any point in the novel. It is *latent*, embodied in the story-as-a-whole, and it takes the adolescent's ability to 'generalise' and 'abstract' to be able to see this. Telling a story ('showing') is the right hemisphere's mode of thinking, of communicating a 'message'; explaining *what the story means* ('telling') is the way that the left hemisphere thinks, and only now can most young people begin to perform this mental 'operation'. To perform it, the capacities of both the right and the left hemispheres are required.

The bulk of the population will never study philosophy, literary criticism or sociology. Most people will never be required to analyse novels or movies once they have completed high school. But many of them *will* think analytically about whether or not the religious beliefs in which they've been raised square with their own convictions, about whether one political party is better to vote for than another. They will start to argue for, or against, questions that are hypothetical: would it be better to decriminalise all drugs of addiction? If my country decides to accept thousands of refugees and asylum seekers, would this be a disaster, or would it lead to a better world? It is in adolescence that most young people start to pay attention to such things. Their thinking may of course be sporadic and superficial. Teenagers can argue passionately with their parents and point out their hypocrisy or their errors of logic – because those arguments serve their own immediate ends.

But for adolescents of higher than average intelligence or greater than average ambition, the big questions of life are often explored more seriously. As Erik Erikson pointed out, adolescence is the great age of idealism.[13] Whatever choices their historical era presents them with – Catholicism or Protestantism (in the sixteenth century), Communism or Fascism (in the 1930s), Islamic fundamentalism or Save the Planet (today) — many young people seek out *something to believe in*, something in which they can embody their vague hopes for themselves and others. Their choice of causes is often as poorly grounded as their initial choices of boyfriends or girlfriends. My atheist mother once laughingly confessed that as a university student, she joined an evangelical Christian organisation 'because of a boy I was chasing at the time'.

Adolescents both want and need to express their powerful, individual convictions somehow. Many girls, with their characteristic bias towards the verbal, have in the past expressed themselves in diaries, or in letters to friends. In the intense world they shared only with one another, the Brontë sisters and their brother Branwell created endless narratives and plays about aristocratic characters in obsessionally detailed imaginary realms — an activity very similar to today's role-playing games. In the 1980s, the celebrated 'Silent Twins' — a pair of West-Indian-born British teenagers who achieved notoriety by getting arrested for arson — seemed literally incapable of speaking except to one another, and communicated their private world voluminously in writing intended entirely for themselves.[14]

Most girls today express their inner worlds in lengthy conversations — now facilitated by the existence of mobile phones, which enable them to be in touch with others almost constantly if they so desire.[15] Those whose bent is towards the visual paint, create graphic novels, or learn the techniques of animation via computer software. Adolescents compose songs, and adolescent performers choose songs that speak to their own feelings. In 1963, 17-year-old Lesley Gore's 'You Don't Own Me' (with its spine-shivering shift from an initial minor key to a wish-fulfilling major) became an anthem for young women struggling to escape the straitjacket of conventional gender behaviour.[16] In 1978, an 18-year-old Kate Bush wove words of longing and obsession from Emily Brontë's *Wuthering Heights* into a haunting melody that took the pop world by storm (she had discovered that her birthday fell on the same day as Emily's, and, typically for a teenager, composed the song in a few hours late at night). Like the ill-fated Sandy Denny's 'Fotheringay', these songs powerfully convey the intensity with which adolescents can experience both hope and despair.[17] Yet when the adolescent songwriter becomes a 'star', it can be overwhelming and even shaming. Kate Bush commented years later that seeing herself perform 'Wuthering Heights' on the video clip that made her famous was 'like watching myself die'. Even the most unlikely individuals are capable of a temporary urge to express themselves in verse while at this age. In the closing years of Tsarist Russia, Joseph Djugashvili was an intense, morose adolescent in Georgia, officially training for the priesthood, in fact reading radical and subversive literature in preparation for becoming a Marxist revolutionary. Like so many adolescents, he 'practised' for adulthood in secret. At the age of 16 this brooding visionary wrote an idealistic poem. It hardly sounds like the sort of thing that Stalin ('man of steel'), would ever do — and so far as we know, he never did it again.[18]

The ability to generalise and abstract not only permits reflection on values and ideas *external* to self (such as politics and religion), but also reflection *on* self. As concrete thinkers, children in middle childhood answer the question 'Who are you?' in fairly 'outside-in' ways. They tell you their name, their sex, where they live, their school grade, what sport they enjoy, what they're good at. Rarely do they describe themselves in terms of personality as adults would see it. Adolescents, however, begin to do so. As they grow older, many of them develop a consuming interest in classifying or labelling themselves, even if to us their classifications and labels appear superficial: 'I'm a fun person' and 'I'm a Pisces' both reflect an ability to abstract, to consider 'what type they fit into'. Adolescents begin to talk and think about how they *feel*, not just about what they *do*. 'I'm really loyal to my friends. It breaks me up when someone that I've trusted lets me down. I'd never do that to them'. They begin to develop a sort of 'relational ethics'.[19] The years between 14 and 17 are the years in which most humans first put conscious effort into introspection. All of us measure ourselves against others, but adolescents do so more intensely and consistently than ever before, and (for some) more than they will in the future.

Adolescents' search for a cause to believe in can be seen as a search for an 'ideal self' – the self that the young person would *like* to be. Heroes, gurus and mentors give a concrete shape to such ideal selves. 'When I'm grown up, I'm going to look like she does'; 'Once I'm out of home, I'm going to push myself to the limit like he did'. So adolescence is when each of us, individually, becomes fully *aware* of our individual selfhood, fully conscious of what distinguishes us from others, as well as what we have in common with them. The left hemisphere, largely responsible for our sense of ourselves as *separate* from the world, has propelled this development – a development that is arguably even more important than the 'scientific' and 'logical' reasoning that so preoccupied Piaget. It can feel exhilarating to be a unique, separate self – but it can also feel very lonely.

Is it surprising, then, that teenagers so readily fall into 'problematising' themselves? New to introspection and inexperienced at reading the behaviour of others, they are only too prone to compare themselves unfavourably to their peers, to imagine that nobody could possibly feel as they do – which, for a substantial number of adolescents, is awkward, self-conscious and confused. Many of these states are temporary products of sudden body changes, hormonal swings and upsurges of startling new emotion. In a few years' time, things will have settled, and life will seem less intense, less overwhelming. But younger teenagers have no way of knowing that. They do not even know themselves very well yet. Their own unpredictability surprises and puzzles them. They are not yet conscious of their own patterns – an awareness that, for most, will start to show up around the age of 30.

In such circumstances, it is natural for adolescents to focus intently on some of their existing temperamental characteristics, and turn them into causes for concern. An anxious 12-year-old boy, scared of the extra social and intellectual demands he fears high school will bring, cannot tell his friends about his fears.

He would feel stupid, and his friends, normal, carefree males, seem blithely unaffected by the same prospects that trouble him. So he becomes obsessed with dirt, and 'has to' wash his hands, up to 20 times a day. A teenage Elvis Presley, temperamentally shy, and always aware of how different he feels from others, constantly combs his hair and begins a pattern of behaviour in which he 'has' to put on his right shoe before his left, his right sock before the left, his right trouser leg before the left.[20] A 14-year-old girl, frightened at the thought of boys and their attentions, and responding unconsciously to her family's unspoken agendas and half-secret secrets, exercises compulsively and begins to starve herself into anorexia.

Each one of these three young people was born with thinner boundaries than the average: their sensitivity makes it that much easier for them to turn their thoughts into obsessions, to overvalue and over-personalise the way others react to them. Adolescence, that time of change par excellence, affects them more profoundly than it does their age-peers whose temperaments are more equable. Shyness becomes even more crippling in adolescence, for now more than ever, being able to 'relate' seems to be the central feature of being a successful person. The intense introspection of adolescents creates a temporary sense that everyone else is as curious about them as they are about themselves, that everyone is looking *just at them* – can even, somehow, *know what they are thinking*. Hence the adolescent overvaluation of privacy, yoked paradoxically to a good deal of public 'display' of what others would imagine to be private. Hence also the temporary preoccupation of teenagers with psychic phenomena. The adolescent Elvis, preoccupied with coincidences, superstitions and astrology, was simply one of many adolescents to develop such interests.

We've seen in earlier chapters how awareness of self and awareness of others develop simultaneously. As teenagers build up their self-knowledge (not only through introspection, but through noticing how they react to different people, and in different situations) they simultaneously begin to realise more about others. They begin to see that if they themselves feel anxious, or ashamed, or guilty, then others might also feel those things – 'theory of mind'. If them-selves feel an urge to keep certain thoughts and feelings private, then others might also have private thoughts and feelings. All of this steps adolescents towards true empathy – the ability to think hypothetically about someone else's feelings, to 'put oneself in someone else's shoes' without necessarily having shared exactly what they have experienced. The full development of such empathic attunement to another person may take much longer, however, as it depends in part on the experience of one's own suffering, as well as on the further brain maturation that occurs in the twenties and thirties. In the absence of hard evidence, I strongly suspect that the capacity for empathy is easier for 'inhibited' individuals with 'thin boundaries' to develop than it is for those whose boundaries are less permeable. If a sensitive adolescent can learn to distinguish between his own feelings and those he picks up from others, he is on the way to possessing an invaluable asset – a key facet of 'emotional intelligence' – that will stand him in good stead later in his life. On the other hand, without the right conditions, a thin-boundaried adolescent may turn all his sensitivity inwards, generating an intense conviction of 'specialness', along with a sense of entitlement to disregard the feelings and needs of others – indications of narcissism.

Friends versus family

The process which Margaret Mahler called separation–individuation is accomplished, not in a smooth, even progression, but in a series of fits and starts. We saw how the two-year-old moves rapidly from pride in her own ability to be independent of mother to panic when she falters, and mother is not immediately there to help her. Gradually, her sense of separateness and autonomy becomes more solid, more reliable, and she can ask her parents for help when she really needs it, rather than pretending, omnipotently, that she can function without them all the time.[21] The automatic 'no!' of the 'terrible twos' is replaced by the growing ability to say 'no' only when it is appropriate, and 'yes' the rest of the time.

A very similar process takes place in the years between 12 and 20, for adolescence 'replays' some of the developmental issues of the early childhood years. Both are periods of very rapid physical, mental and emotional growth. And both are periods when the forces of togetherness and separateness pull powerfully against one another before a new balance is reached. A pre-school child has (hopefully) achieved a sense of separate selfhood, but still *within* the security of a social world she has always known – her family. An adolescent must achieve a fuller, deeper sense of selfhood, and must move, inevitably, *away* from her family, into an existence in which she is fully self-supporting. At least, that is how it is in theory, and how it actually is for *most* of us. To become adult is to leave the nest, to learn to fly solo. What learning to walk is to the toddler, learning to drive is to the adolescent: to drive confers the power to 'get away' literally and symbolically, to inhabit spaces remote from, or unknown to, our parents, to be alone with friends or lovers, and to feel the heady rush of being in sole charge of a ton of machinery travelling at speed down Route 66 into the future – feelings memorably conveyed in the Dixie Chicks' 1998 song, 'Wide Open Spaces'. It is like being born again, only this time you are not a helpless passenger, but the one at the wheel.

Two dynamic forces operate to help adolescents 'separate and individuate'. First, there is the pull of the world external to the family. In many ways, adolescents seem to withdraw the intense feelings that have previously been invested in their parents and siblings, and instead invest them first in friends (usually of the same sex), later in potential (or actual) sexual partners. Friends supply not only fun (often of a kind that parents refuse to sanction), but also empathy of a kind that parents can rarely provide (and if they can, some adolescents cannot tolerate it). 'Your friends know how you feel', say adolescents. (In fact, they know how *they* feel, and that will often suffice to convince you that they understand you as well.) If you are in conflict with your parents, or siblings, friends almost automatically side with you, strengthening your conviction that you are ill-used, deprived and maligned. And friends provide a channel to the seductive world of teenage culture, the culture of 'cool' – a temporary alternative to the world of family-supported, adult-sanctioned values. Within this alternative world you are free to explore – not to explore an unlimited range of options (for the culture of cool is tyrannical and oppressive in its own way) but, at least, options that appear to confer individuality, autonomy and confidence.

Some of these options are in fact simply the pleasures of the adult world, enjoyed subversively or illicitly (alcohol, smoking, drugs, sex). Others are provided directly *by* the adult world, in the form of the commercial consumer culture which today's teenagers engage with and purchase. The fact that this culture is actually created, financed and marketed by adults (who also profit handsomely from it) is irrelevant to most teenage consumers. What matters to them is that 'their' culture is disliked, even hated, by the adults they know (especially parents) and thus serves its real function: to mark the teenager off as separate from her family. In a few years, they will have outgrown most of it, and may be embarrassed by it, but it will have served as a transitional space between the culture of their families and the culture of the wider adult world. They will have felt at home in it at a time when they most needed *not* to feel at home *at home*.

Like two-year-olds, adolescents say 'no' to parents, openly or covertly. Some adolescents seem driven to turn their backs on almost every aspect of the routines, rituals and values that they have been brought up with. To them, their parents seem uncomprehending, stupid, untrusting, rigidly old-fashioned, regardless of whether, by objective standards, these things are true or not. A minority remain stuck in this phase for years, even well into young adulthood. Most adolescents move through it fairly rapidly. As they gain confidence in their new bodies, learn to trust themselves more and judge both themselves and others more realistically, their need to define their selfhood simply by opposing themselves to their parents declines. Some never need to do so in any but minor ways. Many do it in the semi-theatrical manner we observed in Fiona earlier – self-consciously acting the scowling, sullen 'rebel without a cause', with half an eye on how well the performance has gone across.

And there are real battles that adolescents must win if they are to achieve emotional autonomy when they move away from their families into independent life. They must assert their wills against their parents and, at least sometimes, gain concessions. They ought not to gain them too easily, for if parents simply give in to every demand, their children will have no sense of achievement, no victory to savour. 'Good authority' is what adolescents need – a subject we'll return to in Chapter 8.[22] Adolescents must declare their right to opinions that vary from their parents'. They must increasingly carve out a personal and relationship life to which their parents are not privy. The over-intense privacy of early adolescence must give way to a real sense of personal space. Then, and only then, can the late adolescent feel safe enough to begin (tentatively) to share some of her secrets again with her parents – even, perhaps, to ask them for advice.

For many middle-class teenagers, their *room* becomes the symbol of their separate self, the battleground on which their wars of independence will be fought. At 15, Enid Blyton was locking herself in her bedroom to write, struggling to carry on the literary aspirations that had once been nurtured by her father – whom she now no longer saw. She confided her feelings to a diary, but when her mother once entered her room and read some of what she had written, Enid vowed that never again would she record anything but a bland, boring summary of daily happenings. Although socially confident, Enid was an extremely sensitive child, and for the sensitive individual one rejection, one intrusion, is often enough to fix a habit of evasion: Enid's adult diary relentlessly excludes her innermost thoughts and feelings.[23] Today, the diary in the bedroom has largely been replaced by the computer in the bedroom – desktop, laptop or mobile phone. Teenagers can generally rely on their parents knowing less about all things digital than they do, and it is not hard for them to ensure that their Internet chat is hidden from parental eyes. Yet surprisingly often, they do not bother too much, and parents find out anyway – almost as if part of them *wanted* to be found out. It is the same dynamic as occurs in adult affairs: the 'guilty' partner swears that nothing is going on, but the other partner has only to go through his phone messages to find out otherwise. As Freud was aware, we humans are conflicted creatures, caught between impulse and self-control, between desire and fear. We cannot *not* communicate both sides of our inner dilemmas,[24] and while we want to keep our private worlds to ourselves, social media ensure that we will share them with others – who, in their turn, will not necessarily be as trustworthy as we imagine. At this point we need to remind ourselves that young people who were securely attached as infants may need to find out the hard way that others may not be as safe and protective as their parents were!

Exactly like toddlers learning to cope with being temporarily 'on their own' in another room or during a brief parental absence, adolescents and young adults often need to make several 'tries' at achieving independence. Reaching late adolescence in early 1950s Australia, Jill Ker, despite her academic abilities, dropped out of university, flatted, moved back home, worked behind the counter of a store and re-enrolled at university, before she finally found the courage to declare her independence of a mother she saw as increasingly demanding and controlling. Like Jill, many adolescents today retreat to the security of home for a while, until the discomfort of again inhabiting a nest they have outgrown drives them out again, this time, perhaps, for a bit longer.

Physical separation from parents is not necessarily the hallmark of true adulthood. Simply because a young adult remains living at home does not mean that he is 'dependent' or that the family is 'dysfunctional'. In many non-Western cultures, young people stay under the family roof well into adulthood: their marriage and the birth of their children occur under that same roof. It is perfectly possible – though all too rare – for young adults in our own society to achieve emotional independence and lead largely autonomous lives while still physically living at home. But for most, the ability to live separately without running back when the least thing goes wrong means that a measure of functional individuation has been achieved. The task is certainly not complete. But it is sufficient for now.

The cradle of pathology?

Many developmentalists today deny that adolescence is a time of 'storm and stress' and point to findings which show that the majority of young people experience a largely trouble-free adolescence – or at least, claim that they do ('How was school?' 'Fine' 'What did you do last night?' 'Hung out with friends'). But nobody would deny that for a significant minority, puberty and the developments that follow it do trigger serious problems, some of which may persist for many years thereafter.[25] Of course, *any* period of prolonged change, readjustment and stressful emotion will tend to be associated with the eruption of emotional and behavioural problems, and the temperamentally vulnerable will inevitably be most affected by any such period. But in adolescence even temperamentally resilient young people can for a few years be dragged down into considerable distress by processes neither they nor their families can fully control.

Some emotional disorders from which adults suffer show up for the first time during adolescence. As we saw earlier in this chapter, anorexia is typically associated with the earlier years of adolescence, when bodily changes demand the teenager's attention. Others, like schizophrenia and drug addiction, tend to have a later onset, when the issue facing the young person is the challenge of separating from his family. Most adolescents naturally desire independence, but negotiate it only gradually. However, the prospect of living away from their families flings some adolescents into outright panic, just as the commencement of sexual maturing coincides in others with a retreat into the behaviour typical of a younger child. Narrative therapist David Epston used to ask young people, 'Are you more in favour of growing up, or more in favour of growing down?', a question that confronted them humorously with the serious implications of their regressed behaviour.[26] Let me repeat that in speaking of temperamental vulnerability, I am *not* saying that babies are destined from birth to be anorexic, schizophrenic or drug-addicted. Despite regular claims from journalists that scientists have isolated a 'gene for schizophrenia' (or dementia, or depression or anorexia), most experts agree it is misleading to suggest that genetic blueprints are ever as precise as that. But as I've repeatedly suggested, having extremely thin boundaries ('born without a skin' as people sometimes put it) will often mean a personality which is more *likely* to tip over into some form of pathological behaviour, if subjected to the same level of stress that other individuals take in their stride.

The particular *form* of the symptoms that are displayed is once again the product of a complex reinforcement of nature by nurture. My own observation is that obsessive-compulsive symptoms (as opposed to some other ways of displaying intense anxiety) tend to evolve in families where one parent, or sometimes both, are already preoccupied with order, neatness and cleanliness. There is evidence to suggest that OCD is more likely to develop in families where someone (or several) already suffers from the disorder. But the extended family may also manifest anxiety symptoms that take different forms from OCD.[27] Clearly, OCD has a genetic basis, but it seems that instead of a specific 'gene for obsessionality', there is a broader genetic predisposition to *anxiety*, which upbringing and/or parental modelling then encourages. A young Elvis Presley insisted on carrying his own eating utensils with him when he ate out, unable to trust the cleanliness of those provided. Yet this odd behaviour echoed his mother's: she had always kept 'special' dishes for him, which nobody else was permitted to use.

Similarly, anorexia seems very often to evolve in families where food and eating are emotionally loaded issues (for example, if one or both parents are overweight, or if one parent expresses love for her children mainly through cooking for them).[28] There is an observable relationship between the particular problem, and the family 'style' as a whole, though because of their unquestioned assumption that problems are located *within individuals*, many mental health professionals fail to see this, and hence deprive themselves of information that would otherwise make their job easier. Families where people hug pain or resentment to themselves, conceal their drinking or have secret affairs tend to produce adolescents who become depressed, smuggle drugs into their bedrooms or lock themselves in the bathroom to vomit after binge eating. Families where children are provided for materially but starved of affection and attention tend to breed young people who steal and lie *within the family*, though rarely outside of it.[29] Families where people display their hurt or their anger in open conflict tend to produce adolescents who 'act out' their rage and distress by punching holes in walls, smashing objects and even attacking family members.

What we call 'emotional disorder' is a form of mental life which all of us are capable of experiencing if subjected to sufficient stress for long enough. It is very reminiscent of the right hemisphere-dominated thinking of young children, which we described in Chapter 3. In this state, we 'take everything personally' – seeing everything else in the world as related directly to ourselves; we can start to feel as if other people are 'staring at us', or 'looking into our minds'; to give ourselves comfort, we revert to ritual, including repeating things (thoughts, actions or both) over and over again; we mistakenly imagine that simply *thinking* something may make it happen, we lose our awareness of the needs and feelings of others (lashing out at the very people who are trying to help us) and our inner world dominates our awareness of outside reality (as an anorexic is convinced she is 'fat' when in fact she is skeletally thin, or a depressed boy believes he is a failure despite being seen by others as a high achiever).

All of the behaviours and thought-patterns I've just listed can make brief appearances as part of a normal life, but for most adults, they are transitory. They may be triggered by a particularly stressful situation, or by the shock of an unanticipated life event like a serious car accident, a natural disaster or the sudden death of a significant other. Most of us recover our equilibrium as our situation improves, or as we come to terms with what has happened. But adolescence faces many of us with considerable pressures at a time when we have not yet developed our own resources to cope with such stress, and so are particularly vulnerable. As my colleague, Australian family therapist Max Cornwell, memorably quipped, 'All adolescents are borderlines!' (That is, many teenagers *temporarily* behave in the impulsive, risk-taking, self-destructive ways we associate with 'Borderline Personality Disorder').[30]

Fortunately, many adolescents are resilient enough to withstand even severe stress. When Jill Ker was 11, her father died in what the family described as a drowning 'accident'. He had been depressed for a considerable time and had almost certainly taken his own life. Despite the fact that she had been so close to her father, Jill's life was not permanently warped by this loss. But the family as a whole did not cope so well. The facts of the tragedy could not be fully acknowledged; Jill's mother gradually retreated into dependency and overprotecting her children: *she offered them what she wanted for herself.* And when Jill was in her third year of high school ('transformed from adolescent rebellion to genuine intellectual interests', as she puts it) her adored elder brother, Bob, just turned 21, died in a car accident. This second blow could easily have induced another girl to develop depression, anxiety or even delusional thinking. But both Jill and her second brother Barry survived this too.[31] It would only be when Jill came to marry that the after-shocks of her father's death would resonate through her life, as we shall see later in this book.

Addiction and independence

Adolescents (with the notable exception of fat-obsessed anorectics) typically eat heartily. Yet even those who do not suffer from eating disorders sometimes develop strange aversions to particular foods, and cravings for others. Again, hormonal activity probably plays a part in this: for example, eggs, previously enjoyed, suddenly become 'disgusting', presumably because of a temporary shift in body chemistry. But above and beyond such biological effects, adolescence is the time when foods and drinks become intensely imbued with *meaning*. The adolescent's peer culture validates his consumption of Coke, French fries and hamburgers: high-calorie foods, often with substantial fat content. The sugar and salt addictions of the five-year-old continue, but supplemented decisively by caffeine (in coffee, Coca-Cola and the newer 'energy drinks') and, for many, nicotine and alcohol. The teenager tentatively trying her first cigarette may not enjoy it much, but she persists, because she knows that to hold one in her fingers or in her mouth (as once she held a nipple) is a badge of belonging – and an excellent way of concealing anxiety. All drugs combine a component of meaning with a component of self-medication.

Thus are born addictive patterns which, for many, will persist throughout early adulthood, and for some, throughout life. The addictive process is the same whether what is in question is a mild, socially sanctioned substance like chocolate, ice-cream or coffee; a stronger but socially sanctioned drug like alcohol; or an illegal and potentially life-threatening drug like heroin or 'ice'. All these substances alter consciousness to some degree; all become sources of comfort in times of stress; all may dominate the user's entire consciousness. All of them can crowd out sources of true nourishment. As many drug/alcohol workers have noticed, it is the most vulnerable adolescents, whose sense of self is not secure and who are particularly reactive to trauma and change, who are most likely to seek succour in drugs of addiction. These young people are drawn with uncanny precision to substances that offer comfort without nourishment, intense short-term pleasure at the cost of extreme long-term misery, and require ever larger doses to maintain their effects. The drugs are as empty and unreliable as the adolescent himself feels inside. Once again, the outside symbolically matches the inside.

Some teenagers commence addiction to alcohol, marijuana or methamphetamines very early, at 12 or 13 – and not surprisingly, these young people often come from troubled homes where one or both parents are themselves addicted, depressed or violent, leading to unempathic, neglectful or punitive parenting. With drug-using peers, teenagers can escape this harsh and uncaring environment, feel accepted and (at least temporarily) blot out their inner pain. Of course, at this age teenagers are rarely capable of admitting that in so many words – they may not even know it themselves. They do not connect their wish to use drugs of addiction with family events they would prefer not to think about at all. 'How's things at home?' 'O.K.' 'How do you get on with your step-Dad?' 'All right'.

By late adolescence, established addicts have effectively formed an entire lifestyle around their drug use. They may still live at home, but they have little meaningful interaction with family members; they talk mainly to fellow-users, seek money (legally or illegally) only to finance their habit and spend most of each day planning how to 'score' or how to avoid the dealers who are chasing them for money. The world of illegal drug using and dealing can be as empty, unreliable and frightening as the world inside the young user. Developmentalist Erik Erikson saw adolescence as a time of 'moratorium' – an 'on hold' time when young people could explore possibilities without commitment.[32] This is especially true for the young addict. The management of the drug becomes a 'life structure': it is his 'job', his source of meaning, and it provides his most reliable relationships. Few adolescents are ready to face their own pain squarely and, for most, the time for detox – either physical or emotional – has not yet come. The moratorium continues.

The use of life-threatening drugs is at one extreme; at the other is the apparently innocuous, yet highly meaningful, preferences all of us evolve for particular foods, drinks and socially sanctioned drugs. At 17 I went to university, living away from home for the first time. One of the several ways that I marked this step towards autonomy was to shift decisively from drinking tea (my childhood habit) to drinking coffee. There were reality-based reasons for the change (coffee was the peer-approved student drink; it was easier to prepare instant coffee in a college room), but the true dynamics of the change were unknown to me at the time. Switching to strong black coffee appreciably raised my daily intake of caffeine, rapidly creating an addiction. I had been an anxious child, pacing the floor as early as two years of age, and continuing to do so whenever emotionally overwrought. By late adolescence, this restlessness had begun to diminish. But my ingestion of several cups of coffee a day kept it alive, as it were, artificially. Caffeine also perpetuated and intensified my insomnia and my tendency to become elevated ('hypomania' – a milder form of the mania experienced in bipolar disorder). In this way, my drug of choice served to prolong several key features of my temperament, almost as if I needed to hold onto the self that I knew, neurotic and dysfunctional though it was.

Similarly, I suggest, with all of us: the drug or combination of drugs we unconsciously select in late adolescence and early adulthood is exquisitely matched to our pre-existing temperament, intensifying some of its features while masking others. Thus Elvis Presley's lifelong use of amphetamines intensified his temperamental restlessness, counteracted his addiction to fatty foods, restored his energy after all-night partying and provided temporary relief from anxiety (while in the longer term worsening it). Cocaine, like coffee, offers a temporary 'lift' and abundant energy – no wonder it is the drug of choice for always-on-the-go high achievers and stage performers. Crystal meth generates a powerful sense of invulnerability and omnipotence – under its influence, the user feels he can do anything, and get away with it – a clear continuation of the way that normal adolescents often feel, and which encourages them to take dangerous risks, convinced they will escape unscathed.

Paranoia and depression are the dark undersides of many addictive drugs: when the user 'comes down', she starts to feel a restless anxiety, with circling, repetitive negative thoughts, or an overwhelming feeling that the world is out to get her. Even coffee (very mildly) can do this when the caffeine high wears off; so (much more powerfully) can cocaine, so can marijuana and 'ice'.

A self to grow into

However unformed and immature we may appear in late adolescence, the personality that we exhibit by our late teens is basically the personality we will live with for the remainder of our lives. We will *add* a great deal to it – self-insight, wisdom in the ways of the world, greater ability to discipline and channel our impulses, the patience that is born of repeated pain and frustration and disappointment, the confidence that comes from having mastered a difficult job, from knowing sexual delight, from having parented children. We may learn new languages and new ways of comporting ourselves in company. But none of these things will transform us into a different person. None of them will *take away* the structure we have, by late adolescence, erected around the framework of our temperament. Like the evolution of the brain itself, the process of personality development is cumulative, not substitutive; it operates by accretion ('adding on').

In his first year at Military Academy, an 18-year-old George Smith Patton commenced a conscious attempt at 'remaking' his personality. Believing himself 'stupid' because he could not spell, and periodically despairing that he would reach his grandiose ambition to be 'a general by the time I'm 26', Patton believed that he must kill his sensitivity, and train himself for aggression. In front of the mirror, he practised what he called his 'war face' — a fierce scowl. It was also at this point in his life, as he crossed from boyhood to manhood, that he deliberately adopted the profanity that would become his trademark when addressing his men ('We'll go through the Nazis like shit through a goose!'). He forced himself to stand among the targets on the rifle range, exposing himself to the risk of being shot, because he feared that he might be a coward ('counter-phobic' behaviour). In all of these ways, Patton was adding new 'layers' to his existing personality, habits of behaviour which would successfully convince others that he was a tough, hard-bitten soldier — but he never eliminated the softness and the self-doubt that lay beneath. Sometimes we perversely look for deep and hidden motivations, ignoring far simpler ones that stare us in the face. How much of Patton's desperate need to become a 'man's man' was due solely to the fact that he retained into adulthood a high-pitched, squeaky voice that sounded so unlike a 'real soldier's'?

Notes

1 'Newspeak' was the version of English employed by The Party in George Orwell's *Nineteen Eighty-Four* (1948), an English shorn of its complexities and nuances, modelled on Charles Kay Ogden's 'Basic English' (introduced in 1930).
2 *World of Warcraft* (2004) is the world's most successful 'MMORPG' (massively multi-player on-line role-playing game), with over seven million players worldwide in 2015. *Second Life* (launched in 2003) is an on-line virtual world, similar to a MMORPG, but not a 'game' in the strict sense. It is restricted to individuals who are 16 years and over, and is mostly 'played' by adults. SL has its own currency, and has around one million followers worldwide.
3 See Brian Boyd, *On the Origin of Stories: Evolution, Cognition and Fiction*, Cambridge, MA, and London, Harvard University Press, 2009: 104; 163–165.
4 See Chapter 2 Notes.
5 See Irving Goffman, *Stigma: Notes on the Management of Spoiled Identity*, Englewood Cliffs, NJ, Prentice-Hall, 1963.
6 See Lawrence Stone, *The Family, Sex and Marriage in England, 1500–1800*, London, Weidenfeld and Nicholson, 1977.
7 'My Generation' was written by Pete Townshend and recorded by The Who in 1965. Townshend's reflections on this period of his life can be found in his autobiography, *Who I Am*, London, HarperCollins, 2012.

8 The ages typical of the onset of puberty in our own society are not necessarily typical of others: evidence shows that puberty comes earlier in warmer climates; it can differ for different races; and in Europe, at least, age of onset has become steadily younger since the 1840s, a striking development that has been attributed to dietary changes and other environmental factors. The fact that girls who have significant interaction with adult males tend to reach puberty earlier than those who do not (the 'Vandenberg Effect') suggests that we may be seeing another example of epigenetics – a particular environment may 'pull' an earlier unfolding of genetic potential than would otherwise have occurred.

9 Peter Whitmer, *The Inner Elvis: A Psychological Biography of Elvis Aaron Presley*, NY, Hyperion, 1996: 61.

10 'I'm a King Bee' was written and performed by Slim Harpo in 1957, and later recorded by the Rolling Stones on their first album in 1964.

11 See Arthur Applebee, *The Child's Concept of Story*, Chicago, University of Chicago Press, 1978: 94, 100.

12 See Hugh Crago, 'Anna Abridges *Masha*' in *Language Arts*, 66, 3 (March, 1989): 252–266. See also my *Entranced by Story: Brain, Tale and Teller, from Infancy to Old Age*, London and NY, Routledge, 2014: 59–92.

13 See Erik Erickson, 'Eight Ages of Man' in *Childhood and Society*, 2nd Edn, Harmondsworth, Penguin, 1975: 252–255. [First published in the US in 1950.]

14 For more on the imaginary worlds of the Brontës and Jennifer and June Gibbons, see Chapter 4 of Crago, 2014, op. cit.: 113–116.

15 See Judith Milner, 'Narrative Groupwork with Young Women—and their Mobile Phones', *International Journal of Narrative Therapy and Community Work*, 3 (2003): 50–56.

16 'You Don't Own Me' was written by John Madara and David White; although Gore did not write the song herself, it had a strong personal meaning for her, both at the time she recorded it and later in her life. Kate Bush's 'Wuthering Heights' was released in 1978 to a response that Bush found completely overwhelming, and she refused to perform in public for many years as a result.

17 See Mick Houghton, *I've Always Kept a Unicorn: The Biography of Sandy Denny*, London, Faber, 2015: 65–66.

18 See I. Deutscher, *Stalin: A Political Biography*, London, Oxford University Press, 1949: 17.

19 See Carol Gilligan, Nona P. Lyons and Trudy J. Hanmer, *Making Connections: The Relational Worlds of Adolescent Girls at Emma Willard School*, Cambridge, MA, Harvard University Press, 1989.

20 See Whitmer, 1996, op. cit.: 111–112.

21 See *The Psychological Birth of the Human Infant: Symbiosis and Individuation* (with Fred Pine and Anni Bergman), London, Karnac, 1985. [First published in 1975.]

22 See Tom Pitt Aikens and Alice Thomas Ellis, *Loss of the Good Authority: The Cause of Delinquency*, London, Viking, 1989.

23 See Barbara Stoney, *Enid Blyton: The Biography*, 2nd Edn, London, Hodder, 1992: 26. [First edition published in 1974.]

24 'You cannot not communicate' was one of the 'five axioms' Paul Watzlawik introduced in his early work. See Paul Watzlawik, Janet Beavin Bavelas, Don Jackson and Bill O'Hanlon, *Pragmatics of Human Communication*, NY, Norton, 2011. [First edition published in 1962.]

25 It was actually John Watson, the pioneer behaviourist, who first described adolescence as a time of 'storm and stress', although such a conception would have suited those of a psychoanalytic persuasion even better. However, the more recent view has been that we have over-problematised this period. Other things being equal, say scholars like Paul Amato, adolescence need not pose significant stresses for the average adolescent. See e.g. Paul Amato and Alan Booth, *A Generation at Risk: Growing Up in an Era of Family Upheaval*, Harvard University Press, 1997.

26 See for example *Explorations: An E-Journal of Narrative Practice*, 1 (2011): 14–20.
27 See Eric E. Ingram and Joseph M. Price (Eds), *Vulnerability to Psychopathology: Risk across the Lifespan*, 2nd Edn, NY, London, Guilford, 2010: 347–348.
28 Salvador Minuchin, *Psychosomatic Families: Anorexia Nervosa in Context*, Cambridge, MA, Harvard University Press, 1978.
29 See Fred W. Seymour and David Epston, 'An Approach to Childhood Stealing, with Evaluation of 45 Cases', *Australian and New Zealand Journal of Family Therapy*, 10, 3 (1989): 137–143.
30 Max Cornwell, personal communication. 'Borderline Personality Disorder' is a very controversial diagnostic category, and it has been argued that its symptoms most often reflect chaotic, traumatic experiences in childhood or youth. See Michael H. Stone, *Abnormalities of Personality, Within and Beyond the Realm of Treatment*, NY, Norton, 1993: 215–258; Bessel van der Kolk, *The Body Keeps the Score: Mind, Brain and Body in the Transformation of Trauma*, London, Allen Lane, 2014: 136–148.
31 Jill Ker Conway, *The Road from Coorain: An Australian Memoir*, Melbourne, Heinemann, 1989: 114–119.
32 See Eric Erickson, 'Eight Ages of Man' in *Childhood and Society*, Harmondsworth, Penguin, 1965: 252–255. [First published in the US in 1950.]

6

'THE TIDE IS HIGH'

Young adulthood

'Twixt 12 and 30?

When I was an undergraduate in the 1960s, textbooks of developmental psychology stopped abruptly when their human subjects reached the age of 20. This was not quite as absurd as it now sounds, because the years of childhood and adolescence do embody the most rapid, influential and *obvious* unfolding of the mental and physical maturing that is programmed into human beings from birth. However, since the publication in 1950 of Eric Erikson's landmark *Childhood and Society*, developmental psychology has slowly extended its coverage to include adulthood. The years between 20 and 50 leapt into prominence in the 1970s as a result of the work of Dan Levinson, popularised by Gail Sheehey in her best seller, *Passages*.[1] More recently, neurological advances have led to a major correction of Piaget's belief that cognitive development was complete by the end of adolescence. In fact, it seems that brain maturation continues, albeit much more slowly, throughout early and middle adulthood.

I have gradually come to see that it is somewhat artificial to divide adolescence from the first half of young adulthood. After all, prior to the last century or so, most people did not think of 'adolescence' as a separate stage of life, or even have a special word for it – 'youth' was the closest they had, and the term 'teenager' was not coined until 1941. Adolescents already possess most of the mental equipment they will need to function effectively in the adult world, and young adults in their twenties continue to evince the insouciance, lack of self-reflection and conviction of personal invulnerability we associate with adolescence. Schizophrenia, the mental illness most frequently associated with late adolescence, typically develops *between* the mid-teens and the mid-twenties, straddling the transition from late adolescence to early adulthood.[2] Though I have retained the conventional distinction for this book, I have come to think of the period of true youth as spanning the years 'twixt 12 and 30' (not, as crooner Pat Boone once sang, 'twelve and twenty').

'To love and work'

Levinson's *The Seasons of a Man's Life* (first published in 1978) proposed that male adulthood fell into a series of predictable stages, in which longer periods of relative stability alternated with shorter periods in which the individual's 'life structure' would be rebuilt. Echoing Freud's statement that the tasks of adulthood are 'to love and to work', Levinson's life structure is made up of two primary components: relationship and career. In a stable life structure, a man experiences himself as doing useful or meaningful work and advancing within his chosen career. Similarly, he feels valued and supported within a continuing relationship, able in his turn to offer support and nurturing to his partner and children. Stable 'structure building' periods can last up to ten years, but inevitably, says Levinson, are followed by shorter 'structure changing' periods (of five to seven years' duration) in which the man to some extent questions his previous choices, and inwardly experiences anything from mild discomfort to major crisis. Such disquiet may prompt a man to change his career, end his marriage or even suffer a complete breakdown, but in other cases the inner questionings may be set aside, and outwardly life proceeds as before. In the early adult years, Levinson proposed periods of structure-changing in the years between 17 and 23 (the 'Early Adult Transition'), between 27 and 33 (the 'Age 30 Transition') and between 40 and 45 (the 'Midlife Transition'). Thus Levinson's stages of adulthood somewhat resemble the alternating periods of gradual development and sudden 'growth spurts' of childhood and adolescence.

Levinson's pioneering research can easily enough be faulted on details. His original model was based on in-depth interviews with only 40 individuals, mainly middle-class and professional men. It failed to take into account how differently women typically experience their adult lives – 'advancement within a stable career' is very difficult if you also want to bear children and be their primary caregiver, unless employment conditions facilitate it (which, at the time Levinson was writing, they did not). Late in his life, Levinson broadened and adapted his theory, although the overarching concepts of structure-building and structure-changing phases were not significantly modified. By the time *Seasons of a Woman's Life* appeared in 1996, the academic world had already concluded that Levinson's theory was too much of its time – too male-centric, too class-specific and too American. It reflected a stable work environment in which most adults expected to have a single career for life, which is certainly no longer the case, and since 1996, the 'digital revolution' has made for even more far-reaching changes to our expectations of work and relationships. Apart from these valid criticisms, however, Levinson's theory has evoked strong opposition on less rational grounds. Adults don't mind a bit if their *children's* development is viewed in age-related stages, but dislike the idea that their own, adult futures might in any way be predictable. Levinson's ideas seemed deterministic and limiting to many, and still do. Yet even if Levinson was too rigid in his attempts to pin down his developmental stages to precise ages, there is much that is useful in his conceptualisation of adulthood. And, as I shall argue in later chapters, our 'freedom' is more limited than we like to think, and the element of predictability in each of our lives is higher than most of us would care to know.

Indeed, it is precisely as we travel through early adulthood that the patterned nature of our lives becomes more obvious. If our lives at 20 seem like arrows shooting straight ahead into a hazy distance, they will come increasingly to resemble boomerangs, turning as they reach their furthest point from the thrower, and curving back, ultimately to return whence they came. But only around the early thirties do most of us start to become conscious of that. We are still engaged in the great adventure of forging an independent life, making a career, finding the 'right' person with whom to build a stable relationship and raise children. In a carry-over from adolescence, what we are most conscious of in our twenties is our *difference* from our parents – what we are most proud of is our ability to make our *own* decisions, to captain our own ships. Anne Brontë voiced it through her heroine Agnes Grey, almost certainly describing what she had herself felt when she left home for the first time, at 19:

> How delightful it would be to be a governess! To go out into the world, to enter upon a new life, to act for myself, to exercise my unused faculties, to try my unknown powers, to earn my own maintenance . . . to show papa what his little Agnes could do, to convince Mama and Mary that I was not quite the helpless, thoughtless being they supposed.[3]

No longer awkward or surprising – the way it seemed in early adolescence – the body has settled down into predictability and (for most people) dependability. Except for individuals who experience the crisis of accident or the early onset of a chronic illness, young adults usually take their health and strength for granted. For those adults who build their initial life structures around the body and its capacities (manual labourers, models, athletes, sexual adventurers), the effortless way their bodies respond to challenge is usually a source of pride. The people who find a partner and start a family in the early adult years also experience a certain status and confidence that comes simply from having accomplished what society seems to expect. Anxieties about attractiveness do not disappear (and the fashion industry has a vested interest in keeping them alive) but they typically recede somewhat. New responsibilities in the adult world and more confidence in our ability to attract a desirable mate help to restore a sense of proportion about our physical appearance.

For those who form part of the workforce there is often a sense of accomplishment, and a willingness to look forward to a better job some day, better pay, greater challenge or a promotion. Even if the present is humdrum and disappointing, it is relatively easy for young adults to focus on the future: 'when I get a raise', 'when we have children', 'when the kids are at school', 'when we've paid off the house'. With its reserves of energy and resilience still high, the young adult body fuels a more general optimism. Radical movements from the French revolution to the Freedom Rides of the 1960s have depended heavily on the passion and felt invulnerability of young adults. Between 18 and 27, young adults may embrace a cause more completely than they will ever do again. Many will risk imprisonment, torture, even death, certain that their sacrifice will not be in vain, convinced that a new era is about to dawn. As Ashley Hutchings, founding member of the folk-rock band Fairport Convention, put it in 1967: 'It's all to do with youth, and the things that come out of youth. It's the fact that you have this enthusiasm and bravery that you're never able to hang on to as you get older'. It is, in the words of novelist Joseph Conrad, 'the feeling that I could last for ever'.[4] The irony is that we can only fully know and value that feeling when it has gone.

The tide is high

Young adulthood is the high tide of consciously chosen selfhood when, for a short time, the waves of our individuality may lap shores unknown to our families. And typically, this is the time when, as Dan Levinson says, we make our two most momentous decisions – choice of marriage partner, and choice of career – before we are old enough and wise enough to understand the implications of either.[5] Neither marriage nor career is any longer, for many people, the fixed and immutable thing that it seemed in 1960s America. But Levinson remains accurate at a general level: we do make some of the great decisions of life well before we are qualified by experience or self-knowledge to understand fully what we are doing. And perhaps that is the way it has to be. Believing ourselves to be making 'rational choices' about our future (the realm of the brain's left hemisphere), we may in fact be guided by the idealistic, romantic thinking of the right hemisphere, a kind of thinking that prevailed in our early childhood and which has not gone away simply because we now consider ourselves 'grown up'.

Aged 25 in 1922, Enid Blyton is a Froebel-trained teacher, acting as governess to small groups of children, but already publishing verse and stories. By literary standards, her work is predictable and clichéd, but it accurately gauges the taste of ordinary readers. Central to her growing success as a writer is Enid's temperamental trait of persistence, for she has continued to submit her work for publication in the face of hundreds of earlier rejections. Having left home at 18, Enid has turned her back on her family; she will never see her mother again, and her father only rarely. She tells her friends that she was adopted. The protective lies her mother insisted she tell about her father's absence are already repeating themselves in her own 'blanking out' of her family of origin.[6] A four-year-old can deny some naughtiness he's committed in order to avoid punishment; a young adult, however, can create a web of interlocking falsehoods that may last the rest of her life. At 27, Enid marries divorced publisher Hugh Pollock. She appears sexually and intellectually confident, and is already sure that her destiny is to be a successful writer.

Many young adults travel for reasons that appear to need no further explanation than a wish to 'spread their wings' or to 'see the world' (two phrases in which we have conventionally acknowledged this impulse). Young men and women from depressed rural areas typically migrate to cities, for the obvious reason that work is easier to find, and prospects better. And, of course, better-off young people in their late teens and early twenties are typically unencumbered with children or pressing family responsibilities. Travel or temporary relocation seems exciting and adventurous. It is one way that young adults can experience and act out a sense of control over their own lives, even if the distances involved are not great, and the time 'abroad' is brief.

It is 1959, and Australian Jill Ker (later to be Jill Ker Conway), aged 25, has made the momentous decision to abandon a secure future teaching history at Sydney University in order to study for her doctorate at Harvard. Several things have influenced this decision, some calculated and rational, others seemingly driven by deep emotional programming of which Jill is unaware at the time. Many key life decisions have no single 'cause', but originate in the convergence of separate impulses or needs. Jill has been passed over for a position in the Australian diplomatic corps in favour of a male applicant – something that was typical of the times in which she grew up. Because she is a woman, she is convinced, Australia will never reward her talents. She has already formed a favourable impression of the United States as the result of a friendship with a young American. However, there is a more compelling reason still for Jill to leave her own country. Since her father's premature death, Jill has experienced her mother as increasingly dependent, demanding and emotionally manipulative. She feels massive guilt at the thought even of leaving home. As she herself puts it, going to study in America will 'finesse' the whole issue of gaining her independence. 'Doing a geographical' is one of the most frequent ways that young adults attempt to deal with ambivalent ties to parents, family or homeland.

Yet there is another, less conscious reason for her life-changing decision. Shortly before his death, her father had told 11-year-old Jill to 'make something of yourself . . . get a real education, and get away from this damn country for good'.[7] Can it be that she has taken him *literally* to mean she should 'get away' not just from the drought-ravaged western region of New South Wales, but from Australia itself? Certainly Jill, like many Australians of her time, seems convinced that a 'real education' can only be obtained overseas, and certainly she has 'left this damn country for good', for once she reaches Boston she will never again live in Australia.

Only a minority of young adults experience as fierce a desire to escape from home and parents as Jill Ker's or Enid Blyton's, but the impulse is still real. Travel in young adulthood is the logical continuation of the adolescent's urgency to break free of family rules and restrictions. Many young adults do not need to stay away permanently: they spend some time abroad, or in a distant region, and then return closer to where they were brought up. Simply to have been away, to have done something different, has 'got it out of their system'. Perhaps what that really means is that they feel somehow confirmed in their selfhood. Throughout life, the feeling of having 'been there, done that' confers a certain authority, a certain self-confidence.

But the urge to travel in young adulthood is not simply a wish to get away. 'Seeing the world' represents, in part, a need to expose ourselves to challenge: new places, new people, new possibilities, new ideas. It is self-chosen *education*. How profound or how superficial that exposure is depends on the individual concerned. In 1911, many young American army officers expected to spend periods serving outside the United States, even in peacetime. But at the age of 27, the same age that both Jill Ker and Enid Blyton married, Lt Joe Stilwell spent a few weeks in China, then in the throes of the nationalist revolution. That visit would profoundly alter his life. Stilwell felt an instinctive sympathy with the Chinese, noticing their capacity for hard work, loyalty and persistence in the face of great adversity. *He noticed those qualities because he himself possessed them.* He eventually learned their language. He also felt an instinctive frustration with China, which seemed to throw away its opportunities, and to stubbornly turn away from its own advantage. These traits were also Stilwell's own, and in Chapter 9 we shall see how his own life path and the fate of Kuomintang China became inextricably intertwined during the East Asian campaigns of World War Two.[8]

Similarly, we can read between the lines of Jill Ker Conway's account of her early days in America and find an explanation for why she found the United States so much more sympathetic than her native Australia. To Jill, the United States represented freedom, expansiveness, a generous spirit of acceptance, rather than the narrowness, prejudice and ex-colonial mentality that she perceived in her own country. Up to a point, her perceptions accurately reflected a difference between the two national cultures at that time. Yet it is clear that Jill had already formed many of these conclusions about America before she ever went there. Jill's choice of America was in a sense *a choice of one conception of herself and her future above another.*

Other countries, then, represent encounters with parts of ourselves, the more vivid and beguiling because we see them as different and exotic. We fail to recognise that what we have travelled so far to see may well be what we have brought with us. The appeal of 'abroad' (distant countries, new languages and customs, different climates) remains strong throughout the lives of many adults – the tourist industry could not exist without it – and maybe this has something to do with the older parts of our brains, for while the left hemisphere of the cortex thinks in terms of *time*, the right thinks in terms of *space*.[9] After all, isn't arriving in a new land where everything seems new and strange a parallel (however distant and unconscious) to what we experienced when we came into the world? It is as if, by travelling to new *places*, we can transcend *time* – wipe out a painful past, or even return to the hopeful idealism of our earliest child-hood years. Through travel and immersion in other cultures, we enrich ourselves with new experiences and deepen our self-confidence. We make choices that seem exciting and unprecedented. Yet, at this high tide of selfhood, our 'choices' may simply be ways of confirming the choices already made long before by others, and by ourselves.

Choices, choices

It is in young adulthood, typically from the late teens to the late twenties, that most people in our society adopt the belief systems they will live by for the rest of their lives. These ideologies are less superficially chosen than the intense but fleeting enthusiasms we examined in the last chapter. Yet, just as in adolescence, when making these choices we often feel strongly drawn to select affiliations *different* from our parents'. My mother and father, for as long as I could remember, had always voted for conservative political parties. As a child and adolescent, I simply assumed that these were the right ones to vote for, and always sat up on election night hoping that the conservatives would win (which, given the state of Australian politics at the time, they always did). But when I was old enough to vote for the first time, I voted for the party of reform and social conscience, and despite many dissatisfactions with the party of my choice, have since seen no compelling reason to return to my parents' allegiance. My need to be different from them had temporarily overridden the innate conservatism of my 'responsible eldest' profile. Yet, though I chose the opposite side of politics from theirs, my *persistence* in supporting my chosen party exactly paralleled theirs. *It is not in content, but in form* that we display our deepest loyalties.

If, on the other hand, we do remain loyal to our parents' politics – or their religious beliefs – we often enter more intensely into those allegiances than they did and even pursue them further. Sometimes we unconsciously locate one facet of a parent's beliefs or interests and make that our own central focus, so that our practice 'fills out' what is only outlined in theirs. While our father was a tradi-tional churchgoer who rarely spoke of his faith and never attempted to convert others to it, both of my siblings, in early adulthood, adopted evangelical versions of the same faith, made Bible study central in their lives and took very seriously the command to live out their convictions in daily action. In this way they intensified our father's choice, and also successfully differentiated themselves from me, whose choice it was in early adulthood to give up Christianity altogether (a choice that had also been my mother's). Sometimes, though, we neither adopt and intensify our parents' choice, nor 'go to the opposite extreme'. Instead, we compromise, by choosing a set of beliefs that seems ostensibly different from our family's, yet which subtly reflects it just the same. Nowhere is this principle clearer than in the way we choose our careers.

In small-scale, tribal societies, career choice as we understand it did not exist. Roles and duties for both sexes were largely prescribed, and most people were generalists, because there were relatively few specialisms. Life did not change greatly from one generation to the next, and so there was no particular incentive for individuals to move out of their traditional lands, or to seek out new roles. Ambitions and talents were played out within the ambit of the small community itself. Prior to the industrial revolution, career choice was not an issue for the majority of people in Europe either. The accident of birth largely determined one's future – at least for men, since women were generally destined for careers as wives and mothers. If your father was a small farmer, you would probably follow in his footsteps. If your father owned a mill or a store, you would probably join him in that enterprise and continue it after his death. Now that genuine career options do exist for many young adults, however, it is predictable that they will use those choices to balance their loyalty to family traditions with a need to be different. Some young adults will opt for walking 'in their parents' footsteps' – but aim far higher.

In 1948, Margaret Hilda Roberts, 23-year-old daughter of a Lincolnshire grocer, is a young industrial chemist. She applies, unsuccessfully, for a position with chemical giant ICI. The company's report on her interview describes her as 'headstrong, obstinate, and dangerously self-opinionated'. In the same year, she cements her future allegiance, and joins the Conservative Party, embracing a political position that her family would have approved. Within a decade she will be seen as a future party leader.

As with the choice of beliefs, some children will opt for reversing their parents' pattern: 'As a young man, I swore I'd never set foot in the family business!' or, 'If there was one thing I was sure of, it was that I'd never, never be a teacher like Mum!'. The barely concealed anger of such declarations marks them as motivated primarily by a desire to break away, to 'be oneself'. If 'reactive' career decisions like these are not supported by the young adult's own talents and personality traits, then they tend to be unstable. On the other hand, if the impulse to differentiate is reinforced by the young adult's real abilities, then it is unlikely that he or she will waver from that original choice. A grazier's daughter like Jill Ker, who opts for a professional career, may from time to time dream of returning to the land, but realises that such a career would use fewer of the intellectual and creative abilities she has cultivated over many years, and so when the opportunity comes, she declines the chance to run a property.

Similarly, when young adults are content to do what their father or mother did, motivated by family loyalty, or timidity, or both – something that developmental psychologist James Marcia referred to as a 'foreclosed' identity decision[10] – they are likely to experience a crisis either in their thirties, at midlife. By that age, they may experience their original choice as restrictive, and greater self-knowledge and self-confidence may have propelled them into realising 'there's a whole lot more out there than I ever knew when I was 20'. Their new choice of career might then integrate more of their own abilities and potential than was possible for them when they simply 'drifted' into running the family farm, or working in the same factory as their mother.

But the most common pattern of all is the one in which the career choices of young adults unconsciously balance both the 'togetherness force' of family loyalty and the 'separateness force' of self-differentiation within the family system.[11] Thus the son of a minister of religion becomes a psychiatrist or clinical psychologist: a secular 'priest'. The daughter of a union boss obtains a degree in social work – the drive to act for change and justice is still present, but it has taken different forms and attached itself to different causes.

Charles Darwin's paternal grandfather, the first Erasmus Darwin (Charles's brother was named Erasmus too) was a physician, but also a man of science in a wider sense. He espoused radical evolutionary ideas, which he expressed in long poems that were widely read and admired. Erasmus's third son, Robert Waring Darwin (Charles Darwin's father), was virtually expected to be a physician, and was. In his turn, Robert's son Charles also commenced medical studies. Charles experienced his father as rigid and disapproving of his early interest in science. By turning his back on medicine and making a career as a biologist and evolutionary theorist, Charles Darwin 'rebelled' against his father, and yet developed key aspects of his *grandfather's* wide ranging scientific interests – in particular, his devotion to evolutionary thinking.[12] His writings, like his grandfather's, were much read, although highly controversial, and his name became synonymous with the theory of evolution. Charles had 'balanced' his need to differentiate from his father with a career choice that 'followed in the footsteps' of his father's father.

My own pattern of career choice nicely demonstrates how individual talent, family norms and the need to individuate all flow together in an individual's choices through his or her lifetime. Both of my parents were outstanding elementary school teachers and, at an early stage in their professional careers, served as school counsellors, which at that time (the 1930s) meant doing educational testing and offering career advice, rather than therapeutic counselling. By the time I reached adulthood, my father had become an inspector of schools, and my mother a college lecturer in education. As the eldest child, strongly influenced by my parents' model yet aware of wanting to be different from them, I opted initially for a career in teaching, but teaching at university rather than school level. This gave me a sense of 'going further' than my parents, yet it also acknowledged my own deficits: I lacked the social confidence to manage a school classroom. However, my original choice of academic discipline – literature – did not offer me an avenue for intellectual activity that I could fully believe in or make my own. I restlessly explored a number of possibilities, but eventually opted to leave academic teaching altogether, at the age of 30, and retrain myself for a career in – yes – counselling. Career shifts around that age are common, and form part of the evidence on which Levinson postulated his structure-changing 'Age 30 Transition'.

Of course, the counselling that I chose to study was very different from the profession that my parents had taken up half a century earlier. Yet was I not *literally* repeating an element of their pattern, as Jill Ker *literally* interpreted her father's words years later? (I have come to see that these literal repetitions of earlier generational patterns are hints that the older parts of our brains are at work in such decisions. As psychoanalysts would say, they are 'unconscious'.) In the years since my career change, I have spent time as a full-time counsellor, and time as a full-time university teacher. Eventually, I combined both roles — lecturing to university students of counselling. Counselling has enriched my life and made my teaching more sensitive, responsible and functional than it was when I began lecturing. But ultimately, I am probably still at my best as a teacher. And when I look back at my parents' professional careers, I realise that the same was true of them. Both of them were most valued for their teaching abilities, rather than for their administrative skill or their scholarship. The temperamental traits of persistence, sensitivity and emotional expressiveness — which I shared with them — all contributed to my success as a teacher, strengthened by the actual modelling they provided. In a sense, I *knew how to* be a teacher simply from having grown up with them, despite never having seen either in a classroom setting.

In their own ways, both my brother and sister have also followed our parents' model, even though less literally than I. In fact, if we look at the spread of career choices made by a set of siblings, we will often find that it exhibits the same 'variations on a theme' as their inherited *physical* features. The same will be true of their values, leisure pursuits, clothing preferences, tastes in music or reading or food. In all of these ways, our family microcultures seem to imitate the process of variation within a genetic legacy (as Mendel famously demonstrated in his experiments with plants). In all of these ways, we seem to balance similarity and difference, both from our parents and from each other. These observations on career choice are, I should emphasise, my own, and not supported by hard data.

The early adulthood of the painter Vincent van Gogh is a dramatic example of how desperately an individual can struggle with the balance between family loyalty and individuation. Vincent's family included both clergymen and art dealers. His father and his grandfather were pastors of the Dutch Reformed church. He was functionally an eldest child, a brother (whose name he had inherited) having been born dead exactly a year before his own birth. In adolescence, he began his working life as an art dealer like his brother Theo, a job which allowed his own aspirations no outlet. At 22 he was unhappy and unfulfilled, spending much of his time in Bible study in a driven search for answers to his doubts about the meaning of life. He shifted from job to job, eventually committing himself to training for the ministry. But he dropped out of theological studies, opting instead for a short course intended to train missionaries. At 26 he was a volunteer lay preacher, but his superiors saw signs of emotional instability, and he was dismissed.

All of these aborted initiatives suggest what Levinson calls a 'flawed life structure' in early adulthood. The failure of Vincent's efforts to follow the family path led to a decisive career shift at 27 (the earliest Levinson allows the Age 30 Transition to occur), when Vincent began to study art. Interestingly, at this point

Vincent actually returned to live with his parents for a while, almost as if to say, 'I wasn't ready to leave home back then'. The second life structure that Vincent built, this time around art, failed to give him a sense of true autonomy, for he could not sell his work, and he continued to be supported by his brother, Theo. Nevertheless, he continued to paint with driven intensity, completing no less than 40 self-portraits in the last four years of his life. *Relationship* is the second element in Levinson's model of the life structure. Vincent fell deeply in love on two occasions, at 21 and 28, and was rejected both times. He lived for a time with a prostitute in The Hague and, at 31, entered a relationship with a different woman, which ended when she committed suicide. His choices of partners, like his choices of career, had proved abortive. They symbolised his truncated selfhood, and anticipated his own future. He had 'loved and worked' but, by his own estimation, had failed in both. He was dead at the age of 37. An earlier Vincent, his brother, had died: did he therefore 'need' to die too?[13]

The cradle of pathology?

'Flawed life structures' are common enough in early adulthood, but in Vincent's case there was another significant factor: he appears to have suffered from manic-depressive illness (now more generally known as 'bipolar affective disorder' or 'bipolar' for short).[14] Manic-depressive illness belongs to early adulthood, and is most often diagnosed in the early twenties. For most of us, early adulthood (and particularly the period between the late twenties and early thirties) is when, as a result of continuing brain maturation, we start to display 'reflective thought' – looking at our own behaviour and personality in a more objective way than we have previously done.[15] It is a time of life often associated with creative breakthrough – and it was certainly around this age that Vincent opted decisively to pursue his art. In normal individuals, all of this suggests a higher level of co-operation between the instinctive, idealistic right hemisphere of the cortex, and the self-analysing, self-conscious left. In the case of manic-depressive illness, however, that balance fails to develop. Instead, there is an increased likelihood of wildly impulsive actions, overwhelmingly powerful feelings and grandiose visions – a kind of exaggerated parody of the right hemisphere's typical way of seeing the world.

To be fair, many individuals who develop manic-depressive illness start life as temperamentally thin boundaried (exquisitely sensitive to pain and suffering) and high reactive – prone to express their feelings more dramatically than most. Yet the onset of the illness seems to bring a new dimension to that genetic profile: unlike most of us, bipolar individuals may temporarily lose touch with reality, and begin to believe things that, in their right minds, they would never have believed previously – convictions of 'destiny', or 'specialness', convictions that the usual rules do not apply to them. Their thoughts 'race' at a million miles an hour, they have great difficulty sleeping and they drive themselves to extraordinary feats of endurance, whether it be in artistic creativity, or in cleaning and tidying their homes. The wild, windblown cypress trees that Vincent van Gogh painted obsessively in his final years in Provence show us the state of his inner world: vivid, intensely alive, yet curiously distorted, permanently swayed not just by the hot winds of the South of France, but by the gales that tormented his own mind.

Manic-depressive illness has been known to humankind at least since the ancient Greeks, who were the first Europeans to leave us a literature about psychosis (madness). As Ruth Padel points out in *Whom Gods Destroy*, the language used in Greek tragedy to describe madness has shaped the way that we in the West have seen it ever since.[16] The Greek poets described madness as something 'dark' or 'black', something 'put into' people by the Gods, driving them to raving and violence. To Aeschylus, Sophocles and Euripedes, powerful emotions had an existence semi-independent of human beings, outside of their control. They could drive people temporarily 'sideways' or 'outside of their minds'. Today, we still speak of 'black rage' which – rarely, but alarmingly – sometimes propels people to kill others. At the other extreme of the manic-depressive swing, the sufferer's anguish becomes so great that he or she sees suicide as the only option. 'Depression' is far too mild a word for this state, just as 'anger' does not adequately describe 'black rage'. Bipolar illness is a 'mood disorder' – while it may include distorted and unrealistic thinking, manic-depressive illness is primarily about extreme *feelings*, which can dominate rational thought to the point where the suffering person is convinced that she is coping well and feeling good when in fact her behaviour is risky and potentially self-destructive.

What the ancient Greeks described corresponds quite well with the most extreme form of bipolar illness (Bipolar I), in which delusions and hallucinations may occur, but not so well with schizophrenia, and interestingly, schizophrenia seems to have been comparatively rare in the ancient world.[17] Today we distinguish schizophrenia as a 'thought disorder' – taking the affected person into a strange, alienated state in which thoughts are divorced from feelings, indeed, in which feelings may not be consciously experienced at all.[18] In schizophrenia, it is typically *thoughts* that patients experience as being 'put into' them from outside – as in the common delusion that television broadcasts (or, these days, mobile phones?) might contain 'special information' intended only for the patient, 'instructions' as to how they should act (which, as in manic-depression, may even include murderous or self-harming actions). Schizophrenia seems to have become far more common (at least in Europe) from the late eighteenth century, prompting speculations that widespread urbanisation and human alienation from the natural world may have been factors in the apparent increase. Evidence has steadily been accumulating for the effects of melatonin deprivation (due to artificial light) on mental health.[19] Interestingly, Vincent van Gogh's devoted brother Theo survived him by only a year, developing first a kidney condition, and then being diagnosed with schizophrenia. Because manic-depressive illness can be misdiagnosed as schizophrenia, it seems possible that Theo (a lifelong

depressive) may actually have developed his brother's illness. Early family therapists noted that when the 'identified patient' in a family starts to improve, another
sibling will often decline into some kind of illness or emotional disorder, a
systemic variant of Freud's 'symptom substitution' within an individual. Could
this have occurred with the van Gogh brothers?

Some enchanted evening . . .

Falling in love for the first time is one of life's most radiant experiences.
No wonder that most of us remember it lifelong. Typically, it coincides with
youthful idealism, ambition and optimism. Love crowns the time of hope.[20] For
a short while, the celestial light of early childhood again seems to bathe not only
our beloved, but the whole world. Everything seems possible, and whatever
hurts and harms we have experienced in our lives so far seem suddenly healable.
Falling in love is not something that happens only when we are fully adult —
adolescents fall in love just as intensely, and a few people may not do so until
much later — but it is normally in young adulthood that we choose the partners
who will bear, father or co-parent our children.

Sexual attraction happens constantly, and many people fall in love more than
once. But choosing a partner with whom one may ultimately raise children
is different from either of those two things. Other factors, both conscious
and unconscious, enter into the choice. The conscious ones we all know about.
Research has long since confirmed the fact that people generally select partners
from roughly similar backgrounds to their own — similar social class, similar
education levels, similar values. And, at the level of personality, everyone knows
that 'opposites attract'. But even introspective, highly intelligent adults may be
unaware of the less obvious things that dictate their choice of partners. Today,
when serial monogamy is common, young adults may have a number of live-in
sexual relationships before they suddenly *know* who they will commit themselves
to, the thought of permanence and children already dimly present in their minds.
How *do* they know? What is it, 'across a crowded room' on 'some enchanted
evening' that makes them so sure, even though they may only just have met
the person concerned and know little about them?[21] 'Cupid's arrow', said the
Romans, echoing the Greek belief that love was akin to madness. 'Chemistry',
we say. It amounts to the same thing. We speak of 'falling' in love, as we speak
of 'falling' pregnant, both expressions suggesting something over which we have
little control, perhaps even something 'put into us' from outside, influencing
us even though we 'know' (the left hemisphere knows) that it may be harmful
for us.

Biologically, all that is necessary for reproduction is a single act of sexual
intercourse. But culture extends and enlarges upon the structures and purposes of biology. Typically human, we add powerful *meanings* to the biological
power of sexual attraction, and create enduring social structures around them.
Before the European eighteenth century, 'love' was not thought to have a great

deal to do with marriage. Marriage existed for the stable upbringing of children, and to create a viable economic unit within which those children could grow into productive adulthood. Many marriages today, it must be said, are very like this in practice. But there has been a huge shift over the past two hundred or so years in the way in which we *think* about love and marriage, and how we think has greatly altered how we feel and behave. Today, love is seen as a *vital* component of marriage and parenting, and the original biologically based attachment bond between mother and child has been extended to encompass other bonds and other feelings.

Always prepared to look an uncomfortable truth squarely in the face, Freud said that marriage is essentially an adult replay of five-year-old allegiances: that, typically, men marry someone who reminds them of their mother, and women someone who reminds them of their father. But what if our chosen partner looks nothing like our opposite sex parent? In our literal-minded way, many of us assume that this destroys the validity of Freud's theory. Of course, it is not necessarily at the level of *physical* appearance that the template operates, although sometimes it actually does. The logical implication of Freud's view is that our unconscious would 'program' us to choose a partner who resembles *the parent we remember from early childhood* – a parent who would have looked much younger, and probably more attractive, than the parent of our later childhood and adolescent memory. Moreover, this parent template will have been formed by an immature, egocentric consciousness, which (as Melanie Klein believed) would have idealised some aspects of our young father or mother and, perhaps, demonised others.[22] Klein called this 'splitting', and maintained that an infant might well experience her mother or father *as two entirely separate beings*, one nurturing, kind and good, and the other damaging, malevolent and evil. I used to rebel against this particular aspect of Melanie Klein's theory, but as I've grown older and wiser, I have found it increasingly credible. After all, fairy tales embody exactly this kind of 'split' (the kind mother dies, and is replaced by the 'wicked' 'stepmother'). And I have to say that it is surprisingly easy for many adults to behave in exactly this way. When the person they initially fell in love with proves to be fallible and imperfect, they act almost as if they were dealing with *two completely different individuals*, instead of a single human being with both loveable and dysfunctional aspects. (Typically, such adults describe their partner, or ex-partner, as 'bipolar' or 'schizophrenic' – a wild misuse of the terms, but one that eloquently expresses the 'splitting' they experience with the other.)

In Priscilla Beaulieu, Elvis Presley chose to marry a teenage girl who significantly resembled his mother as a young woman. And he chose her shortly after his mother's premature death. Like Elvis himself, Priscilla had experienced the early loss of a significant other (in her case, her father) and, like him, she had developed an over-close relationship with her mother.[23] Such exquisite matches are not rare: they are common. But what about women who marry men who are more like their *mothers* than their fathers (and vice versa)? And what about same-sex couples? Among the many who have re-stated Freud's theory and broadened its application somewhat, Harville Hendrix contended that we unconsciously choose someone whose personality resembles the personality of one (sometimes both) of our parents/caregivers (not necessarily the opposite-sex one) and that our relationship with our chosen partner *will therefore replay the precise conflicts that we had as children with that parent* (and the conflicts our parents, as adults, had with each other). Thus a committed relationship becomes either an opportunity to resolve those same issues differently or an invitation simply to repeat, at the same level of frustration and disappointment, the conflicts experienced in our families of origin. Many couples in therapy can relate to this idea, albeit with understandable reluctance.[24] It gets more mysterious still. Our chosen partners do not simply repeat the *personalities* of our parents, which is something that, logically, we might be expected to be partly aware of at the time of our choice. We also seem programmed to select a partner on grounds that we could not possibly know at the time we made our choice.

When 27-year-old Jill Ker fell in love with Canadian professor John Conway, she found herself attracted to a man 18 years older than herself, a man who was old enough to be her father. His personality and background certainly resembled her father's in a whole range of ways. She knew before she married John that he had 'black moods' and carried a revolver in case he decided to end it all. But, convinced that she and John were 'two mature adults' who were making a rational choice to be together, she somehow avoided seeing the full implications of his regular bouts of depression. John's 'moods' (in fact, bipolar disorder) replicated not only the depression in which her father had (almost certainly) taken his own life, but the paranoia and suspicion into which her *mother* had gradually sunk after losing both her husband and her son.[25] Perhaps all of us see such shadows on the horizon of our happiness, but it is easy to understand why we would turn our gaze elsewhere. 'Repression' of unwanted, emotionally intolerable information does not only happen in early childhood. After all, if we saw the full implications of our partner choice, would we be able to carry it through? Does our DNA 'know' more than we do?

My grandmother Ethel, born in 1879, lived to be 84, and suffered from dementia in her final years, eventually being unable to remember even the names of her own sons. But when those three sons married (in 1930, 1937 and 1944 respectively), they can have had no reason for imagining that their mother would one day lose her memory. Yet her eldest and youngest sons both chose partners who would develop dementia, and her middle son developed it himself. Moreover, the two sons who 'married dementia' were the two who had allied themselves strongly with their mother in childhood, developing a corresponding dislike of their father, whereas the one who developed dementia himself was more strongly allied with their father. My father and my eldest uncle could not possibly have known that their fiancées would one day suffer from dementia, any more than they could possibly have known that their mother would – yet in some sense, they 'knew before they knew'. I believe that we all do, though most of us, understandably, deny it.

This knowing comes from a level deeper even than that of the individual 'unconscious' that Freud envisaged. I call it *biological knowing*. I think that when we, as assemblages of genes, encounter another human being whose assemblage of genes is 'recognisable' by ours, or somehow senses its compatibility with ours, then we feel a 'rightness', a 'fit'. We feel at home with that person because we are, almost literally, 'at home' again. The right hemisphere of the cerebral cortex, closely interconnected with the reptile and mammal 'brains' that lie beneath the cortex, thinks by associating like with like. It is programmed to respond to things – individual people in this case – that seem familiar, but it does not consciously reflect upon those similarities. It just prompts us to act on them. What I call a 'protective, projective trance' operates while we are in love, shielding us from the full realisation of these uncomfortable similarities.

'Opposites attract', we say, and indeed, that seems to be so. We choose a partner who offers some of what we lack, and hence 'completes the circle' for us. Thus my father, a somewhat awkward country boy, chose my mother, a sophisticated city girl (at least, she seemed sophisticated to him, although her worldly wise veneer was actually skin deep). Mum, an impulsive person who often blurted out the first thing that came into her head (like her own father), chose my Dad, a reserved man who kept his deepest feelings to himself. She loathed his family of 'narrow' conservative Methodists; he felt uneasy with her cripplingly shy atheist mother. Yet for all the surface differences, the two of them were very alike. Deep down, my mother was no more confident than my father; he too could 'put his foot in his mouth'; and she also (as I found out too late) could hold on to bitterness and disappointment lifelong. Both hid 'thin-skinned' fearfulness and reactivity beneath an acquired veneer of social confidence. Pioneer family therapist Murray Bowen seems to have been the first to point out that we tend to choose partners who are at the same level of emotional maturity, the same level of 'selfhood' as we are.[26] They may *look* totally different from us; they may have a very different *personality* from ours; to the outside world, they may appear much more 'together' than we are, or much less. But underneath all of those apparent differences, there will be an underlying similarity, a 'match' at the emotional level – just as when we choose a book, a job, a religion or a political party that 'matches' our own personality.

Faced with such examples, people commonly say 'oh, it's just a coincidence', arguing that a handful of anecdotes proves nothing. Yet I have seen such repetitions in biography after biography of famous individuals, and in family after family of ordinary people whose lives are undocumented except in the process of therapeutic assessment. The genetic matches between families seem the norm, not the exception. Often, we fail to notice them, simply because we rarely think beyond the couple themselves to the genetic and cultural patterns of their respective kin. Why should we, when our entire culture glorifies the passion of romantic love and disdains the family-arranged marriages still common in India and many other cultures? Yet there may be far less difference between an arranged marriage and a love match than we think. In a love match, the couple must deal with the unloveable realities of each other as the 'trance' wears off; in the arranged marriage, the couple have to learn to love (or at least accept) the realities that they may initially have found unloveable. Both kinds of marriage will break down unless the partners can learn to tolerate the less-than-ideal.

It would seem that when we choose the person who will be the mother or father of our children, we unconsciously select an individual whose future adult life is more likely than not to unfold in a way that repeats symbolically – or even quite literally – the life of one or both of our parents. Time and again, marriages come apart when one, or both, of the partners is at the precise age of one or both of their parents when *that* marriage fell apart. It is why one partner develops a life-threatening illness at precisely the age that *his* or *her* father or mother developed a different (but equally life-threatening) condition – or died in an accident, or lost their job or left home.[27]

The phenomenon may seem a little less odd, a little less disturbing, if we look at the same process in a very different context. Choice of stories, for example. Devoted readers, who know what they want from a novel, decide whether or not a new book is 'their sort of story' very rapidly. Regular readers of women's romances cast their eyes rapidly over just a paragraph or so, and then they 'know'. Yet a paragraph or two from the first page of a 150-page novel cannot possibly contain enough information to tell them that, can it? How can a few hundred words of introduction or scene setting, quite possibly with no action, and maybe even no main character yet, tell a reader what the book is going to be like?[28]

Well, they can, and here is why. In anything that human beings create, they embody themselves. Literally, to *embody* means to 'make something into a body', as *incarnate* means to 'make into flesh'. Just as individuals choose a home or a garden in their own image (often incorporating childhood memories without realising it, as we saw in Chapter 3), so authors write *themselves* into every page, every paragraph, of the novel they create. The book is an external image of *them*, a symbolic 'body'. Emily Brontë's personality, her inner preoccupations, are 'written in' to her choice of words, her way of building sentences, her metaphors, her themes. Gustav Mahler's first childhood composition (he was just five) was entitled 'Polka, with Introductory Funeral March' – the incongruous juxtaposition of gaiety and gloom that would characterise all his adult symphonies was already present before he even started his schooling. Writers and artists do not do this by conscious choice: it just happens. In the case of a book, when a practised reader reads just a short sample of writing, she either instantly recognises the 'personality' it embodies as a match for her own, or she instantly realises that there is no match, and puts the book down.

It would seem, then, that we choose stories in much the same way that we choose life partners: largely at a level below consciousness, and yet with an exquisitely developed instinct for picking up the cues that signal a matching 'personality'.[29] So, too, do we choose friends and so, too, in my view, do employers choose staff – not really on the basis of the advertised selection criteria, but largely on the basis of an instinctive sense that 'she/he is like us'. So accurately does this latter process operate that organisations may repeatedly select similar types of personalities whenever staff vacancies occur and thus 'reproduce' their organisational style in each new generation of staff, just as a family reproduces itself in its children. Existing staff who fail to fit that style tend to leave, or are deliberately pushed: they no longer fit.[30] Much of the foregoing is, of course, speculative. There is no 'hard evidence' to confirm it, yet nor is it 'scientific' to dismiss a hypothesis simply because we cannot yet prove its validity, or don't want to risk our scholarly reputations trying to do so!

If our key life choices are indeed less conscious, more instinct-driven, than we think, then what is the purpose that does drive them? I look to Darwin's evolutionary theory for my tentative answer. The purpose of biological organisms is simply to reproduce themselves. In order to reproduce, each organism (each human being) must select a suitable partner. At the level of biology, any partner is 'suitable' provided that he or she belongs to the same species, is fertile and is available for copulation. But humans have built a complex structure of customs, ideas and emotions on that simple biological foundation, and so the basis of *our* choices must be vastly more complex also. My hypothesis is that we are instinctively motivated to choose our partners in order to re-create our family gene pool – and in choosing us, our partners re-create *their* family gene pool.[31]

What do the words 'I love you' actually mean? For many men, and some women, they simply signal strong sexual attraction ('I want you' might be more accurate). In the novel and movie *Love Story*, the words 'I love you' meant 'never having to say you're sorry' – a comforting illusion which my brother wittily destroyed when he said, 'Love means having to say you're sorry over and over again'.[32] In terms of Panksepp's work on the neurology of feelings, there is no 'primary emotion' that exactly correlates with 'love': rather, love seems to be a mix of the sexual instinct ('lust') with the protective 'care' that bonds parent and child ('I'll always look after you').[33] As we saw earlier in this book, love is the *adult* version of infant attachment – expressed not just in terms of gazing, holding and cuddling, but in terms of genital sexuality as well. Love is not just about sexual attraction, but also about vulnerability and protection. Fundamentally 'I love you' really means (or *should* mean) something like, 'I feel safe with you. I can risk being vulnerable with you, showing my shame and my weakness to you'. 'Intimacy' can only exist as a by-product of vulnerability – something that often makes heterosexual relationships difficult, because men have traditionally been raised to conceal their vulnerability, and women to 'use' theirs to gain attention and protection. But when both partners can admit to each other the doubt and fears they really feel, trust tends to grow, and the attachment bond is strengthened. Ideally, each can 'look out for' the other, and each can allow the other to take care of him or her at times of need, while also being able to function independently at other times. If things go well, we feel most fully ourselves in this strange blend of infant dependency and adult autonomy. Of course, things don't always go well, and that is something we'll explore in the next chapter.

And so it is that when the tide of our individuality is highest, it is also on the turn. Between 20 and 37 most of us are already making the choices that will ensure that our families will repeat themselves. Our marriages, and our careers, will replay the scenarios we grew up with – not necessarily literally, of course – and our children will re-create them once again. This is not weird or tragic; it is not 'uncanny' (as people often say) but predictable; it is not necessarily either good or bad; it is simply the way we are.

Notes

1 Daniel J. Levinson, with Charlotte N. Darrow, Edward B. Klein, Maria H. Levinson and Braxton McKee, *The Seasons of a Man's Life*, NY, Ballantine, 1978; Gail Sheehy, *Passages: Predictable Crises of Adult Life*, NY, Dutton, 1976; Daniel J. Levinson, with Judy D. Levinson, *The Seasons of a Woman's Life*, NY, Ballantine, 1996.
2 Schizophrenia is very rare below the age of ten, and after the age of 40. Age at onset for individual males ranges from 16 to 25 (average 18); for females, the average age of onset is 25, and the minority who develop the condition after 30 are much more likely to be female than male.
3 Anne Brontë, *Agnes Grey*, London, Folio Society, 1991: 21–22. [First published in 1857.]
4 Ashley Hutchings, quoted in Mick Houghton, *I've Always Kept a Unicorn: The Biography of Sandy Denny*, London, Faber, 2015: 122; Joseph Conrad, 'Youth' in *Youth, Heart of Darkness, The End of the Tether, Three Stories*, London, Dent, 1923: 36–37.
5 Levinson, 1978, op. cit.: 102.
6 See Barbara Stoney, *Enid Blyton: The Biography*, 2nd Edn, London, Hodder, 1992: 29–53. [First edition published in 1974.]
7 See Jill Ker Conway, *The Road from Coorain: An Australian Memoir*, Melbourne, Heinemann, 1989: 64.
8 See Barbara Tuchman, *Sand Against the Wind: Stilwell and the American Experience in China*, NY, Macmillan, 1970.
9 See Iain McGilchrist, *The Master and his Emissary: The Divided Brain and the Making of the Western World*, London/New Haven, Yale University Press, 2009: 32–93.
10 See James Marcia, 'Ego-identity Status' in Michael Argyle, *Social Encounters*, Harmondsworth, Penguin, 1973: 340–354.
11 'Separateness force' and 'togetherness force' are terms coined by family therapist Murray Bowen. See Michael Ker and Murray Bowen, *Family Evaluation: An Approach Based on Bowen Theory*, NY, Norton, 1988: 59–88. It could be argued that the 'separateness force' described by Bowen is in essence the typical perspective of the brain's left hemisphere, whereas the 'togetherness force' would represent the perspective of the right. See McGilchrist, 2009, op. cit.: 203.
12 For details of Darwin's family, see Janet Browne's *Charles Darwin: Voyaging*, London, Cape, 1995; and Frank Sulloway, *Born to Rebel: Birth Order, Family Dynamics and Creative Lives*, Boston, MA, Little, Brown, 1996.
13 Details of Vincent van Gogh's life from Philip Callow, *Vincent van Gogh: A Life*, Chicago, IL, Dee, 1990; and from Bernard Denvir, *Vincent: The Complete Self Portraits*, Philadelphia, PA, Running Press, 1994.
14 I have used the older term 'manic-depressive illness' because it more specifically conveys the twin 'poles' of the illness – manic 'highs' and depressive 'lows'. In this I follow Kay Redfield Jamison, an international expert on the illness, who has also written eloquently about her own experience of the disorder in *An Unquiet Mind: A Memoir of Moods and Madness*, NY, Knopf, 1995.
15 See Kurt W. Fischer and Ellen Pruyne, 'Reflective Thinking in Adulthood', in Jack Demick and Carrie Andreoletti (Eds), *Handbook of Adult Development*, NY, Springer Series in Adult Development and Ageing, 2003: 169–198.

16 See Ruth Padel, *Whom Gods Destroy: Elements of Greek and Tragic Madness*, Princeton, NJ, Princeton University Press, 1995.

17 The DSM distinguishes Bipolar I (the 'psychotic' form of manic-depressive illness) from Bipolar II (extreme mood-swings between elation and suicidal depression, but without overt psychosis). See *Diagnostic and Statistical Manual of Mental Disorders*, 5th Edn (*DSM-V*), Arlington, VA, American Psychiatric Publishing, 2013. To the extent that bipolar illness includes delusional thinking, and (in Bipolar I) may include hallucinations, it overlaps with schizophrenia, but where 'mood stabilising' drugs can revolutionise the lives of bipolar patients, the medications currently employed for schizophrenia, although they eliminate overt psychotic symptoms, seem less effective in enabling sufferers to lead fully productive, creative lives.

18 In brain scans of persons with schizophrenia there is evidence of 'an abnormal but overactive left hemisphere' compared with the right (see McGilchrist, 2009, op. cit.: 53; Michael R. Trimble, *The Soul in the Brain: The Cerebral Basis of Language, Art and Belief*, Baltimore, MD, Johns Hopkins University Press, 2007: 114–115).

19 Exposure to artificial light suppresses melatonin, and can disrupt the 'circadian clock' that governed human sleep patterns prior to the coming of powerful artificial lights that enabled people to work all night in factories. For relevant recent research, see Martha U. Gilette (Ed.), *Chronobiology: Biological Timing in Health and Disease*, Progress in Molecular Biology and Science, Vol. 119, Oxford, Elsevier, 2013.

20 The phrase is taken from the title of C. P. Snow's *bildungsroman*, first published in 1949, the third of Snow's 'Strangers and Brothers' sequence.

21 'Some enchanted evening': the song is from Rogers and Hammerstein's *South Pacific*, 1949. It was the most successful song in the show, where it appears several times, and has been constantly re-recorded since.

22 See Melanie Klein, 'On the Theory of Anxiety and Guilt', *Envy and Gratitude and Other Works, 1946–1963*, London, Vintage, 1997: 34–35. [Essay first published in 1948.]

23 See Peter Whitmer, *The Inner Elvis: A Psychological Biography of Elvis Aaron Presley*, NY, Hyperion, 1996: 308–315.

24 See Harville Hendrix's 'imago therapy', as explained in *Getting the Love You Want*, Melbourne, Schwartz and Wilkinson, 1988.

25 See Jill Ker Conway, *True North: A Memoir*, London, Hutchinson, 1994: 64–108.

26 Bowen's theory of partner choice. See Ker and Bowen, 1988, op. cit.; see also Bowen's original formulation of this hypothesis in his *Family Therapy in Clinical Practice*, NY, Aronson, 1979: 265.

27 See Averil Earnshaw's theory as explained in her *Time Bombs in Families*, Sydney, Spencer Publications, 1998; a somewhat different perspective on the same phenomenon was independently evolved by Anne Ancelin Schützenberger in *The Ancestor Syndrome: Transgenerational Psychotherapy and the Hidden Links in the Family Tree*, London and NY, Routledge, 1998. [First published in French in 1993.]

28 See Janice A. Radway, *Reading the Romance: Women, Patriarchy and Popular Literature*, London, Verso, 1987. [First published in 1987.] See also Hugh Crago, *Entranced by Story: Brain, Tale and Teller, from Infancy to Old Age*, London and NY, Routledge, 2014: 147–152.

29 See Crago, 2014, op. cit.: 147–152.

30 See Hugh Crago, 'Programmed for Despair: the Dynamics of Low Morale/High Burnout Welfare Organisations', *Australian Social Work*, 41, 2 (1988): 31–35.

31 As far as I know, this hypothesis is my own (though I am sure others must have thought of it) and was first advanced in the earlier version of this book, *A Circle Unbroken*, published in 1999.

32 See Erich Segal, *Love Story*, NY, Harper & Row, 1970.

33 See Jaak Panksepp and Lucy Biven, *The Archaeology of Mind: Neuroevolutionary Origins of Human Emotions*, NY, Norton, 2014: 245–310.

7

'THE MAKER AND THE MADE'

Committed relationship and parenthood

At some stage in their young adulthood, most people form a committed relationship and have children. For some, this means the traditional marriage-for-life. At the other extreme, an adult relationship may endure only long enough for a pregnancy to result, so that the stable relationship is between the baby and one parent, usually its mother. Some babies may never know either of their biological parents. This chapter deals with the situation as the majority of people experience it: a long-term (but not necessarily lifelong) heterosexual relationship, often a formal marriage, with children. I am well aware that this is not the only pattern, nor am I implying that it is the only emotionally healthy one. The ability to stay in an intimate, caring relationship is usually an indicator of emotional stability, but we can all think immediately of people who are anything but stable, anything but emotionally healthy, yet who stay forever in relationships that to most people would be torture. Equally, we can all think of emotionally healthy individuals, gay and straight, who choose to remain single all their lives.

In my experience, the dynamics that characterise gay and lesbian couples are not significantly different from those of heterosexual couples – at least, not at the level of the largely unconscious emotional processes with which we shall be concerned here. Of course some things are different if you are in a same-sex relationship, but most of those differences come from the way others react to you, and the pressures the external world exerts on your relationship. Similarly with the issue of having children. The fact that a couple has reached the state of parenthood via an unconventional route (adoption, IVF, sperm donation, surrogacy) does not necessarily change the dynamics of their parenting. Because we are not simply products of our biology, we can experience joy and despair over a child whether it is biologically 'ours' or not, whether we have given birth to it or not. As we have seen repeatedly, humans react as strongly to the symbolic as they do to the literal.

Forming a stable relationship and having children is part of the emotional 'work' of early adulthood for most of us, part of 'building a life structure'. At the biological level, the family reproduces itself by giving birth to new family members. Simultaneously, cross-generational patterns of meaning, feeling and behaviour also repeat in fairly predictable ways. A committed relationship is a stressor, one of the greatest challenges any of us will ever face. Living long term with another person, sharing key decisions, raising children together – these things are not easy. Building a family demands a lot of two individuals who are likely to be both very similar, and very different. If they cannot find common ground, if they are unwilling to meet each other half way, then their relationship will falter, and the family they start may be compromised. In Chapters 2 and 3 we examined the development of the infant and child within the family – but largely from the child's point of view. In those chapters, we were concerned with how the family environment interacts with the child's genetic temperament. Now it is time to alter our focus, and see how the coming of children affects the personality and selfhood of their parents. But first, we need to return to marriage, a dramatic example of the way we humans react to the symbolic world of words and meanings as if they were 'real'.

What marriage really means

Engineer Bennie and his retailer partner Gina had lived together pleasantly and comfortably for seven years. Both of them had been unsuccessfully married before, and neither was in any hurry to rush into a new commitment. But it had gone so well, for so long, that they overcame their caution and set a wedding date. Within weeks of the ceremony their relationship had begun to slide downhill and, by the time they came to counselling, they both felt it was irretrievable. It took them a year of slow, painful work to let go of one another. Their dream of a happy, loving relationship had somehow vanished over the horizon as soon as they walked down the aisle.

Seven years is an unusually long time, but apart from that, Gina and Bennie's story is typical of many. Couple after couple get on fine while they live together, doing everything that married people do and yet, when they are formally married, suddenly find that they can't stand one another, even though they say 'nothing has changed'. Something *has* changed, though. Being married *means* certain things to each of them, meanings which in turn produce different attitudes, and new behaviour. Stories like Gina and Bennie's are not confined to the ranks of the formerly married. Nor are they unique to the many who live together before deciding to marry. Everybody knows the young couple where one or the other suddenly begins to panic as soon as the wedding date is set, the stories where the bride is left at the altar (or occasionally it is the groom). Such stories are not restricted to those who opt for church weddings; civil ceremonies attract the same behaviour. The one element common to all such stories is the decision to *marry*, as opposed to continuing in some less formally sanctioned relationship.

Women often mutter that men are scared of commitment. But of course, women can be scared of commitment too. Some people will tell you that, for them, marriage means being 'tied down', others say that for them it means giving up their freedom of choice, or losing a sense of being in control of their lives. For others again (though they may not articulate it) marriage means being 'drowned' – losing their identity. Whatever label people put on their feelings, we can be reasonably certain that for all of them marriage represents an invisible but powerful dividing line between one thing and another, between one kind of existence and another. Anthropologists refer to 'liminal' phenomena (from the Latin word 'limen', meaning 'threshold'). When humans encounter such 'thresholds', anxieties rise high, conflicts erupt and emotional problems are triggered. Going to school involves crossing such a boundary; so does leaving home to set up independent adult existence. Getting married constitutes another boundary, a sort of electric fence with the power to give anything from a mild tingle to a lethal shock.

Edwardian playwright James Matthew Barrie was an extreme case of failure to negotiate this particular boundary. His most famous book is full of (to us) embarrassingly sentimental talk about Mothers, and how desperately important a Mother's Love is. It should not surprise us, then, to learn that Barrie was deeply attached to his own mother, who dominated his life well into adulthood. Having failed to achieve emotional separateness from her while she was living, he married a witty, attractive actress within a year of her death. It was a prescription for disaster. As if he felt disloyal to his mother, he was unable to respond sexually to his new wife. Did he, perhaps, feel as if his wife really *was* his mother – (as with Elvis Presley, this would have been the 'saved' mother he remembered from early childhood)? Was he homosexual, but unable to admit it even to himself – which at the time would have been easy enough to understand? Whatever the explanation, his 'Tinkerbell' was bewildered, frustrated and resentful – eventually, she left him. Barrie reverted to a bachelor existence, and seemed to feel safest in the company of pre-pubertal boys. And his most famous and enduring contribution to our consciousness? *Peter Pan*, the often silly, yet haunting and disturbing story of a boy who could not grow up, memorably re-created by the late Robin Williams in the movie, *Hook*, and presented even more poignantly in the prequel *Pan*. When Barrie wrote Peter Pan's story, he wrote his own.[1] And he was not the only individual who has experienced intimations of incest when he or she marries a partner who at a deep level re-creates a Lost Mummy or Lost Daddy.

Conventionally, we think of marriage as going forward into unexplored territory, but it is also, more profoundly, a going *back* – back into a forgotten heartland of our being. It is as if a married couple is dimly aware that they now occupy the same psychic space their parents once did. If your parents were happy together, then moving into the roles they occupied 20 or more years before can be deeply confirming, and generate optimistic expectations. Behaving as your father or mother behaved in a happy relationship does not (usually) constitute a problem. It just happens, and because things on the whole go well you do not question it, or even notice that this is what you are doing. He comes home grumpy after a bad day at work: you 'know' (because you saw your mother do it thousands of times) that the right thing to do is to leave him alone, or get him a beer and ask him to tell you what went wrong, or whatever. When it is she who is distressed, he smooths things out for her in the way she prefers. And so the potential trouble-spot is simply bypassed, without either really being aware of it.

But if your 'saved' memories of your parents' relationship are of tension, fear, anger or sadness, then things take a very different course. Consciously, of course, you may be determined to have a totally different kind of relationship from your respective parents', just as (in the last chapter) we saw people determined to break decisively with their parents' career, politics or beliefs. But by the Tinder-Box principle, such reactive decisions usually end up producing the outcome they attempt to avoid. Unwittingly, each of you begins to behave, and to feel, in ways that reflect the feelings and behaviours of one of your parents in relation to the other. What was swallowed whole in early childhood is regurgitated a quarter of a century later. What you most dreaded is happening all over again – to *you*.

It is not simply that once we experience adult commitment we begin to repeat the patterns of our *parents'* relationship with each other. We are also repeating the patterns of our *own* earliest relationship *to* one of our parents, and perhaps that is the more fundamental level of replication. As we saw earlier in this book, very young children begin to form an 'attachment strategy' in the first year of life: they learn a (reasonably) reliable way of getting at least some of what they need from their attachment figure. In doing so, they learn a *pattern of interaction with another person*, a 'template for relationship', an 'internal working model' as John Bowlby called it.[2] The insecure-avoidant child learns to suppress her feelings of anger or sadness and focus on the smiling compliance that she knows her attachment figure will reward ('Good girl!'). The insecure-ambivalent child, by contrast, learns to escalate emotional displays (including both anger and help-lessness) and so gain attention from his attachment figure – even if it is critical, punitive attention, he is at least being taken notice of! Securely attached children, by contrast, are fortunate enough to have parents who interpret their behaviour accurately, and willingly give them what they need. These children's feelings elicit an appropriate response – at least most of the time – and so there is no need for them to intensify the expression of those feelings to gain parental attention, as the ambivalent infant does. Nor do they need (like avoidant infants) to suppress the full range of their emotional expression in order to feel loved and accepted.

As we saw towards the end of Chapter 6, 'opposites attract', and in clinical experience this holds good for attachment strategies too. Thus avoidant adults (apparently confident and reliable, apparently easygoing and tolerant) tend to select ambivalent adult partners (apparently spontaneous, emotionally open and exciting), failing to recognise that they are also impulsive and unreliable. Gender stereotypes also play a part here: the ambivalent attachment style can look 'desirably feminine'; the avoidant style can look 'admirably male'. In doing so, both insecurely attached partners set the scene for a re-enactment of their own infant struggles to feel emotionally safe. As long as things go well, the avoidant-ambivalent couple will enjoy each other's company: the ambivalent partner will lean on her partner when needy and distressed, and the avoidant partner will supply the 'strength' and reliability she needs. But if relational stress escalates, the avoidant partner's easygoing attitude will give way to contempt for his partner's 'weakness', and the ambivalent partner will feel shut out emotionally, or even abandoned. She will ramp up her own emotional display in a desperate attempt to regain access to him, angrily accuse him of 'never showing me what he feels' or collapse into weeping or self-destructive behaviour. Faced with this, the avoidant partner will withdraw even further, losing touch not only with her feelings, but with his own, and substituting the more reliable satisfactions of work or sports for the relationship he has come to distrust. And so it continues.

Ambivalent-avoidant parings are by far the most common type that couple therapists see. Such couples were described by early family systems theorists as 'the pursuer and the distancer'.[3] The 'pursuer', who moves in (angrily or pleadingly) towards the other in the hope of gaining connection and a renewed sense of safety, is displaying the insecure-ambivalent strategy. The 'distancer', who withdraws either physically or emotionally or both (keeping vulnerability hidden from the partner) has learned the 'avoidant' strategy. The more insistently the pursuer moves close, the more the distancer feels overwhelmed and moves away. Trainee family therapists are coached to engage the pursuer in an exploration of her own feelings and needs, rather than to join her (it is usually 'her') in 'pursuing the distancer' (which would simply alienate him further). Once the distancer's trust has been gained (and that may take a while), there will be an opportunity to even things up.

Of course, securely attached adults sometimes form a relationship with an avoidant or an ambivalent partner, but more commonly, one securely attached individual is attracted to another. Therapists don't see these couples all that often, because secure couples experience less relational distress, and cope better with it when it does occur – largely because their earliest experience has been that they *can* trust their attachment figure. Securely attached individuals are not free of emotional problems, nor are their relationships always rosy, but they find it easier to *keep talking about* the issues that separate them, without assuming that these differences spell doom for the relationship. In fact, this is the major difference that John Gottman found between couples who stay together and those who split up – it is not that 'successful' couples do not have real and enduring differences (they get as mad at each other as couples who end up splitting) but simply that these differences are not perceived as final.[4] Anger, to secure couples, simply does not *mean* what it means to unhappy couples. Once again, the significance we humans attach to a behaviour counts far more to us than the objective reality.

None of this means that the rules of these inadvertent 'games' cannot be altered – they can. But *each of us is most likely to have unconsciously selected a partner who will play the game according to the rules we are familiar with.* Our patterns of interaction in the present can easily become so entrenched that we lose sight of our potential for being different. What we know becomes all we know, and we cling to it, fearing the very changes we crave. Indeed, when our partner does begin to change, or starts to act in a way that we have always said we would prefer, we may angrily dismiss the new behaviour as 'just a show' or 'too little, too late'. Even worse, sometimes couples do not even *see* the new behaviour, so sure are they that their partners will never give them what they need. Relationship counselling cannot magically change that pattern. But it can steady couples as they 'trial and error' their way, like little children learning to walk and talk, towards interactions that are less destructive and more enriching.

For many people, the realisation that they are 'locked in' to a seemingly unalterable, dysfunctional pattern with their partner tends to happen around the time of Levinson's 'Age 30 Transition'.[5] Many extramarital affairs happen at this age, and many marriages end, as individuals tell themselves that they 'married the wrong person' and that an exciting new partner will change everything. Sometimes it does, but mostly it does not because, by the law of attraction, we all tend to be drawn once again, like filings to the magnet, into a similar relationship dynamic. The new lover may *look* very different from the first. He or she may *appear* different in personality. We may even select someone who seems the exact opposite of our first partner, just as we consciously try to adopt the opposite life choices to those of our parents. In extreme cases, though, individuals will select again and again partners who not only resemble each other in personality, but also in physical appearance. They may even have the same *name*. It's more common than you'd think!

When Bennie remarried after his painful divorce from Gina, he married, this time, a woman much older than himself. 'Old enough to be his mother', people muttered cruelly. She looked very different from the younger, plump, emotional Gina. But when I sat with Bennie and his new wife, I realised that one key element of the old pattern was still alive and well: Bennie had once again hooked himself up with a woman who knew what she wanted, and would forthrightly tell him so, in whose presence he felt inadequate, unable to assert himself, unable to express his inner doubts. That was how he had felt with Gina. That was how he had felt with his mum. It was all coming around again. And he felt powerless to stop it happening.

To blame our partners for our stuckness is natural, but it is supremely unhelpful. Our first caregiver was our mirror, in whose responses to us we saw our own worth, and learned about our own selfhood. If our romantic partner has now taken the place of our early caregivers and become the guardian of our selfhood, it is almost inevitable that we will see in him or her aspects of ourselves that we dislike and disown. When we see these features we want to make them go away. It is easy, and natural, to see our partners' weaknesses, to point out their immaturity. It is vastly harder to see the ways in which those weaknesses are also our own, the ways in which our own 'maturity' is superficial.

Every couple therapist knows a variant of the relationship where one partner is so obviously more 'together' than the other. The woman weeps as she talks about her problems. She is overweight, she can't drive a car, she has panic attacks when she goes to the supermarket, she can't control her children and she relies on her husband for everything. She is inarticulate and seems unable to cope with her own feelings. The man is trim, talks fluently and insightfully about his wife's difficulties, appears caring and compassionate, seems to have everything under control. Murray Bowen's belief that individuals select partners who are at the same level of 'self-differentiation' as themselves seems hard to square with the 'facts' of this couple.[6] But wait a few months. With some professional help, the woman has gained confidence, and now ventures from home with aplomb, is learning to drive, feels better about her parenting, talks rationally about her feelings. And who has gone to pieces? The man. He's having anxiety attacks, he's even putting on weight. Why? His apparent confidence, emotional maturity and mastery all depended on her inadequacy. As long as she was sick or weak, he could be well and strong. Nurses perform this role all the time: compared with a bedridden, helpless patient they feel strong, calm and coping. So, for that matter, do therapists! In their private lives they may be anything but patient, empathic and non-judgemental! Bowen referred to the kind of competence and confidence which depends upon another's deficit as 'pseudo-self'.[7] By contrast, 'solid self' does not evaporate when one partner begins to change.

Many relationships break up because one becomes convinced that the other is entirely responsible for his unhappiness. It is safer for him to believe this than to entertain the devastating thought that he himself might be imperfect or lacking in some way. The Wicked Queen in 'Snow White' did not like it when her magic mirror showed her a picture of Snow White as 'the fairest of them all' instead of reflecting her own face. Her solution: to kill her young rival. Most of us would not remotely contemplate such a solution. Yet the tenor of many separations is that of symbolic death. 'My feelings for him are dead', people say. 'There's no life left in the relationship'. A baby neglected or abandoned may literally die: our adult metaphors betray the screaming child within us, struggling for survival. Of course, some relationships need to end, for compelling reasons – they have become emotionally or physically abusive, and mutual destructiveness has become entrenched. Many others *need* not end – the partners have enough going for them to make a good-enough relationship. But, in the latter cases, the partners often lack the emotional maturity to see that yet.

In young adulthood, fuelled by our reserves of optimism, the lure of the romantic and the new is often too strong. 'In another country' (that is, with another lover), all will be different and better. And of course, if one or both partners come from a family in which the template for marriage involves a split, then the compulsion to repeat the pattern is very strong. It is what our parents did. It seems somehow 'permissible'. Social shifts reinforce this. Over the past half century (my adult lifetime) divorce has become vastly easier, and both serial monogamy and *de facto* unions are much more widely accepted than they once were. Humans are enormously influenced by what others do, and if we are aware that lots of couples split, we will feel greater 'permission' to emulate them, and correspondingly less shame or self-reproach if we do. Like every innovation that human beings create (social as well as technological), 'no-fault divorce' has the potential to be both creative and destructive, both 'good' and 'bad' in its effects.

When marriages do dissolve, adult humans again repeat the attachment behaviour they displayed in early childhood. Those of us fortunate enough to have experienced secure attachment in infancy manage to separate in a reasonably mature way. We cope with the pain, we try hard not to blame our partners for everything, we refuse to recruit our children to take sides. But those who have experienced 'ambivalent attachment' as children cling desperately to their partners, just as they once did to their mummies. Over and over again, men say, 'but I just can't *understand* why she left me!' Their plea sounds like a wish for rational explanation, so the natural tendency for friends, and even professional helpers, is to offer one. But the explanation falls on deaf ears, because these men are simply using the rational language of the brain's left hemisphere to give voice to the primitive panic and grief that accompanies the loss of an attachment figure. 'Mummy' has gone, and the man, for all his adult intellect, simply cannot comprehend that she might have had needs and feelings different from his own. He doesn't 'get it' (as we say). He obsesses, texts her 20 times a day, drops around and pleads to be let in, sends her presents, even writes her letters of enormous, dysfunctional length. She, as unsure of her decision to separate as he is, desperately wants 'space' to 'get her head together'. The 'space' she says she wants is the chance to experience herself as a stand-alone person. If she began to experience that, she might begin to grow up emotionally, and she might (or might not) start to feel differently about the relationship. But he, as if compelled from some deeply buried part of himself, simply cannot let her have that separateness. Clinging harder and harder, he effectively drives her away. And so, the couple *co-operate to separate*, unconsciously help each other to do what they, individually, could not manage.

'The maker and the made'

What is it, exactly, that happens when we make love? Sex is intensely pleasurable, yes, and if we were to believe much of what we see on television or on the Internet, then pleasure would be virtually all sex was about. But that is an adolescent view of sex, which some of us never get beyond. What does it really mean, to lie in the arms of the one we have chosen, and who has chosen us? Unclothed, we temporarily shed the symbolic veneer of civilisation. Surrendering to our bodies' needs, we participate for a little while in the instinctive pleasures that animals experience: we can briefly 'switch off' our oppressive, ever-present self-consciousness, and re-enter the 'embodied' consciousness of the right hemisphere, a feeling of intense aliveness and meaningfulness. Pressed against the naked body of an adult human, we may even experience, after orgasm, something akin to what we felt when we first emerged from our mother's womb.

Of course, most of these things can be experienced in any act of sexual intercourse, with any partner. But when they are experienced with the one who 'feels right', who 'feels special', whom we want to bear or father our children, then something much more profound can occur. A door is opened onto pre-verbal feelings and fantasies. The acts of urgency and tenderness that pass between us revive the ancient hungers and satiations of infancy. In such coupling, we are simultaneously both mother and baby, both 'the maker and the made'. The phrase is that of Australian writer Judith Wright, whose poem 'Woman to Man' movingly conveys the way that the act of birth resonates with the act of conception and, in turn, with the act of our own conception.[8] Sex in this context is the most infolded, the most recursive of all human acts. In it, we temporarily lose not only the boundaries between our own and our lover's body, but the boundary between generations. No wonder, then, that prolonged intimacy of this kind can be terrifying as well as wonderful. Is this, perhaps, why so many relationships that begin with passionate sex change, within a year or two, to ones where the 'passion' goes mostly into bitter, mutual recrimination? No wonder that the lovers who once 'couldn't keep their hands off each other' now find the very thought of touching distasteful, and sex unthinkable! The craving for love and closeness has been replaced by a craving for 'justice', for the 'betrayer' to be punished. To that imperative some couples will sacrifice all their financial reserves (fighting their ex-partner through the courts) and, much worse, their own children's emotional well-being. It is perhaps the most tragic outcome of a failed relationship, and one that often leaves the grown-up children with lasting bitterness or, worse, with a powerful invitation to do the same in their own relationships.

An aside on sexual abuse

Why would anyone be frightened of closeness? Either because they have never had it, or because they have had too much of it, too soon. Perhaps in infancy, intimacy with mother alternated with abandonment, a scary rollercoaster of exhilaration and despair. Perhaps a father, a brother, an uncle or a family friend abused them at the age of three or four. Sexual invasion at a very early age, when a child's sense of its own boundaries is not fully formed, will almost certainly have a more profound effect than abuse at an age where the body and brain are more mature. Those abused so early not only have predictable difficulties with trust and intimacy; they may also find it hard to know their rights as autonomous individuals, and even have trouble separating their own feelings from the feelings of others around them. In my clinical experience, so-called 'psychic' women often prove to be survivors of early abuse. Their lack of boundaries, which may hamper them in other areas of life, actually enables them to be intuitively aware of what is going on inside other people. It is not 'magic'; such people simply possess thinner, more permeable boundaries than the rest of us. We need to remember that thin boundaries make us more sensitive to *everything*, and sometimes that can be useful.[9]

Negative experiences at these very early periods of life are particularly hard to overcome later, because the earlier the experience, the more likely it is to have vanished from awareness into the unconscious memory bank, where it lies, full of power to influence our present relationships but unavailable to conscious introspection. This does not mean that we can never overcome early traumas; simply that it is long, hard work, requiring great patience and persistence from us and from our helpers. Because of the power of early experience, later traumas tend to happen to those who are already traumatised.[10] I am aware that this sad truth has often been viewed as an example of 'blaming the victim' (as in, 'She was asking to be raped' or 'He's an accident waiting to happen'). Yet to assert that, once traumatised, we are more likely to incur renewed trauma, is not to blame anyone. Repeating patterns are not a matter of morality or blame, but of the logic of our emotional lives.

Very often, a sexually abused pre-school girl grows into a young woman with the high-pitched voice of a four-year-old. Her manner may seem winning and delightful, but her every way of being offers tiny but real clues to her vulnerability. Early abuse may lead to a frozen fear of intimacy, to a blatant parading of sexuality, or sometimes, to a powerful mix of the two which is utterly alluring to many men. Marilyn Monroe exemplified such a combination. If our manner screams, 'I've been hurt', we attract those who will hurt us. It is not our fault. It does not in any way excuse our abusers. But it happens. And so women who have been sexually violated in childhood often marry men who will violate either them or their children. Abuser and abused 'recognise' each other, unconsciously. The cycle in which the abused and traumatised tend to be re-abused and re-traumatised is simply one case of the principle of selection that governs almost all marriages. Unconfident people attract those who need to feel competent and confident. Sick people attract those who feel fulfilled by caring for them. Early trauma or loss of one kind 'draws' a partner who will re-traumatise them, probably in response to early trauma or abuse in his own history.

Of course, not all women abused in childhood go on to partner an abuser. Some, in a further demonstration of the Tinder-Box principle, select a man who they sense will never violate their trust in that way – and thus create a different sort of problem for themselves. Mary had a violent, alcoholic father. Her first spouse was also violent, and a substance abuser. Her current partner is a gentle, somewhat passive man who 'goes with the flow'. Because of his own previous marriage to a woman who was angry and violent, he fears to say what he feels in case he attracts rage or a physical attack. His reticence seems to Mary like a rejection, and she complains that there's 'no chemistry' between them, and questions whether he 'really loves her'. This woman has successfully escaped from abuse, but into another untrusting relationship. Yet if the man can learn to risk communicating more of his feelings (intimacy grows with mutual self-disclosure) and if the woman can put aside her assumption that his wariness about disclosing his feelings necessarily means that he does not want her, then this couple may be able to decrease the likelihood that their children will repeat the pattern of abuse or mistrust.

Men who, as children, were treated in an inappropriately sexualised way display adult behaviour just as predictable as that of female sexual abuse victims. Gladys Presley, mother of Elvis, was a highly religious woman, and there is no evidence of overt sexual activity between her and the son who shared her bed until he was 12. But for human beings, the symbolic 'becomes' the real. Desire need not be acted out to be communicated. Look at how Elvis behaved later. As 'the King', he enjoyed sex with many women, relationships which were brief and exploitative in the way that is typical of the sexual behaviour of many men who have been abused in childhood. Oddly, however, he would never sleep with a woman once she had been pregnant. And with his serious girlfriends, Elvis behaved with exaggerated respect – or fear. He would typically lie in bed with them, in a darkened room, but not touch them. Surely here is a *literal* adult re-creation of how the young Elvis had behaved in bed with his mother? Regis, Juanita and finally Priscilla (all three of them teenagers when they met Elvis) were younger versions of his mother. No wonder sex with them was something fraught with holy and frightening implications. Elvis's magnetic appeal to an entire culture, just like that of Marilyn Monroe, was based in his own powerfully ambivalent feelings about sex, his peculiar combination of adult desire and childhood taboo.[11]

A baby, maybe . . .

For most people, having children seems natural. It is what their biology urges on them. It is also – or has been until very recently in human history – what their society urges on them too. A childless woman was referred to as 'barren'. An infertile man was 'sterile'. The harshness of these terms makes the underlying biological judgement clear. At a level beyond biology, however, we humans create additional meanings for procreation. We all know the pathetic cry of the self-doubting girl who falls pregnant at 15 or 16, 'because I wanted someone to love me'. *Having* a baby is the closest she can come to *being* a baby again. But for many more people, men as well as women, having a child completes the circle of selfhood in some dimly understood but very real way. As parents, we somehow feel more whole – even though, ironically, those of us who most need to feel whole are often those least ready to parent a child. The inability to have children is not necessarily solely a genetically determined matter. In yet another example of the way genetics and environmental factors potentiate one another, childlessness, or difficulty in having children, often points backwards to determinant events and traumas not only in our own lives, but in those of our parents.

Enid Blyton, happily married for six years, consulted her gynaecologist as to why she had been unable to conceive. He told her that she had 'an undeveloped uterus', which (as she remembered it later) he had likened to that of 'a girl of 12 or 13'. Was this seeming 'developmental arrest' purely genetic? Or was there some relationship between the failure of Enid's uterus to develop and the traumatic departure of Enid's father when she was precisely that age?[12] Remember, too, that Enid's private 'storytelling', the origin of her creativity as a writer, also commenced at 12 or 13. Was it, somehow, as if her storytelling took the place of her reproductive capacity? Certainly, when she did eventually manage to have two daughters, they always had to take second place to her writing, and four-year-old Imogen did not even understand that the lady she was brought to spend an hour with each afternoon was actually her *mother*. Many writers behave as if their books were more important to them than their real children (if they have them), or as if the books were substitutes for the real children they never had.

Jill Ker Conway, too, encountered a biological impediment to having children. Severe endometriosis made it impossible for her to conceive, and since she and John had no wish to adopt, she remained childless. Is it coincidental that Jill's mother had herself been diagnosed with benign uterine growths at the time of Jill's conception – the same condition which had at first convinced her that she should attempt to abort baby Jill? Did Jill and her mother share an inherited vulnerability in the reproductive system? Quite possibly. But think further. Jill had felt alienated by her mother, powerfully resentful of her mother's manipulation and dependency. Maybe her inability to have children removed her from the terror of becoming a mother like her own? And did it not also recon-firm her well-established life structure as a successful career woman in a man's world?[13] To say that Jill's endometriosis was 'caused' by these factors rather than by an inherited biological deficit is to fall into the typical human error of 'either/ or' thinking. Once again, we can only say that if we feel certain feelings strongly enough, for long enough, they cannot but become part of the total context in which our bodies grow, or fail to grow; develop disease, or successfully resist it. Jill Ker Conway's inability to have children was a personal tragedy; it also had a compelling emotional logic.

For those who do reproduce successfully, the birth of the first child is often a high point of young adulthood. Women, indeed, are socialised to see it so ('The wedding day, then the children, and after that, it's all downhill' said one sadly). No wonder if the reality of a new baby can come as an anticlimax, or bring with it numbing postnatal depression. Women who suffer from the latter are often unaware that their own mothers endured a similar experience. We do know that babies can be profoundly affected by a mother who is emotionally unavailable in the crucial first weeks or months. Is it so unlikely that such a baby might somehow 'record' or 'save' feelings of longing, of an 'absence' where a loving presence should be, and that those same infant feelings might well up again when her own adult situation as a new mother of a vulnerable, demand-ing child triggers them? Or could there be an explanation at the genetic level?

We'll see in our next chapter how epigenetic research is beginning to suggest that there is.

For virtually every new mother, the agony and the delight of giving birth leave an indelible mark. Simply to have given birth is a massive achievement, a great fulfilment, a sort of 'rebirth' in itself. Men must find other ways of feeling that they have 'faced the ultimate' and come through. Physically dangerous contact sports and 'extreme' activities like skydiving or abseiling are common forms in which men (and some women) pit themselves against fear, and experience the exhilaration of surviving. And then there is war. War comes at much the same stage of life for men as childbirth does for women: early adulthood. 'God help me, I was only nineteen' runs the refrain of an Australian ballad about a conscript in Vietnam in the 1960s.[14] The words speak eloquently of young soldiers' unreadiness, their unpreparedness for the enormity of what lies ahead. As a young woman experiences her body being torn open in childbirth, so the young man may experience the tearing open of his body through wounding. Even worse, he has to witness the tearing open of other bodies, perhaps as a result of his own actions. War, like birth, confronts male humans nakedly with their incredible physical vulnerability, with their intense wish not to die and with their capacity for dealing death to others. Like birth, battle exhausts and depletes. As repeated childbirth takes away youth from women, so combat and all it entails takes their youth from men. They come back changed forever, haunted perhaps by what professionals now term 'post-traumatic stress disorder'. For some men, battle also exalts – but battle gives birth to no new life. There is no baby, formed in our own image, to renew our hope and negate our mortality. For many men, as for my grandfather Victor, who fought on the Western Front not long before Patton did, it is 'downhill all the way' once the war is over.

When the first baby is born – or adopted – things begin to change for every couple. Why? A baby makes a two into a three, a dyad into a triangle – with a triangle's natural tendency to form into a 'two against one' alliance.[15] Giving birth and breastfeeding are intensely emotional things, returning the adult mother to body memories of her own infancy, re-creating in her, perhaps, sensory memory traces of her own mother's way of being with her. Two bodies are intimately linked, and both derive sensual pleasure from their contact and closeness. The third party, the baby's father, cannot be part of this in quite the same way. For some men, perhaps for more men than care to admit it, their exclusion is painful. 'Here is the woman who made these soft cries of pleasure to *me*, who called *me* "baby", now speaking in the same lover's voice to someone else!' No wonder men can be jealous of their own children and, especially, for obvious reasons, of their baby sons. Freud was simply telling it like it was (and is). For some men, perhaps more men than can remember it, the sense of exclusion they feel as new fathers wakes up a much earlier sense of being cast out. It can re-awaken primitive jealousy of a new baby brother or sister. But for men there may be more to it than that. As feminist psychoanalyst Nancy Chodorow pointed out some 30 years ago, both boys and girls start life being held close to a woman's body. But boys eventually need to *turn away from* the warmth, softness and safety of the body that nurtured their first years *in order to start thinking of themselves as male*. They learn that they must act 'tough', stop crying and abjure softness in order to be *perceived* as male. Although their maleness is a source of pride, it begins in loss. No wonder they feel this renewed 'exclusion' from the mother–baby dyad so keenly.[16] Of course this is not quite as true now as it was when Chodorow wrote – but traditional stereotypes of maleness have by no means died out completely.

If the coming of a baby injects tensions into relationships, or intensifies tensions that were already present, then the baby itself comes to play a part in how those tensions are dealt with. All babies seem to 'absorb' and resonate with their parents' feelings to some extent, but a baby who is temperamentally thin boundaried is, I believe, far more likely to do so. Thick-boundaried babies, resilient enough not to absorb their parents' tensions in this total way, may nevertheless be drawn into the evolving couple relationship later, in more overt ways. A parent who feels let down by her partner, or treated unfairly by him, naturally turns to the child with whom she is allied (often her son, sometimes her daughter) for comfort, reassurance and, as the child grows older, emotional support. It is gratifying for children to feel that a parent trusts them and turns to them in this way, although such a responsibility can also make them feel anxious and burdened. Some parents, experiencing their partners as disappointing or frustrating, pour all their energies, their love and their dreams into one or more of their children. The child is, as it were, 'appointed' to live out its parent's needs and ambitions, and it may be difficult for that child later to feel like an entirely separate, autonomous person. This is almost certainly what happened with *Peter Pan's* J. M. Barrie and his mother. After her father's death, Jill Ker's mother seems more and more to have treated Jill in this way. Elvis Presley seems to have been cast by his mother from the very beginning in the role of surrogate husband and, as long as she lived, the two cooed to each other in 'baby talk' reminiscent of lovers. No wonder Elvis had such fragile selfhood, and could tolerate so little reality around him. Graceland became a real-life Neverland, an endless cycle of 'fun' and avoidance of responsibility, in which an adult Elvis hid himself from the world as totally as Gladys had once done in her home – and the 'Memphis Mafia' (Elvis's male companions) were the Lost Boys.

Very strong parent–child alliances, especially those which exclude the other parent from the magic circle, can produce adults with unshakeable faith in themselves. Indira Gandhi was 'her father's daughter', and so is Aung San Suu Kyi. A whole string of famous men – among them Freud, Hitler, Lyndon Johnson and Bill Clinton – grew up knowing that they were their mother's favourite (or only) son. The intense protection and patronage of a parent (occasionally another relative like Patton's aunt) creates a child whose confidence in his own rightness convinces not only himself, but others as well. No wonder these children often grow up to become charismatic leaders. If people nearly always do as you wish when you are a small child, when you become an adult you will expect those in authority over you to do the same. If they refuse to accede to your desires, you will assume that you ought to be able to take their place – or simply remove them. Such a sense of being 'born to rule' can be both a huge asset and a massive liability. Children who are already, at a deep level, unsure of who they are, can be encouraged by such grand parental investment to develop the 'inflated balloon' self of the narcissist. Even those who escape that fate will still have difficulty in adulthood seeing themselves realistically.

The circle curves back

When parents experience problems with one or more of their children, these problems are to a degree predictable. I am not talking about those parents who, against all odds, have a severely developmentally handicapped child in an otherwise healthy family, and must rise to the enormous challenges this child poses. I am speaking of the trials and tribulations of the average parent, with average children. Here, a complex interaction occurs between temperament, attachment, birth order and family structure, in which, as so often in human systems, one factor potentiates another in a cycle that rapidly becomes self-perpetuating.

We might think that caregivers would tend to repeat, with their own children, the particular attachment strategy that they themselves developed in infancy, but, as Patricia Crittenden points out, the evidence does not bear this out. The greatest cross-generational continuity is between securely attached parents and securely attached infants. Securely attached parents are more likely to have children who are securely attached – but not necessarily, of course, since as we saw in Chapter 2, the child's temperament may make it harder for a secure attachment to develop. But research shows that parents who displayed insecure attachment as infants often did *not* produce a child with the identical strategy to their own. A parent who herself was insecurely attached may give birth to a temperamentally 'easy' child, enabling that child to become more securely attached than her mother was. Or an insecure-ambivalent parent may have a child who grows up avoidant, instead of ambivalent. Clearly, much depends on the child's temperament as well as the way it is parented, and the reassuring evidence is that many children can grow up securely attached despite having one or both parents who were not.[17]

Parents' birth order position can also affect the way they parent their own children. Eldest children who marry other eldests find that rules and limit-setting come naturally to them in parenting, but they may have corresponding problems in the area of inappropriate strictness – they may, for instance, *over-react* to rebellious adolescents, which simply intensifies their rebellion. On the other hand, youngest children married to other youngests may have more difficulty setting limits and maintaining appropriate rules, perhaps because they themselves were never placed in charge of younger siblings, or because their own parents imposed fewer limits on them than on their older siblings. They may even tolerate extremes of chaotic and unrestrained behaviour in their own offspring without realising that anything is wrong, until the children's patterns of behaviour are so entrenched that trying to impose boundaries becomes a major enterprise.

Many of us resonate more intensely with the child whose birth order position is similar to our own. This may mean that we regard that child more highly, and look more indulgently upon her or his weaknesses. Or it may mean that we find this child the most 'difficult', and are at a loss as to how to cope with behaviour that, in another child, would not pose a problem. If this child, whose birth order position mirrors our own, is also *temperamentally* similar to us, and develops the same attachment strategy, then things become more complicated still. It is as if we are witnesses to a replay of our own childhoods, but this time with the roles reversed: and we must watch ourselves 'from above', as once our parents watched us. Such dynamics create powerful invitations to parents to become what professionals call 'over-involved'. It is easy for psychologists and doctors to use this label, far less easy to do something constructive about it. To learn objectivity when the subject is a child who painfully reminds you of your earlier self is one of the hardest lessons life can demand. No wonder most of us learn it slowly, and imperfectly, and some of us fail to do it at all. Most of the doting parents of the famous individuals we listed at the end of the last sub-section could have been diagnosed as 'pathologically over-involved'. But they were probably viewed by those around them as 'wonderful mums' (or, less often, dads), especially since their 'overprotected' child whose 'grandiosity' they had encouraged went on to become famous and admired!

The Tinder-Box principle dominates our attempts as parents to solve the problems of our problem children. Our natural tendency, as in almost every significant aspect of our relationship life, is to see the *other* person (in this case, our child) as the source of the problem. The more we concentrate on the child's behaviour or personality, seeking to change it (or shield it from potential harm) the more the child will unconsciously resist our attempts to make it over into someone different, and will sense its similarity to us. When the child reaches puberty, it will increasingly challenge what it perceives as our hypocrisy: 'how come you want *me* to control my temper when you can't do it *yourself*?' It is particularly painful, even frightening, to see our son or daughter exhibit the traits we most dislike in ourselves – so frightening that many parents deny completely the correspondence between their own 'shadow side' and the problematic behaviour of their child. This denial 'freezes' their ability to act differently. And so we either do to our child what our own parents did to us, unaware of the parallel or – because we *are* aware of it – we attempt to do something completely opposite (with similar lack of success).

When child or family therapists suggest that if parents change their attitude and/or their behaviour, this will in turn help their child, many of them tend to hear the suggestion as a criticism: 'you think *I'm* to blame, don't you!' Sometimes, parents will rationalise, 'how on earth can *me* coming to counselling make any difference to *her*? It doesn't make any sense to me!' These parents confuse *accepting responsibility for change* (which as an adult is our proper role) with accepting *responsibility for the problem* (for which neither we nor our child are solely responsible). So wedded are we to the idea of autonomous, self-contained individuals that we fail to recognise that within a close, complex human system like a family, everyone's behaviour is bound to impact on everyone else. Our children are at some level aware, not only of what we say and do, but also of how we feel about ourselves. Any change that we effect in ourselves, whether or not it appears directly relevant to their behaviour, cannot *not* 'ripple through' to them. Those of us who can accept this truth are often in a position to make a real difference to our children – and to ourselves.

The hardest challenge of all comes when the 'problem child' is the child of an absent father or an absent mother, and here we come to the issue of family structure. As we saw with Trenton in Chapter 4, it is irresistible for the custodial parent to blame the child's behaviour on 'his father's (or mother's) genes'. It is irresistible, because it is partly true. But only partly. The 'problem child' probably *has* inherited some temperamental vulnerability from the parent who has now left the scene. But (we fail to remember) the child's temperament embodies an equal genetic contribution from the parent who still cares for him/her – or, to be more precise, from that parent's family gene pool. It is just too easy to place all the genetic eggs in one basket, when there are two involved. It is just too simple to see the manifest faults in our ex-partner, when our own weaknesses were part of what led us into a relationship with that partner in the first place. And, to complicate things further, our own behaviour in the present is usually part of the problem.

Just as we failed to find an effective way of dealing with our partner's behaviour in the days before our child was born, so now we may find ourselves locked into the same struggle with our daughter. Once, we felt powerless to draw the line with an intimidating or violent 'ex'; now we feel equally powerless when faced with intimidating or violent outbursts from our son. Our child's attitudes and actions elicit from us actions and attitudes which simply carry the pattern into a new generation. It is true that we cannot bring back the 'missing' father or mother, and we cannot heal the gap torn in our child's circle of selfhood by the mystery of an absent parent. Such things create emotional black holes which inexorably suck emotional 'matter' into themselves – a principle that extends well beyond missing biological parents. As a particularly insightful member of my women's therapy group said recently,

> If you don't get any feedback from your family when you're little, if they just don't see you, or recognise what you're feeling, then you end up giving *yourself* the feedback – you fill the empty space with stuff about how bad you must be.

And if it is a missing parent who fails to 'see' you then it is entirely understandable that even a temperamentally resilient child is likely to tell herself that she must be a very bad person, for Dad/Mum to go away and not seek any contact with her.

But such destructive processes can, with effort and persistence, be reversed. Custodial parents can accept responsibility for their own present behaviour, and begin to alter it. And, as they do so, they may also be creating the opportunity for the child to develop a more realistic, flexible view of the missing parent – who has usually been a potent presence within the 'difficult' child's mind, despite not being physically present at all. While the unsuccessful parenting of children reminds us painfully of what is unresolved in our own lives, successful parenting gives us a matchless sense of fulfilment, and even more so if we have managed to avoid with our child at least some of the negative consequences of our own upbringing. Either way, the experience of parenthood confronts us, even more radically than does marriage, with our deepest insecurities. However much we may turn our heads away, we cannot but be aware that the circle has swung back, that now it is our turn to feel what our parents once felt. The brash confidence and optimism of young adulthood falters in the face of such awareness, repeated again and again over the years of our childrearing. We begin to develop greater humility, greater self-awareness and greater respect for what our own parents experienced. When we hear ourselves speak to our children the words that hurt us so much in our own childhood, we realise that we must start to grow up. Nobody is going to 'kiss it better' for us. If we want things to be better, it's up to us to do it by ourselves.

Notes

1 Biographical information about J. M. Barrie comes from A. J. Birkin's *Barrie and the Lost Boys*, London, Constable, 1979. Also very useful for deciphering the traces of Barrie's personal preoccupations in his most famous work are *The Annotated Peter Pan: The Centennial Edition*, edited with copious notes by Maria Tatar, NY, Norton, 2011, and Jacqueline Rose's influential *The Case of* Peter Pan *or The Impossibility of Children's Fiction*, London, Macmillan, 1984.

2 See John Bowlby, *Attachment and Loss, Vol. 1: Attachment*, NY, Basic Books, 1982. [First edition published in 1969.]

3 See e.g. Philip Guerin and Katherine Buckley Guerin, 'Theoretical Aspects and Clinical Relevance of the Multigenerational Model of Family Therapy' in Philip Guerin (Ed.), *Family Therapy*, NY, Gardner, 1976. Harriet Goldhor Lerner's *The Dance of Anger: A Woman's Guide to Changing the Patterns of Intimate Relationships*, NY, Perennial, 1985, offers a soundly based, readable treatment of this concept on pp. 57–61, 191.

4 A popular account of Gottman's research is summarised in John Gottman and Nan Silver, *The Seven Principles of Making Marriage Work*, London, Weidenfeld and Nicholson, 1999: 1–24.

5 See Daniel Levinson, with Charlotte N. Darrow, Edward B. Klein, Mariah H. Levinson and Braxton McKee, *The Seasons of a Man's Life*, NY, Ballantine Books, 1978: 84–89.

6 See Murray Bowen, *Family Therapy in Clinical Practice*, NY Aronson, 1978: 265. This principle is not supported by hard evidence: Bowen simply asserted it. On the other hand, it would be a very hard proposition to research in any meaningful way, and it certainly rings true in my own clinical practice with couples over some 30 years.

7 See Michael E. Kerr and Murray Bowen, *Family Evaluation: An Approach Based on Bowen Theory*, NY, Norton, 1988: 103–105.

8 Judith Wright, 'Woman to Man' in *Collected Poems, 1942–1985*, Sydney, Angus & Robertson, 1994. [Poem first published in *Woman to Man* in 1949.]

9 See notes to Chapter 2, and particularly Ernest Hartmann's *Boundaries in the Mind: A New Psychology of Personality*, NY, Basic Books, 1991.

10 See Bessel van der Kolk, *The Body Keeps the Score: in the Transformation of Trauma*, London, Allen Lane, 2014.

11 See Peter Whitmer, *The Inner Elvis: A Psychological Biography of Elvis Aaron Presley*, NY, Hyperion, 1996.

12 See Barbara Stoney, *Enid Blyton: The Biography*, 2nd Rev Edn, London, Hodder, 1992: 81. [First edition originally published in 1974.]

13 See Jill Ker Conway, *True North: A Memoir*, London, Hutchinson, 1994: 132–133.

14 'I Was Only Nineteen' was written by guitarist John Schumann, and recorded by Australian folk-rock group Redgum in 1993. Its powerful lyrics incorporated the actual words of Vietnam veterans.

15 See Murray Bowen, *Family Therapy in Clinical Practice*, NY Aronson, 1978: 306–307.

16 See Nancy Chodorow, *The Reproduction of Mothering: Psychoanalysis and the Sociology of Gender*, Berkley, University of California Press, 1978.

17 See Patricia McKinley Crittenden, *Raising Parents: Attachment, Parenting and Child Safety*, NY and London, Routledge, 2012: 117–118. [First published in 2008.]

8

'THE MIDDLE OF THE JOURNEY OF OUR LIVES'

In a dark wood

As far as biology is concerned, reproduction is the primary task of adult life. Once we have replicated ourselves, we are dispensible. Many insects die once they have reproduced, and the males of some species always do so. Having children keeps us young (although for the women who bear them, it also 'makes them old'). In the last two hundred years, we have prolonged adulthood far, far beyond the life expectancy that prevailed before the industrial revolution. When the Brontë children were growing up in the early 1800s, the average adult in their local community could expect to live to be just 25. In the light of this, the fact that their two older sisters had died in childhood, that Emily, Anne and Branwell all died before the age of 30, and that even Charlotte only reached 38, seems less an extraordinary family tragedy than simply an example of the ordinary misery of life at the time. Had they been growing up today, the Brontë siblings could have expected to enjoy at least double the lifespan they had then – although the temperamentally vulnerable Branwell and Emily may still have died young (like Jimi Hendrix, Janis Joplin, Brian Jones, Keith Moon, Sandy Denny, Jim Morrison and other passionate young performers of the 1960s). It is as if we have added an entire 'life' after early adulthood. To complicate things further, women can now delay childbearing into their forties, or even later. To begin to deal with this 'second life' is the task of what Daniel Levinson called the 'Midlife Transition', popularly (if somewhat misleadingly) known as the 'Midlife Crisis'.

When having children is no longer an issue, humans must find other meanings to sustain continued living. It is a struggle, and some do not make it. Midlife, for both women and men, is ultimately about a transition from a biologically driven life to a life driven by meaning, a transition from the sexual to the spiritual, from literal, physical reproduction to reproduction of ourselves in less direct, more symbolic ways. From now on, the air is thinner, the tinkle of cow bells in the valleys falls away below us, and the top of a cold mountain looms. Gustav Mahler portrayed this musically in his sixth symphony, composed at the age of 44.[1]

Eliot Jacques, the psychoanalyst who introduced the term 'Midlife Crisis' in 1965, believed that the crisis could begin at any time from the early thirties on.[2] Levinson proposed that the 'Midlife Transition' would occur somewhere between the ages of 40 and 45 for men and an almost identical range (40–46) for women.[3] Since then, even those scholars who remain loyal to the 'ages and stages' model of adult development would probably agree that we need to be more elastic about the transition's dates of onset and termination.[4] Some individuals seem to experience their 'crisis' as late as the early fifties (Levinson considered this to be the *next* age-related structure-changing period, and called it the 'Age 50 Transition'). It has also been argued that the whole idea of a midlife transition is culture-dependent – but perhaps it would be more accurate to say that the phenomenon is a product of a society preoccupied with change, innovation and individuality – what Ken Wilber calls 'egoic consciousness'.[5] It may well be that as traditional cultures (like those of India and China) are increasingly Westernised, people will begin to report 'midlife crises' where once the idea would never have occurred to them.

Looking back, I was not aware of any 'crisis' in my early forties, though I did change jobs and I did move to a different state. For me, the period of self-questioning, heightened anxiety and mild depression did not begin until I was around 54, when I entered long-term therapy to help me find out why I seemed to keep making the same mistakes over and over again. A few years after beginning this exploration, I was fortunate enough to regain a permanent academic position for my final eight years of salaried employment. Interestingly, I noticed that this paralleled my father's career at a very similar age. Having failed to gain the promotions he felt he deserved, he then accepted a role at the same level but with more independence, giving him the chance to be 'captain of his own ship' for the final eight years of his working life.

The death of youth

Sustained by our superior diet (at least for some) and by modern medicine's routing of illnesses like scarlet fever and tuberculosis, which once carried off children and young adults in droves, most of us are still physically healthy and energetic in early middle adulthood. Long gone are the days when a 40-year-old might already have been considered on the threshold of old age. But even those of us who have put sustained effort into maintaining our bodies in good running order are conscious that we can no longer expect of ourselves what we could 20 years before. Undue exertion makes us pant, our backs 'go out' more easily, we no longer recover so readily after partying. Our youthful 'organ reserves' (the 'bounce-back' capacity of our heart, liver, lungs and so on) are now diminishing. We cannot run as fast, lift such heavy weights, keep going as long. Our society still casts men in the roles of physical workers, athletes and hard drinkers, and so such limitations tend to affect them more than females. Men whose identity has been bound up with their body's strength and endurance can feel loss and self-doubt for the first time in their lives when they must retire from sports teams, moderate the physical demands they place on themselves – and drink less.

They find themselves looking at younger men with envy, and at younger women with desire. The popular stereotype of the middle-aged man leaving his wife for an 18-year-old is true only of a small minority, but there is a symbolic truth in it for most men. A much younger woman represents the youthfulness that they themselves have lost, and her femininity represents the softer, more nurturing qualities they have typically neglected within themselves. Midlife men are no exception to the rule that if we don't feel it inside, then we try to marry it, or at least, mate with it. But try telling that to a 45-year-old man who is desperately in love with a 20-year-old! In his forties, and married with a large family, Charles Dickens courted a young actress, Ellen ('Nellie') Ternan (whose story is movingly told in the 2014 movie *The Silent Woman*). Interestingly, when he met her, Nellie was almost the same age as his 'first love', Maria Beadnell, with whom he had been desperately infatuated as a young man. But Dickens would never have admitted that he was seeking 'lost youth' or trying to contact his 'inner femininity'! Most of us do not give up our illusions any more readily, and many men need to go through the affair, even the remarriage and the starting of a second family, before they are ready to acknowledge what seems so obvious to others.

Where men mourn loss of strength and endurance, women feel more keenly the loss of their body's elasticity and shapeliness, their youthful, unlined skin. They may still be good looking, they may still be capable of bearing children (though the risk of doing so is now increasing), but the onset of menopause is, for many women, a message about loss, change and the need to redefine self. Despite reassuring promises from journalists that midlife is a time of peak sexual responsiveness and new energy for career as childrearing recedes, women whose primary source of identity and meaning has been their ability to bear and mother children often experience menopause as a time when green softness hardens into brown husk. A 45-year-old client of mine once referred bitterly to 'this time of your life when everything's falling down all over the place'. She was talking about her body. Men do not bleed monthly, do not bear children and so do not experience the beginning of a new season of life in such a dramatic, embodied way. They can still, after all, *beget* children well into old age. Yet the waning of sexual self-confidence that many midlife men experience suggests that they, too, sense the cold winds blowing.

Genetically programmed signs of ageing vary widely in their age of onset (my wife's family began to grey in their thirties; my father's family had scarcely a grey hair before 60). But, by the middle forties, the vast majority of faces are showing signs of change. Repeated small insults to the body (too many broken nights, too much sun or wind, routine illnesses) gradually erode the smooth, elastic skin of youth. When major traumas occur in midlife – chronic illness, accident, torture, the experience of prolonged anxiety and stress – they etch their lines deeply and permanently.

People used to say (and Enid Blyton's characters repeated it endlessly) that you should be careful, because if the wind changed while you were scowling (or adopting some other unpleasant facial expression) it would be fixed forever. That moralistic superstition carries a kind of poetic truth. Smile enough, and our face smiles permanently; sneer enough, and the sneer eventually becomes engraved. By midlife, the face of many a career politician is showing a characteristic split – one side of the mouth turned down, the other up, one eyebrow raised, but not the other. Such observable distortions are a physical testament to political leaders' skill in evading questions, and their willingness to do 'about-turns' on controversial issues. By midlife, the pursed mouths of women who have disapproved too much of themselves and others proclaim judgement and disapproval even when, temporarily, they do not feel it.

As for the face, so for the body. Our bodies are metaphors for our selfhood, for its triumphs and its battles lost. How we stand, how we walk, where we bulge with unwanted fat, where we cave in on ourselves, hunched forward under the weight of our emotional burdens – all of these things are public statements to others about who we have become. If the unconscious mind is the hidden *mental* repository of everything that has ever happened to us, the body is the visible, tangible repository. In the words Bessel van der Kolk used for the title of his book on trauma, 'the body keeps the score'.[6] If a person's prevailing facial expression is contradicted by her prevailing gestures, if the shape of the body contradicts how it is in motion, then we know that some conflict, some unresolved dichotomy, is present within the individual concerned. It cannot be otherwise.

Yet although our bodies are open books to be read by those who can interpret them, we collectively agree to keep this knowledge hidden. We see the politician's eyes move shiftily from side to side as she avoids the honest answer, yet somehow we pay attention to the content of her words and not to what her eyes are saying. Is it because we so desperately want to trust, that we fail to acknowledge the lies and evasions? In everyday life, with our intimates, we do the same. Though we register and respond unconsciously to each others' bodies and idiosyncratic movement patterns, we consciously attend mainly to words, and to overt facial expressions. A brief smile can sometimes override the permanent sneer on the face of the sneerer, words of apparently sincere praise or flattery can cancel out the facial indications of insincerity. Those individuals whom psychiatry terms 'sociopathic' (con men and women – with some politicians among them) can continue to delude us, not only because they are skilled in impression management, but because they know that they can trade on our gullibility, our strong need to be told what we want to hear.

With the entrenchment of prevailing expressions on the faces of midlife adults there comes, for many of us, a point at which we begin physically to resemble one or both of our parents more closely than before. With the shrinking of the fat that may have disguised the resemblance in youth, the lines and wrinkles that appear on our faces may start to remind us of our parents. Conversely, *increasing* fat may round out our faces to bring about the same resemblance. But there is more to it than those purely physical changes. After all, have many of us not undergone similar experiences to our parents, and coped with those experiences in much the same ways?

Secrets, lies and synchronicity

Perhaps, then, it is natural that midlife is the age at which many people become preoccupied with discovering more of their personal past. Those adoptees who have not already sought out their birth families (typically, this seems to happen in the twenties and thirties) will often do so now; those who have grown up with an absent mother or father will feel the stirrings of a wish to meet them, or know more about them.[7] Similarly with non-adoptees: in young adulthood, many of us were happy to accept unquestioned the half-truths and evasions with which we grew up. If our parents did not talk about a particular relative, or a particular bit of the family past, then we, too, simply ignored it. By midlife, this has changed. Now some of us, at least, want to *know* what was concealed, to uncover what was kept hidden, to understand what previously seemed inexplicable. People talk of needing to 'discover their roots', to locate their family or ethnic heritage in time and space, and this is certainly part of it, but ultimately, I suspect, what we need is to complete *ourselves*. It was at 48 that prominent feminist author Germaine Greer began a quest to find out the truth about her father's life and, in so doing, to understand some of the disowned parts of herself. What she found was not what she had expected, and it brought certainties that were deeply disconcerting. She concludes her book *Daddy, We Hardly Knew You* with the words, 'In finding him, I lost him. Sleepless nights are long'.[8]

Following Carl Jung,[9] Levinson claims that we actually *need* this inward turn, this period of preoccupation with self, in order to grapple with the tasks of midlife: to come to terms with the loss of youthful dreams, to set new and more realistic goals for the second half of our lives, and to build a life structure that will sustain us through the next phase of our adulthood. In Levinson's scheme, midlife adults can deny or defer this emotional quest (postpone the 'structure-changing' work), but there will be a cost: their lives will rigidify, their selfhood will be diminished and, sooner or later, they will have to face a period of even greater turmoil and disruption, a true *crisis*. My own sense is that those of us whose temperaments incline them to introspection (mostly, but not solely, those born with 'thinner boundaries')[10] will be more likely to experience the midlife transition (or any of Levinson's other transitions for that matter) psychologically or spiritually. For them, midlife will be an invitation to self-doubt, conscious experimentation, concern with the reality of death and the meaning of life. It will offer the possibility of both personal growth, and the temporary emotional overload which we call 'breakdown'.

By contrast, those whose attention has always been focused outwards, and especially those who are temperamentally uninhibited (have 'thicker boundaries') often deny having experienced any inner crisis at midlife. What they will tell you instead is that in their forties their business collapsed, or they lost their job, or their adolescent son or daughter began using drugs, or one of their parents died suddenly. They see no connection between these external events and the fact that they themselves were traversing the midlife years at the time. And indeed, why should they? Wouldn't it be just as true to say that as we get older, the chances of our encountering unemployment, illness or loss of a loved one are statistically higher? Some would say that having adolescent children is itself a crisis, and if one is 40 or 45, the death of a parent is obviously on the cards. Most people would probably agree that external misfortune at midlife is just a coincidence. Of course, the 'hammer blows of fate' can happen to anyone at any stage of life. Yet I wonder whether something else may be going on.

Our inner calendars

Popular thinking features 'the big 4–0' as a landmark birthday, one on which we are expected to celebrate extra hard (and accept commiserations for the loss of youth that it supposedly signifies). In 1923, Captain Joe Stilwell had just spent another period in China, at his own request, as military attaché and language officer with the American Legation. On his fortieth birthday, shortly before he headed home to the United States, he wrote in his diary, 'Here it is. Middle-aged man now'.[11] Whether or not people claim to notice or care about such landmarks, they can hardly fail to be aware of them. Out of sight, out of mind, we seem to have an inbuilt 'personal calendar', almost like a biological clock which chimes dimly in the hidden recesses of our minds, reminding us of how much time has elapsed, how much (roughly) we have left. Such semi–conscious calculations are probably based on a generalised sense of family life-expectancy, and a specific consciousness of how old our parents are (or were, when they died).

Significant events in the lives of our parents figure heavily in our hidden calendars. Thus the early death of a mother can hardly fail to leave a trace on the growing consciousness of her children. Charles Darwin's mother died when he was only eight, C. S. Lewis's mother when he was nine. They remembered how old they themselves were when the loss occurred, but it is unlikely they thought about *their mother's age when she died*, since younger children are far less aware of their parents' ages than they are of their own. Even when, as adults, we revisit the early loss of a parent, we may not 'take in' the information that she died when she was 38, 40 or whatever. Perhaps we do not do so because it frighteningly reminds us that we ourselves may now be approaching that same age. But in some part of our mind, it seems the calculation has already been done for us.

We 'know' that 40 is going to be a difficult time for us. Only when we are forced to stop and think about it do we explicitly make the connection: 'Oh, yeah, that's right, Mum must've been 40 when she had her heart attack!' Of course, the predicted difficulties do not necessarily materialise. We reach 40, and despite our apprehension, nothing happens. Only rarely, in fact, do we *literally* repeat a crisis in an earlier generation by, say, dropping dead of a heart attack ourselves. But it is not uncommon to develop some milder symptoms, or to undergo a different *kind* of life crisis.

An untimely parental death is a dramatic example of the internal calendar, and it is easy enough to see the connection, because a parental death is also something that cannot normally be denied or covered up. But what about less public events in the lives of our parents, events of which we were less aware at the time they were happening? What about times of acute tension between our parents, due to the infidelity of one (or both) of them? What of a mother's or father's depression, never named or discussed openly? As we know from earlier chapters, children are aware, at some level, of such things, and the younger they are, the more likely they are to 'save' whatever unresolved emotions are in the air around them. As we've seen earlier in this book, infants can and do absorb some of the feelings and anxieties that surround them (as psychoanalysis has always asserted) even though they do not understand in an adult way what has given rise to those feelings, or consciously remember what was going on at the time. Could it be that we also register and store within our data bank our parents' *age* at the time of this tension or anxiety?

Australian psychiatrist Averil Earnshaw seems to have been the first to draw attention to the specifics of such time-links across generations, although in Europe, Ann Ancelin Schutzenberger's work (published slightly later) has independently explored a very similar territory. Earnshaw's hypothesis was that significant life events in our lives are age-linked with significant events in the lives of one of our parents. These events need not be blows or misfortunes like the onset of serious illness, accident or loss of a loved one. For Earnshaw, significant events can include creative breakthroughs, marriages, gaining important new career positions, or moving to a new home, a new country or a new professional field. From her observation, the correlation often seems to be between such events in our own lives, and something that was happening to our (usually) same-sex parent at the same age, *and that 'something' is often our own birth, or the birth of a younger sibling* when we ourselves were still very small. Thus Jane develops a tumour at 33, and although the tumour proves ultimately to be benign, she begins to re-evaluate her life and her marriage. Her mother was 33 at the time when she gave birth to Jane, 'nearly dying' of complications. Her mother has never talked about this much, and Jane had not connected her own illness with the trauma her mother experienced while giving birth to her – why should she? So, is it that a baby somehow registers and 'stores' (in a manner inaccessible to later conscious recall) physical, observable indications of its parent's age at a particular, crucial time in its own life? That seems to defy credibility, given the very limited sense-capacities of a newborn baby. Or is it that something more profoundly biological is going on?

Mainstream evolutionary theory has always maintained that characteristics acquired by individuals in their lifetime cannot be passed on genetically to their offspring. The belief that acquired characteristics could be inherited was known as the 'Lamarckian heresy' (Lamarck, a contemporary of Darwin, believed passionately that they could; Darwin did not). Yet recently, the new science of 'epigenetics' (how genes are 'switched on and off') has suggested that Lamarck may not have been as wrong as has been thought. What we are beginning to see is that, in a way, *both* Darwin and Lamarck may have been right. Traumatic events in the life of an individual *can* result in the attaching of 'tags' to genes, chemical adhesions that leave the gene itself intact, but which influence the likelihood of that particular gene being 'turned on' – and that these chemical tags can, in some circumstances, be transmitted intact to the genes of that individual's children.

Rachel Yehuda's research team at Mount Sinai medical school in New York has been releasing the results of an ongoing series of studies of Holocaust survivors and their offspring, studies which seem to confirm that the massive trauma suffered by survivors could, indeed, be passed on to their descendants, in the form of molecular marks ('tags') that alter the *expression* of particular genes – making it much more likely that these genes will be activated in their offspring.[12] If this continues to be confirmed, we will, at last, possess a *biochemical* explanation for how 'trauma can be passed on' from parent to child, even though the genes themselves, and their sequence, remain intact. Earlier in this book, I said that those who suffer trauma are particularly vulnerable to being re-traumatised. Now we can see how, in a cross-generational context, a traumatised parent may pass on to his or her children a heightened vulnerability to trauma, via chemical 'tags' that increase that child's vulnerability to stress. Of course the problems experienced by the children of Holocaust survivors can be explained in other, more conventional ways.[13] But as we've already noted, it is far harder to explain the *age-related* 'generational repeats' described by Earnshaw and others. Yehuda's research may in time provide a key to unlock that mystery also. If genetic tags resulting from parental environment can alter the expression of these particular genes, they can also alter the expression of other genes – with implications that offspring may be more vulnerable to particular health risks, for example.[14] So the observation that adult children may experience health crises at the same age as a parent experienced similar or related crises may, in time, be confirmed by further epigenetic research. At the very least, such observations cannot any longer be dismissed out of hand.

Our point of departure for these speculations, however, was the problem of explaining why non-introspective individuals tend to experience a midlife crisis, not in the form of internal events, but of *external* events over which they appear to have had no control. Remember the principle that what individuals do 'on the outside' offers clues to what is going on for them on the inside. The classic psychoanalytic theory has it that when individuals cannot acknowledge or come to terms with their inner feelings, they 'act them out', that is, *they do to other people*, or the world around them, *what they themselves are experiencing inside*. All very well, you will say, but there's a big difference between a teenage boy deliberately smashing public property (because he privately feels 'smashed' and worthless) and a midlife adult who is a helpless victim of accident or retrenchment. Well, on the face of it, yes. But is the adult really a 'helpless victim'? Or has his own behaviour set up situations in which crisis is more likely to beset him?

The man who loses his job may also be the man who sets great store by principles and refuses to compromise with his employers (I know, because I was such a person!). The man who suffers a serious car accident is also the man who has driven *himself* relentlessly for years, and who knows that under stress, his reflexes are poor. In these scenarios, a deeply buried fear of the midlife period could provoke risky actions (perhaps triggered by a genetic 'tag' linked to a serious parental crisis at that age) that set the man up for probable disasters of an external kind. The same buried fear could, in another adult, provoke a much more internal process, equally unconscious in origin, but leading to more introspection and greater awareness of long-hidden feelings. Midlife does not transform our personalities. What we have always done, we usually continue to do, only perhaps with a more forced, desperate quality than before. Let's look at the midlife period of a woman who, lifelong, denied her own pain and grief, and instead, acted out her inner conflicts in the way she handled key relationships.

When Enid Blyton married Hugh Pollock in 1924, she married a man who was older than she, and who had a senior role in publishing, enabling him to mentor her writing. Like Jill Ker's choice to marry John Conway, this looks like the choice of a 'father' – though no doubt both Enid and Jill, under the sway of 'projective, protective trance', would have been unaware of it. At some point, Hugh began to drink in secret (we don't know why). Following the outbreak of World War Two, he rejoined the army. Like her mother before her, Enid resented her husband's absence, suspected him of infidelities and (unlike her mother) herself flirted with other men. This culminated in a serious affair with a London surgeon. She and Hugh had been married for 16 years in 1940, and their eldest daughter, Gillian, was nine. When Enid and Hugh saw each other for the last time, prior to their divorce hearing in 1942, Gillian was 11: just a year younger than Enid herself had been when her father had left her mother. Enid had repeated, quite closely, the pattern of her mother's marriage, selecting in Hugh a man whose 'weakness' she had come to despise – only she had 'dumped' him first, without waiting for him to dump her (as her father had done to her mother).

It was Enid who, having found a new lover, insisted on a divorce, which Hugh did not want. Once she had obtained a legal dissolution of her marriage, she cut her children off completely from any contact with their father. The secrets and lies she insisted upon repeated the secrets and lies of her own childhood. Her second marriage (again to a considerably older man) would be a happy and stable one, and Enid herself would be well content with it. But the impact on her second daughter, apparently more temperamentally vulnerable than her sister, was considerable. Many years after her mother was dead, this daughter, Imogen, emerged to tell her painful story, which newspapers worldwide excerpted under the gleeful headline, 'Enid Blyton, the Unloving Mother'.[15]

Between 1919 and 1939, George S. Patton experienced a prolonged period of instability that stretched over 20 years. Several factors were involved, of which his stage of life was only one. He was 35 when the Great War (as it was then called) ended. Now deprived of the chance to display his extraordinary talent for military leadership, Patton became angry and depressed. Wartime had meant rapid promotion to the acting rank of Colonel, but now he was reduced to his pre-war permanent rank (Captain), which felt to him like an insult, even though he knew that the same thing was happening to all of his contemporaries. As a result of these *external* events, Patton experienced what Levinson would describe as a 'flawed life structure' from his late thirties to his late forties. He became preoccupied with losing his looks, constantly enjoining his wife Beatrice to 'not get fat' and to avoid grey hairs. In Patton's case, Beatrice was Patton's 'mirror' in an almost literal sense. (Elvis Presley, almost 30 years later, would behave almost identically with his wife Priscilla.)

In his late forties and early fifties, Patton's depression and anxiety flowered into a full-fledged crisis. He had a short affair with a woman 'young enough to be his daughter' (in fact, she was his younger daughter's *friend*), which strained even Beatrice's extraordinary tolerance. After the same daughter's wedding, Patton leapt onto the roof of the couple's going-away car, firing his pistols into the air. There could be no clearer example of the way the passage through midlife often resembles the passage through adolescence. In both stages, oppositional, antisocial and bizarre behaviour marks inner turmoil. Beatrice even bought her husband a book on 'change of life in men' – which Patton promptly burned! Patton was typical of those who are too rigid to remake their life dream in the midlife years. He clung desperately to the future he had always planned for himself and, fortunately for him, the advent of another war would give him a second chance to achieve it.[16]

Crisis and creativity

In striking contrast to the short, tumultuous life of Mozart, his contemporary Joseph Haydn lived a long, stable and fulfilling life. In secure employment with his princely patrons, the Esterhazy family, Haydn enjoyed a comfortable lifestyle, ran an orchestra and was free to develop his creativity over many years. His marriage was unhappy, but Haydn looked elsewhere for the affection and support his wife did not provide. Almost certainly, Haydn had an 'easygoing' temperament with a positive attitude to life – although had his career been less smooth, he may have displayed more dissatisfaction and angst. His music was in the *galant* style fashionable at the time – meaning that it was, on the whole, upbeat in mood, written predominantly in major keys, full of joy and (Haydn's characteristic addition) humour. Yet between 1766 and 1775, his symphonies changed dramatically. For the first time in his life, he chose minor keys in preference to major ones (no less than six of the symphonies of this period were in minor keys). The music itself is more serious, it conveys darker emotions more frequently and in greater depth than in his previous symphonies. But these were not the only changes. Haydn's new works were also more daring musically, less predictable. His most famous work of this period, the symphony popularly known as the 'Farewell' (1772), even includes a piece of 'acting out' unprecedented in Haydn's career. As the symphony draws towards its end – unusually, with a slow movement rather than an upbeat, faster one – the members of his orchestra, two by two, closed their music, picked up their instruments and walked quietly out of the room, while the rest continued, eventually leaving only two violinists to play the final notes before they, too, departed. It was, so the story goes, a broad hint to Prince Esterhazy to let his court musicians depart on their long-delayed holiday, but it was also a theatrical gesture on Haydn's part that in its own quiet way calls to mind Patton's behaviour at his daughter's wedding. The 'ebbing away' of the music could even be seen as symbolic representation of the gradual giving-up of life. (It was 137 years later that Gustav Mahler concluded his ninth symphony in a similar way, with most of the orchestra falling silent, leaving only a single high note on the strings to fade imperceptibly into silence.)

After 1775, Haydn's symphonies reverted to the *galant* style, and although his later works grew longer, richer and more complex, he never returned to the feelings that he had expressed in what musicologists call his *Sturm und Drang* symphonies (the German words mean 'storm and stress' – the same phrase John Watson applied to adolescence). Is it purely coincidental that those symphonies correspond with Haydn's mid-to-late thirties and early forties?[17] Haydn is only one of many creative individuals whose work went through a profound transformation during what we might call the 'extended midlife period': novelist Charles Dickens, and artist Paul Cézanne among them.[18] The examples we have just explored suggest that the relationship between enhanced creativity and the midlife period is real enough, but that it cannot be pinned down as narrowly as Levinson's work would suggest. Creative breakthroughs may occur both before and after the period from 40 to 45, and establishing exactly what year a particular creative development occurred is often problematic. Is it the first draft or the final published work that we choose to date? However, there is abundant evidence that both enriched creativity, and in many cases Jung's 'inward turn', does occur within creative lives, which seems to run from the mid-thirties to the late forties.

Most people's selfhood is not bound up so obviously and centrally in their creativity, yet if creativity is to find expression, it will often do so at midlife. At the same age as George Patton was at the peak of his depression and eccentricity, his wife Beatrice completed a novel, *Blood of the Shark*: it was her only attempt at creative writing in a life otherwise devoted to bringing up her children and soothing the wounded ego of her fame-obsessed husband.[19]

Midlife in the family life cycle

If adult partners begin having children somewhere between the ages of 20 and 25, then by the time they reach their forties some or all of these children will be adolescent. Although such a pattern is by no means universal (especially now that many women defer having children until their late thirties or early forties), it is still very common. The consequences for the parents are considerable. At the very time that they are becoming aware of their own waning youth, their children will be bursting with it: energetic, hopeful, seemingly capable of anything. Even those adolescents who are manifestly 'drifting', unable to sense their own potentials, or unclear as to their direction in life, are at least *young* – and urgently experimenting with self-chosen (and often risky) ways of feeling good about themselves. At the very time that both sexes acknowledge the lessening of their peak physical attractiveness, their children are intensely aware of their sexuality, and nearing their most attractive age. Kept dependent far longer than their physical maturity necessitates (as we saw in Chapter 5), adolescents frequently 'push the limits' of parental control. For many parents, this challenge to their authority, whether mild or massive, comes at the very time when their confidence in themselves and their own powers is waning.

It is not difficult for adults to assert their moral authority over pre-adolescent children – they are still bigger and stronger than their offspring. Most parents can get their ten- or 11-year-olds to do what they want, despite spirited opposition at times. But when your offspring are as tall as you are, physically almost as strong and determined to get their way, it all becomes much more difficult. Those parents who have relied on reasoning with their children suddenly come face to face with a 'child' whose cognitive abilities match or surpass their own. While there are many families in which adolescent children continue to do pretty much as their parents expect, their *potential* for going their own way, and for leading a life of which their parents know little or nothing, can still be an implicit threat. Those parents who have relied on threats and actual beatings to enforce their will are now confronted with a young person confident enough to laugh in their parent's face.

Faced with the challenge of their offspring's adolescence, many parents respond with 'more of the same' (or, as early family therapists tellingly put it, 'more of the same wrong solution'). If they dealt out physical punishment before, they try stronger beltings now; if they shouted before, they shout louder now; if they pleaded or reasoned, they do so more lengthily and intensely now; if they spied and intruded before, they now do it more compulsively. The most common result of such tactics is to evoke even more opposition from the teenager, and parents are often in despair as a result, especially when painfully aware that their teenage son or daughter is doing exactly what they themselves did at the same age, and is apparently about to make the same mistakes. Parents try to prevent this outcome – but without admitting fully their own motivation for so doing. 'It's for your own good' is often, in reality, 'It's to make *me* feel less guilty'. 'Don't make the mistakes I made' should read, 'I made these exact same mistakes *and I've felt really awful about it ever since*'. All of these evasive messages amount to '*You've* got to change, but don't expect me to' – an invitation to the adolescent to resist vigorously. Like the King in 'The Tinder Box', these parents end up inviting the very scenario they most wish to avoid.

Typically, problematic behaviour in teenage children draws the same split response from their parents/step-parents that we've already observed in earlier chapters: one of the adults will be 'tougher' on the young person, acting in an authoritarian and often punitive manner ('She's only got herself to blame – she's gotta learn some self-discipline!') while the other will be more sympathetic, seeing the adolescent's difficulties as reflecting emotional distress rather than a deficit of character. This often leads to the empathic parent adopting an over-permissive attitude to the young person (a father secretly gives his daughter money, even though he knows it will probably maintain her drug habit). The split between the stance of the two adults strongly resembles the internal split that Melanie Klein hypothesised occurred in infancy: one parent/caregiver demonises the adolescent, focusing on his 'bad' or unacceptable behaviours; the other refuses to take seriously the adolescent's abusive or risky conduct. Both see only a *part* of the young person, not the complex, contradictory 'whole'.

In fact these two opposed attitudes, with their associated value systems, can be found in how individuals respond to almost any kind of political, social and moral challenge. As American psychologist Silvan Tomkins argued 40 years ago in his groundbreaking work on human emotions, the 'tough' stance is associated with the 'normative' personality, organised around rigid boundaries between right and wrong, and a somewhat distrustful, negative attitude towards others. The normative individual (whom I think of as the 'Warrior') reacts with *disgust* to others' expression of distress. The 'soft' stance, which Tomkins calls 'human-istic', is packaged with a view of human nature that embraces more complexity, more 'shades of grey'. The 'humanistic' individual is more likely to trust others and embrace differences rather than reject them, and reacts with *empathy* to those who express distress (and, by extension, to those who breach moral codes or 'get into trouble').[20] I call this type the 'Social Worker'.

The result of this split between caregivers is nearly always unhelpful. The acting-out or troubled adolescent may feel reassured that she has one parent who covertly supports her, and this empowers her to 'hate' the punitive, authori-tarian one. At a deeper level, the adolescent will feel *less* safe than if both his/her caregivers were united in their stance. Where parents/caregivers are divided, adolescents will experience a 'loss of good authority' – a loss they will be affected by without even realising it. 'Good authority' was a concept advanced by British psychoanalyst Tom Pitt-Aikens, whose career included extensive consultation to institutions that dealt with 'delinquent' youth.[21] Pitt-Aikens defined good authority as that combination of firmness and fairness that has always characterised leaders whose staff, subordinates or colleagues admire and respect them. In parenting, good authority means setting clear (but reasonable) limits on children's behaviour while they are still living in the family home, and responding to the breaking of those limits with understanding, but also with the imposition of pre-announced consequences. Good authority means love but not permissiveness, firmness but not unfairness. Parents who embody 'good authority' do not agonise too much over whether or not they are doing the right thing by their child, and because of their own sureness about their role, they communicate quiet confidence, not defensiveness or anger. Their kids grumble and complain, but underneath, they feel respect, as if to admit 'They love me enough not to take shit from me'. Pitt-Aikens explains that parents are most likely to feel this sureness when their own parents displayed it towards them. But if the family history over the past few generations demonstrates a gradual erosion of 'good authority', then the parents of the most recent generation are likely to experience a major crisis as they attempt to respond to their children's disturbed and disturbing behaviour. Parents whose upbringing was authoritarian and judgemental, or overly permissive and uncaring ('neglectful'), will falter when it comes to parenting their own kids. They will confuse abusive punishment with 'protection', and neglectful permissiveness with 'love', because they did not experience 'firm but fair' parenting themselves. To my mind, Pitt-Aikens' views are a corrective to the current tendency for parents to want to be their children's 'best friends'. The wise parent is not afraid to act in a way that will provoke a young person's anger or resentment, because he or she knows that the anger will be temporary, and that the teenager will, underneath, feel valued and cared about.

In my clinical and personal experience, the extent of teenage rebellion, and the specific behaviours that a particular teenager adopts, usually correlates with the values and behaviours of the family itself. If you yourself drink and smoke, but seek to prevent your children from doing the same, they are likely to rebel by doing exactly what you forbid them, because your own behaviour has already sanctioned it. If you yourself are deeply moral, your teenage children may act out a certain level of 'immorality', but it will be circumscribed by a strong boundary beyond which the child will never go, unless under extreme provocation. If you yourself became pregnant as an adolescent, if the baby was adopted out, and you never spoke of it to your own children, there is a fair chance that one of your adolescent daughters will repeat your pattern, because your own anxieties will propel you to behave towards her in such a way that your daughter will be driven to it. The time-linked cross-generational patterns we mentioned earlier in this chapter seem more powerful and pervasive in families where things are kept secret, and shames are not talked about openly. (The copper castle in which the King shuts up his daughter in 'The Tinder Box' is, perhaps, a metaphor for this kind of secrecy: a hard, metallic wall around the softness of human longing and hurt.)

Teenage 'symptoms' often correlate accurately both with what parents *openly* do and with what they *secretly* desire and fear. Teenage rebels may go 'one better' than parents in behaviours that are openly sanctioned (you drink and smoke, your son uses marijuana or amphetamines); they may also do what you wish you could do, but do not dare ('girls just wanna have fun'). But in either case, the invisible limits are always set by the extended family's range of demonstrated behaviour, and by its overt values. My extended family has had its share of 'teen rebels', but scarcely one of them has ever been in trouble with the law. So, if you want to know how far your adolescent rebel is likely to go, look not only at the range of your own behaviour, both as an adolescent and now, but also at what your relatives, on both sides, have done with their lives. Just as our children's temperaments will reflect the spread of the genes they have inherited from both sides of the family, so their behaviour as teenagers will reflect the 'spread' of the examples and models the extended family provides. Again, this is my own hypothesis, and to my knowledge, untested scientifically.

When love can't be shared

I have dwelt so far on overt power struggles around teenage rebellion, because this is the sort of situation that most often brings midlife parents to seek counselling, but of course, there are many families where no such acting out occurs, and yet there is real pain for parents just the same. Normally, when an adolescent grows up sufficiently to move away from home and to form a serious relationship, it is cause for celebration. But some parents interpret their child's leaving home as a statement that they, the parents, are no longer needed, no longer important. If the adolescent develops a strong attraction for a boyfriend or girlfriend, the parents see this, somehow, as a rejection, a betrayal of their own love — a 'narcissistic wound'. Such parents are governed by the either/or thinking we discussed in Chapter 2: 'If she loves him, she can't love me any more'. Once again, the predictable parental response is either to hang on harder than ever (as Jill Ker's mother did), or to let go with bitterness, so that the now-adult child and the parent may be alienated for years. Living on the other side of the continent, or the world, may 'finesse' the issue of leaving home (as Jill thought) but it does not solve it. 'Distance and silence do not fool an emotional system', observed family therapist Murray Bowen in his laconic Southern way. Bowen called this attempt to escape from family of origin conflict 'cut-off'.[22]

As our children re-enact the dramas of our own adolescence, or go beyond the limits our own parents imposed (which were, after all, the limits of a very different time and place) — as they spread their wings and fly, we often fail to remember that the whole purpose of parenting is to enable this moment. Their struggle for independence, bloody though it may seem to us at the time, is what *needs* to happen if our children are to become viable, autonomous adults. To do our job properly, we need both to struggle for control and, gradually, to let go. If we fail to struggle for control, our children will feel no firm ground beneath their feet, and no solidity in their own autonomy: as in caesarean section, they will have been 'lifted' into adulthood without the struggle and challenge of birth. If we fail to let go, then our children will go into their own reproductive cycle still unsure of where they begin and we end, still dominated by their own parents when they need to become parents themselves. No wonder, then, that even when things go reasonably smoothly with our adolescent children, we so often feel challenged to the core of our being for those few years, no wonder that self-doubt creeps in as our old tactics fail and we are forced to find new ways of relating to these newly equal people whose failings remind us so painfully of our own. We have to say goodbye to the cute toddlers and tractable, trusting school children we knew only a few short years before.

And at the very same time in our lives, our own parents are ageing. They may be hale and hearty 60-year-olds, with 20 or more years of life remaining to them, but they are visibly slowing down, visibly divesting themselves of responsibilities, becoming more and more *our children's grandparents*, rather than *our parents*. Or they may be already frail: physically deteriorating with some incurable condition, or in the early stages of dementia, needing us to care for them as once they cared for us. In these latter cases, the impact on the midlife adult is obviously far greater than in the former; it is greater again when one or both parents die before we ourselves reach 50. If the ageing of a parent reminds us of our own responsibilities, the death of a parent provokes more radical reversals, uncomfortable new awareness. Now we are alone. There is no generation 'above' us, in our own branch of the family. The buck stops with us. The death of a parent inevitably reminds us of our own mortality. How our parents die – well, or badly, or a human mixture of the two – provokes uncomfortable speculations about how we ourselves will handle that 'last migration'. And if our own youthfulness is already under question, parental death will often trigger a very substantial re-orientation indeed. The loss of those who brought us into the world and nurtured us to adulthood can make us acutely conscious of many other losses, among them the loss of our young adult dreams. If our careers have failed, if our children have disappointed us, if our needs for recognition or achievement have not been fulfilled, then the death of a parent can wake up all our longing, and all our despair. Or it can, conversely, drive us forward into renewed and enriched life.

As he entered his midlife years, Sigmund Freud felt he had failed to make the great discoveries that he had hoped would bring him fame. The death of his father in 1896, when Freud himself was 40, threw him into inner turmoil. Gloom, depression, disturbing dreams, powerful feelings he had not felt for years – the whole of his early childhood seemed to surface again. He struggled to confront his own demons, to analyse his own unconscious preoccupations, to make sense of his own irrationality. Typical of both Freud's radical honesty and his grandiosity, the founder of psychoanalysis analysed *himself*. And that is how psychoanalysis began: in the Midlife Crisis of its founder.

Suspended between the youth of our children and the ageing or even the death of our own parents, what wonder is it if so many of us experience some degree of unease and self-questioning at midlife? Perhaps the wonder is that so many of us manage to traverse the years between the mid-thirties and the late forties so calmly. But whether we are forced to confront our own fears and doubts head on, or are enabled by our life circumstances to put off facing them a while longer, something will have changed that we cannot deny. As we turn 50, for the vast majority of us, less lies ahead than lies behind. '*Nel mezzo del cammin di nostra vita . . .*' wrote Dante in the opening lines of his *Divine Comedy:* 'Midway on life's journey, I found myself in a dark wood, where the path ahead was lost'. The Bible saw human life expectancy as 'threescore years and ten' (i.e. 70), so Dante probably wrote those words around the age of 35. However, since he died in his mid-fifties, he had indeed reached a fourteenth-century equivalent of 'midlife'. Of course he did not, at 35, know when he was going to die. But maybe his inner calendar was already telling him that he had reached the halfway point?

Some of us are already afraid. Facelifts, hormone replacement therapy, affairs with much younger partners, the impulsive conception of 'midlife babies', retreat into sleeping pills, antidepressants or compulsive work – whatever route we take, it will only delay the inevitable. Others among us develop a richer, deeper experience of life, and a greater willingness to take life as it is and make the best of it, rather than longing for the moon. The 'vision splendid' of Wordsworth's youth has faded into 'the light of common day', but with that fading can come realism, wisdom, tolerance and appreciation. Those who shift career in their forties to work in a caring or nurturing role with people (nursing, child care, counselling) often prove outstanding in comparison with younger trainees. Why? Because they have lived long enough to appreciate what can be changed and what can't, they are ready to accept people as they find them, rather than treating them as human 'material' on which to stamp their own heroic image. At 50, we begin to look, not just to our personal future, a horizon that is coming daily closer, but to the future of those who will survive us. We are ready to begin forging a legacy.

Notes

1 Mahler's sixth symphony was composed in 1903–1904, between the ages of approximately 42 and 43.
2 Eliot Jacques, 'Death and the Midlife Crisis', *International Journal of Psychiatry*, 46 (1965): 502–513.
3 See Daniel Levinson, with Charlotte Darrow, Edward Klein, Maria Levinson and Braxton McKee, *The Seasons of a Man's Life*, NY, Ballantyne, 1978; Daniel Levinson, with Judy Levinson, *The Seasons of a Woman's Life*, NY, Ballantyne, 1996.
4 See the work of David Blanchflower, British labour economist, whose research on the 'wages curve' across the adult lifespan led him to a large-scale study, in collaboration with Andrew Oswald, of the rise and decline of happiness in adult life. They found that *well-being reaches its lowest point in the mid-to-late forties*, before increasing again with retirement. See David G. Blanchflower and Andrew Oswald, 'Is Well-Being U-shaped Over the Life Cycle?' NBER Working Paper No. 12935, February, 2007.

5　See Ken Wilber, *Up from Eden: A Transpersonal View of Human Evolution*, Boston, Shambhala, 1981; new edn, 1996: 179ff.

6　Bessel van der Kolk, *The Body Keeps the Score: Mind, Brain and Body in the Transformation of Trauma*, London, Allen Lane, 2014.

7　A 2012 survey conducted by the Australian Institute of Family Studies, which canvassed responses from adults born between 1940 and 1980 (and onward), indicated that the majority of adoptees had first made contact with their birth family (usually their biological mother) between the ages of 20 and 39, suggesting that the search for the birth family typically belongs to early adulthood. See 'Past Adoption Experiences: National Study on the Service Response to Past Adoption Practices', Research Report, 21 August 2012).

8　Germaine Greer, *Daddy, We Hardly Knew You*, London, Hamish Hamilton, 1989: 311.

9　As Levinson points out, Jung never made a comprehensive statement of his views on adult development, but midlife 'individuation' is dealt with in *The Archetypes and the Collective Unconscious*, Collected Works IX part one, Princeton, NJ, Bollingen, 1959, and also in his autobiographical *Memories, Dreams, Reflections*, NY, Pantheon, 1963.

10　See Ernest Hartmann, *Boundaries in the Mind: A New Psychology of Personality*, NY, Basic Books, 1991.

11　See Barbara Tuchman, *Sand Against the Wind: Stilwell and the American Experience in China*, NY, Macmillan, 1970: 89.

12　See R. Yehuda, S. P. Daskalakis, A. Lehrner, F. Desarnaud, H. N. Bader, I. Makotkine, J. D. Florey, L. M. Bierer and M. J. Meaney, 'Influences of Maternal and Paternal PTSD on Epigenetic Regulation of the Glucocortical Receptor Gene in Holocaust Survivor Offspring', *American Journal of Psychiatry*, 171, 8 (2014): 872–880.

13　See Moshe Lang, 'Silence: Therapy with Holocaust Survivors and Their Families', *Australian and New Zealand Journal of Family Therapy*, 16, 1 (1995): 1–10.

14　See Kate Yandell, 'Fat Dads' Epigenetic Legacy: Children with Obese Fathers Show Epigenetic Changes That May Affect Their Health', *The Scientist: News and Opinion*, 7 February 2013 (www.the-scientist.com/?articles.view/articleno/34307/; accessed 2 November 2015).

15　See Imogen Smallwood, *A Childhood at Green Hedges*, London, Methuen, 1989.

16　Carlo D'Este, *A Genius for War: the Life of George S. Patton*, London, HarperCollins, 1995: 358, 363–364.

17　For biographical and musicological details on Haydn's *Sturm und Drang* period, see Jens Peter Larsen, with Georg Feder, *Haydn* (New Grove composer biography series), London, Macmillan, 1980: 90–95; James Webster, 'Historical and Chronological Notes' to Joseph Haydn, The Symphonies, Vols 6 and 7 (Academy of Ancient Music/ Christopher Hogwood), L'Oiseau-Lyre, 1994; 1996.

18　See Hugh Crago, *Entranced by Story: Brain, Tale and Teller from Infancy to Old Age*, NY and London, Routledge, 2014: 155–186.

19　D'Este, 1995, op. cit.: 357.

20　See Silvan Tomkins, 'The Right and the Left: a Basic Dimension of Ideology and Personality' in R. W. White (Ed.), *The Study of Lives*, NY, Atherton Press, 1963: 389–411; Tomkins updated this earlier work in his chapter 'Script Theory' in J. Arnoff, A. I. Rabin and R. A. Zucker (Eds), *The Emergence of Personality*, NY, Springer, 1987: 152–217.

21　Tom Pitt-Aikens and Alice Thomas Ellis, *Loss of the Good Authority: The Cause of Delinquency*, London, Viking, 1989. The same authors have also written *Secrets of Strangers*, a fascinating case study of a single family of 'juvenile criminals'.

22　Michael E. Kerr and Murray Bowen, *Family Evaluation: An Approach Based on Bowen Theory*, NY, Norton, 1988: 271–276.

9

LEGACIES

Midlife to late adulthood

At the top of the tree

A dozen men and women sit around a polished table, across which drift copies of documents and minutes. All are aged somewhere between their late forties and their late fifties. Their voices are relaxed, authoritative. Now close to the top of their various professional hierarchies, their slow, deliberate speech is shaped by their body weight, and by the less tangible weight of their years of experience. Yet every now and then, out flashes a barbed joke, a not-quite-concealed look of disgust or irritation. Power is being dealt and shuffled around this table: power now, and power over the future. The men's faces are lined, though their expressions are mostly bland and confident. The women are some-what younger, on average, and rather less ravaged by time – or perhaps they've just looked after their skin better. Hard, absorbed, frustrating discussion goes on for the better part of two whole days. Around this table, rules are being set, structures determined, decisions made. I wonder whether, with their easy confidence, these power brokers were born with 'thick boundaries' and few inhibitions (Kagan's 'low-reactive' temperament),[1] or do some of them, at least, cloak their high sensitivity and reactivity with a sense of narcissistic entitlement? It would be interesting, too, to know how many of them were born the eldest in their families. (In Paris in 1793, 12 men calling themselves the Committee of Public Safety sent thousands to the guillotine. No less than seven of them were first-borns.[2])

Despite their air of assurance, there are numerous small signs that these people are in physical decline. At coffee breaks, the men queue up to use the lavatory, joking about the diminished capacity of their bladders. Discussing where to have dinner, two of the women immediately announce, 'I don't want a late night – I'm exhausted'. Sleep comes less easily now, and guilt and worry – never admitted to colleagues, of course – often haunt the hours after midnight. Addressing each other around the table, several have momentary memory lapses, and cannot remember a word, a key fact or even the correct name of another member of the group, with whom they've met several times before. One argues energetically for her pet project, despite indications that the cause is already lost. When her arguments fail to carry the day, she shrugs off the reverse without apparent distress. In adolescence, she might have felt like crawling into a hole; in her thirties, she might have questioned her judgement. No more: like armoured vehicles, these people charge ahead regardless of obstacles. Beneath their dignity and assurance hides a ticking biological clock. The diminishing years that remain to them lend urgency to their drive to get what they want, not in three years' time, but *now*.

'And other palms are won . . .'

More than ever before, our society worships youth, yet the middle-aged and the elderly still occupy most positions of authority, just as they have done throughout human history. For those who lead their professions, who head businesses and corporations, and who govern states and nations, the years between midlife and old age are when they come, finally, into the full exercise of their powers, wield the greatest influence over the most people, and generally achieve the height of their fame. Historically, nearly all of these 'elders' have been men. And men, lacking the biological fulfilment of bearing children, still seem most driven to achieve rank and power. Now, however, men are increasingly being joined in high office by women.

Margaret Thatcher was 54 when the Conservative party stormed back into government in Britain in 1979. Outside the door of No 10 Downing Street, she offered reporters a gracious, carefully rehearsed victory speech: 'Where there is discord, may we bring harmony. Where there is error, may we bring truth. Where there is doubt, may we bring faith. And where there is despair, may we bring hope.' Her wording deliberately echoed the phrases of a prayer called 'Make me an instrument of Your peace'. Within a few years, though, Thatcher had become one of the most hated prime ministers in Britain's history, famous for discord, not harmony, and (for many people) despair, not hope. Even the Queen, who kept her personal opinions to herself, was known to dislike her. The 'dangerously self-opinionated' young lady of 1948 had become the 'iron lady' of the 1980s. The changes she had made to her self-presentation in her forties, the concerted attempt to erase all traces of her Lincolnshire accent, to make her vowels ape those of her privately educated, upper-class Conservative colleagues, were changes to the 'outside'. On the inside she had remained as she had always been: fiercely determined to win, completely sure that she was right and prepared to brook no opposition in imposing her own values on the country that had elected her.

War interrupts the young adulthood of many men, and those that it fails to kill are often condemned to a permanent state of 'moratorium'. But for the men who rise to high command, the coming of war has a very different sort of meaning. The chance of being killed is much less than it was in their twenties when they were front line soldiers. Now close to the summit of their careers, and generally in their fifties or sixties, they see war as their last great opportunity for success or failure. A general lives most intensely, exhaustingly and completely during war. Let's look at two commanders at work during the years 1939–1945, both Americans, both destined to achieve the four stars of full general. In their contrasting personalities, and in their personal triumphs and interpersonal disasters, we can see just how intractable a shape personality can assume by late adulthood.

Not surprisingly, given his earlier propensities, George S. Patton emerged as the most glamorous and controversial US field commander of World War Two. The 1970 George C. Scott movie was titled simply *Patton* – the producers could rely on everyone knowing who that meant. With his ivory-handled revolvers, his love of decorations and insignia, his reputation for profanity and his crude, flamboyant gesture of 'pissing into the Rhine' as the Third Army struck into the heartland of Nazi Germany in 1945, Patton seemed the epitome of the rough, hard-bitten soldier, single-mindedly pursuing his own glory. The reality, as we have already seen, was far more complex.

Patton had been 57 when he led the US Seventh Army in the 1943 landings in North Africa, soon confirming the faith of his superiors Dwight Eisenhower and George C. Marshall, and establishing a reputation as an aggressive, imaginative leader who, like his German opponent Rommel, toured the front in an open vehicle (as once he had exposed himself to risk on the rifle range at West Point). Yet almost immediately after his triumph in the subsequent invasion of Sicily, Patton came close to engineering his own demise. By long military tradition, no officer was permitted to strike an enlisted man, but when Patton found two of his GIs in hospital suffering from so-called 'battle fatigue' (we would now call it post-traumatic stress disorder), he dramatically slapped their faces and accused them of cowardice. *What we hate and fear in ourselves, we hate and punish in others.* Pattton could never be called a coward, but there is little doubt that he felt the shame of 'failure' on many occasions. Called to account for his extraordinary action, Patton reluctantly apologised in person to his entire army. His long-term friend Dwight Eisenhower was infuriated by Patton's inappropriate conduct, but shrewdly recognised that he could not do without his greatest asset on the battlefield.

Were it not for the slapping incident, Patton would almost certainly have commanded an entire army group in the Normandy invasion. Still he outshone his superiors, achieved dramatic armoured breakouts which took his troops all the way across France, decisively defeated Hitler's last counter-offensive in the Ardennes in 1944, and carved his way through Germany in the last weeks of the Third Reich. In very large measure, he had achieved the fame he had so long sought, gained the overwhelming loyalty of his men, the constant attention of the press and the respect of his German opponents. Yet he survived only a few months as Military Governor of Bavaria, his eccentricities and public gaffes ensuring him a reputation as 'crazy'. Once again, he simply refused to be bound by the rules that governed other men. Like Donald Trump in the 2016 Republican primaries, Patton seemed to glory in his outspokenly 'incorrect' opinions – a sure sign of narcissism. As in 1919, he was in despair at the thought that there were no more battles to fight, no more glory to be gained. Eisenhower, who had protected him almost as faithfully as his Aunt Nannie had protected him 50 years before, could no longer excuse his conduct. Patton was relieved of his command, and shunted sideways to a safe but inglorious position in charge of a military history unit. He was contemplating resignation from the army when his spine was severed in a car accident, not long after his sixtieth birthday. Spinal paralysis was not the heroic end he had craved – but it terminated his life almost as effectively. Patton epitomises all those men whose 'work is their life', and who mysteriously die within a year or two of retirement. He had turned 60 only six weeks before he died. It has subsequently been claimed that Patton was actually assassinated by his own side because of his conviction that the United States must fight the Russians immediately[3] – a view that was, at the time, highly embarrassing to his superiors.

General Joseph Stilwell ('Vinegar Joe' as the press nicknamed him because of his acid remarks) was in many ways the exact opposite of Patton. Where Patton commanded in the high profile campaigns in Europe, Stilwell remained for most of the war in the unglamorous theatre of South-East Asia. There were no stunning victories to be gained here. Where Patton commanded his own countrymen, Stilwell, who had always longed to lead Americans into battle, commanded mainly troops of the Kuomintang government of China, nominally under his leadership, but in fact constantly withheld from him by Chiang Kai-shek.

When Japan invaded China in 1937, 54-year-old Colonel Stilwell had achieved a reputation as a man of action, initiative and personal integrity, who routinely led his own troops in training runs, was impatient of incompetence and attracted loyalty from at least some of his subordinates, while achieving a reputation for being uncooperative and irascible towards his superiors. It was a profile quite similar to Patton's, but without Patton's need for constant external reassurance of his own importance. Stilwell had a healthy interest in advancement, but he obviously felt faintly embarrassed by his own ambitions. His 1943 entry in *Who's Who* was six lines long; Patton's occupied 33. Where Patton wore his General's stars in every possible place on his uniform (one subordinate counted 28 of them), Stilwell had to be *ordered* to restore his insignia to his plain uniform so that his rank could be recognised by his own men. Originally, he was to have commanded the same allied landings in North Africa which offered Patton such opportunities for success. Yet Stilwell accepted a posting to China in 1942, saying, 'I'll go where I'm sent'. That his mentor George Marshall valued his specialised knowledge of China was sufficient for Stilwell. Stilwell somehow knew that he belonged to China, and China to him. The 'marriage' made years before was about to be consummated.

Stilwell was given an impossible task. Chiang Kai-shek was far more interested in maintaining his own power base than in defeating the Japanese invaders. Stilwell, who understood so many things about the Chinese, could never understand Chiang's willingness to tolerate defeat after defeat, his preference for keeping troops weak and divided rather than allowing Stilwell to train them into a modern, efficient striking force – which might then owe no loyalty to Chiang. Nor could he appreciate the Chinese emphasis on saving face. In his outspoken American manner, Stilwell kept trying to confront Chiang with the corruption, dishonesty and inefficiency of his own generals. Chiang did not want to know, and resented this foreigner, humiliatingly forced upon him as the price of US military and economic assistance. Stilwell had learned fluent Chinese, but he never learned to tell diplomatic half-truths in order to get more of what he wanted. Stilwell's war was passed in constant frustration, with hopes raised only to be dashed again and again.

He was true to his personality type, established long years before: conscientious, dedicated, rigorously honest, yet rigid, stubborn, irritable, with no time for flattery and small talk. (When we recall Freud's theory of the 'anal' origins of obsessionality, it may be amusing to note that in his private diary, Stilwell described negotiating with Chiang as 'shovelling the manure heap'!) Like so many of his type, Stilwell seemed to be locked into an almost automatic conflict with authority. For him, truth was a higher principle than personal advantage, more important even than winning wars. He cut off his nose to spite his face.

The one tangible achievement of Stilwell's war was the re-opening of the Burma Road, a vital source of supplies for Allied troops fighting the Japanese in Burma and in China itself. The work was long, hard and slow, and then the Pacific war was brought to an abrupt end by the bombing of Hiroshima and Nagasaki, not by anything Stilwell had achieved in the steamy jungles of Burma. And at the end of it, Stilwell went home to his wife and family in California. Only a year after Patton's life was cut short by a car accident, Stilwell suddenly collapsed from cancer – perhaps the secret, inward sign of years of frustration? While stress does not 'cause' cancer in the strict sense, it is now accepted that continued stress weakens the immune system, and thus makes disease more likely to occur. We might hypothesise that Stillwell's body inhibited the development of the cancer as long as he still had a vitally important job to do. Intriguingly, Stillwell, an 'inhibited' personality type, died of an *internal* process (cancer): uninhibited, extraverted Patton died in a sudden *external* event (as violent as if he had died on the battlefield).

What is evident in the final chapters of both Stilwell's and Patton's lives is the extent to which their years of destiny embodied repetitions – often *literal* repetitions – of earlier crises. Patton's life had been a veritable palimpsest of willed and unwilled 'accidents'. If no war were available to create the likelihood of his death, he would act to create around him conditions of almost equal risk. He had a pattern of indiscretion, and had a number of times been admonished and reprimanded before 1943. Public apologies were not new for him either.

He even risked his marriage in the same way as he had done before, resuming, in his final years, the affair which had caused Beatrice enormous suffering and great bitterness during his prolonged midlife crisis.

Not only did the 'slapping incident' in Sicily recycle predictable elements from Patton's personality and behaviour, it also eerily echoed an essay he had written as a boy of 16, in which he had censured the Athenian commander during Athens' unsuccessful invasion of *Sicily* during the Peloponesian Wars as *'unfitted' for his post*. It is possible that Patton picked out the theme of 'unfitness to command' at that early stage because he was acutely conscious of his own destiny, and painfully aware of his own deficiencies. But did he later need to 'enact it' in a literal way during his own invasion of that same island? Similarly, Stilwell's insistence on telling the truth, and his inability to suffer fools gladly netted him many enemies on his own side. To the narcissistic Chiang, Stilwell's realistic opinion of his own capabilities was intolerable rivalry: yet Stilwell seemed as incapable of altering his tactics as Chiang was of accepting criticism. And Marshall continued to support Stilwell, as he continued to support Patton, until the bitter end.

The mystery of repeating patterns

Famous men and women supply many examples of significant repetitions, not because they are any different from the rest of us, but simply because their lives are matters of public as well as private record. Similarly, many of us undergo the same changes, and feel the same feelings at different stages of our lives as Gustav Mahler did – only we do not leave behind great works of art that chart the course of our inner journeys. Our letters, photographs and accumulated artifacts are mostly thrown away when we die and, even if retained, are hardly ever interpreted as evidence of our inner struggles and triumphs. When I examined the history of my father's family of origin, I found many examples of repetitive patterns both in their actions and the ways in which they talked about their lives.[4] Few of my elderly relatives being introspective, and most of them highly suspicious of 'psychologising', they considered my analysis 'rubbish', and one or two were forthright enough to tell me so. I believe each family contains such evidence, but each family, if they see it at all, sees it as unique, because they usually have no basis for comparison. It is not unique.

In 1834 or 1835, 60–year-old German artist Caspar David Friedrich painted an enigmatic picture known as *Die Lebensstufen* ('The Stages of Life').[5] It is clearly intended to be allegorical – that is, the objects and people in the picture 'stand for' something other than just themselves. The picture shows an ocean in fading daylight, looking out to sea from a rocky shore. In the foreground are five human figures: closest to us stands a man in a long cloak and a tricorn hat typical of the previous century; further into the picture's space a younger man (his son?), in the later-fashionable stovepipe hat, looks round and gestures ambiguously to him; the two children playing with their mother on the rocks close to the water's edge are probably this younger man's family – the old man's grandchildren? In the distance, five ships are visible, at varying distances from the shore, the two closest ones clearly turned towards the land. Their sails hang limp in the still air of evening. The ships take over where the human figures in the foreground leave off. Clearly, we are being asked to think of arrivals and departures, of journeys into new worlds, of farewells. Our lives float out to sea, into an enigmatic night on a windless ocean. Friedrich died, in diminished health which left him no longer able to paint in oils, only a few years after he completed this picture. It is hard not to see 'The Stages of Life' as an artistic 'last testament', a statement not just about his own life – he has been identified as the 'old man', and the other figures are probably members of his own family – but about the life course of human beings in general. The painting is full of mystery and ambiguity. Are the ships approaching land, or departing? Is the old man warning, or waving farewell? Is the younger man angry with his father, or worried? Are the little children gazing at their own future? In much the same way, in families across generations, the past becomes the future, and the future swings around to conform to the past, and while we know bits and pieces about how our ancestors acted, we can only guess what they were thinking and feeling, or what their actions meant.

In part, we fail to recognise the repetitions and resonances in our families because to do so, we need to make particular kinds of comparisons. We may compare our own childhoods with those of our children, or our adult lives with those of our parents, but less often do we compare our childhood with our parents' childhood – let alone with our *grandparents'* childhoods, of which we often know little, and understand less. There is much that grandparents are not going to tell their grandchildren, and even if they did tell us, our ability to make sense of their stories would be limited: we were not there: how could we fully understand their experience? To my amusement, I notice that today's young people often use the phrase 'the olden days' (which once indicated a time *centuries* past) to mean 'when Mum and Dad were kids'! Similarly, it is believed that in the 1970s (or even 1980s) 'children were expected to be seen and not heard'! Our lack of historical perspective prevents us from fully appreciating what we are told by our elders.

As a society, we notice when certain particular behaviours repeat across generations, *because they are painful and distressing.* We have learned to recognise a 'cycle of abuse' or an 'intergenerational transmission of violence', meaning that those who grow up with violence or sexual violation tend to perpetrate it on others, or (alternatively) choose as partners those who do. But it is not only abuse, trauma or 'dysfunction' that repeats. *Everything* repeats, like a set of variations on a musical theme, like genetic variations within a single plant species, only we fail to realise the original theme in its superficially 'different' form. When patterns of loving childrearing, secure attachment, temperamental resilience and courageous adulthood repeat, we do not describe them as 'cycles of resilience' or talk about the 'intergenerational transmission of love'. Yet that is what they are: intricately self-reinforcing circuits between genetics, environment and meaning that, most often, ensure that those who start happy and secure will raise another generation to be the same, and that those who start life less secure and less trusting will (often, though not always) hand on their own pattern also.

My clinical experience, combined with my reading of many biographies and family histories, suggests that dysfunctional patterns repeat most insistently and most literally in families which lack both *flexibility* and *access to outside influences*. Such families may isolate themselves geographically or ideologically from the rest of society through, for example, a rigid set of religious or political beliefs, or through a choice of occupation that permits contact only with those of similar background. Some families may be *forced*, through migration, war and disease, into such isolation. Rigid beliefs, which permit no questioning, also favour all-or-nothing, good-or-evil explanations for traumatic events (as in Silvan Tomkins' 'normative' personality type),[6] explanations which, in turn, increase the likelihood of a literal repetition of those traumas. Such families, which form little worlds unto themselves, are uncannily similar to 'island' ecosystems, in which organisms inbreed and develop certain genetic characteristics in isolation from a wider gene pool. Temperamental factors like extreme sensitivity and low tolerance for change contribute to the perpetuation of such isolation, of course.

Within the individual, as within the family, it seems to me that *conscious awareness* (bringing the left hemisphere's detachment to bear on instinctive or unquestioned phenomena) is one way to avoid the literal repetition of destructive and constraining patterns. Only when we allow ourselves to *notice* what we do, only when we allow ourselves to *think about* our present behaviour in the light of our past behaviour – and the behaviour of others in our family, past and present – do we give ourselves the chance to exert some control over the patterns of our lives. It is often said, truthfully enough, that awareness is all very well, but it doesn't change behaviour. My answer to that is that the promotion of conscious awareness needs to happen in a context of *safety*: a context where individuals, or even whole families, gradually feel trusting enough to permit themselves to feel and talk about what has always seemed so overwhelming that it could not be addressed. Such a context can be provided by good psychotherapy; sometimes it can also be provided by a balanced, self-aware person within the family, who is patient enough to stay with the process for as long as it takes, sensitive enough to know when to back off, and able to be a disinterested observer of others: in Murray Bowen's words, a 'non-anxious presence'. Such individuals would once have been tribal elders, the wise old men and women of the community. The sad thing is that those individuals and families who would most benefit from such a presence are also the least likely ever to avail themselves of it.

All mammals (except, it seems, domestic cats!) possess what ethologists call a 'forgiveness system' – a set of hard-wired behaviours that kick in when a creature needs to 'apologise' to another and restore good relations[7] (Bonobos, notoriously, have an equivalent of 'make up sex'!). In human families, forgiveness is often in short supply: feelings of betrayal and bitterness can continue for many years, as each new generation accepts unquestioningly the previous generation's anger and hurt. Recognising that old patterns may be influencing our own behaviour in the present can be a necessary first step in a uniquely human 'forgiveness system' in which, sometimes, old wounds can be healed and some level of trust restored. But for this to occur, all of us have to be prepared to admit our own fault instead of simply blaming others for theirs. And exposing our vulnerable necks to the teeth of our foe is not something that most human beings find easy!

The new and the old

We cannot *not* be who we are, and by 50 or 60 the paths of our conduct and our decision-making are worn so deep that to willingly step aside from them is very difficult indeed. It simply does not feel 'right'. Perhaps it is partly our awareness (at this age) of our own predictability that makes many of us somewhat cynical. For the enthusiasm and idealism of youth, we substitute weariness and irony. It becomes harder and harder to believe in a leader, a faith, even a new job. We complain that things are not as they once were. The contracting world we see around us mirrors the sense of our own shrinking, the fading of our own lamp. Yet the shrinking can concentrate our energies, and the flame may flare more brightly as the candle melts away.

In early childhood, we discovered ourselves by discovering other people and places. By venturing away from mother, we learned to stand on our own feet, and to realise that she had an existence independent of us. In middle childhood and adolescence, we expanded this awareness to a realisation that our parents – and everyone else – had inner lives independent of ours (theory of mind), might feel things quite different from what we felt (or conversely, might feel exactly as we felt). In young adulthood, we discovered new aspects of ourselves by travelling to new places, living in new ways, adopting new values and meeting people very different from ourselves. It was the *differences* that were exciting, the sense of newness and unpredictability. By late adulthood, for many of us, this has changed. We may still welcome difference, and we may even court it. Yet when we do experience the new, it is more likely to remind us of something familiar than to excite us with its total strangeness. By late adulthood, many people have settled into familiar routines in their daily lives, in their mental lives, even in their leisure and entertainment preferences. We may enjoy jetting off to distant places for that trip we've long promised ourselves, but pre-booked hotels (and tourist guides we can complain about) have replaced the excitements and risks of cheap accommodation, trying to get by in another language, or finding our own way around strange places. The comforting predictability of life becomes more important, the unexpected or spontaneous harder to embrace.

In late adulthood, we tend to relive whatever part of our life most associate with hope, optimism and satisfaction. For some of us, that may be a carefree childhood or adolescence, but for most, it is the years of our twenties, when everything seemed possible, and the world was at our feet, when we backpacked around South-East Asia without a qualm or took off for a year or two of study in another country, trusting that we'd get temporary jobs in hospitality sufficient to provide enough money to 'do the tourist bit' as well. When I spoke with my father's sisters and sisters-in-law – women born in the first quarter of the twentieth century, for whom a career was briefly possible before marriage and childbearing – I found that, for most of them, it was the years of early adulthood that glowed most richly. Those years had been their 'time of hope', when their individual powers were put to the test and not found wanting, when they felt they had made their mark on the world – usually, through a period in the paid workforce. For too many of these women, though they may have enjoyed mothering and family life, that time never came again. Even when young adulthood has been a time of suffering, fear and deprivation, it can be looked back on, in late adulthood, with nostalgia. For many of the old people interviewed by Ronald Blythe in the 1970s for his superb *The View in Winter*, it was the war years that had taken on this meaning. 'I was there. I know' they say proudly. 'You young people have had it easy: you'll never understand what we went through'. Campaign medals recognise the principle that sometimes (and maybe more often than we realise), simply to have lived through something may, in time, come to feel like an achievement.[8]

In youth, when we noticed difference rather than similarity, we also encountered pain and dissatisfaction precisely because of our insistence on looking *outside* us for the source of any distress we might experience. For most of us, the irritation and conflict of the early years of marriage were caused largely by the frustration of our wish for our partner to be more like ourselves. Unable to accept the surface differences, and in denial of the deeper similarities between us, we create much of our own disharmony. Driven by our hormones and the fierceness of our needs, we fight over everything, and take every disappointment and every slight personally. By 50 or 60, some of us are more prepared to accept what we have, and to value our partners for who they are, failings included. The result is that their *familiarity* – and the familiarity of our children, and our friends – becomes a source of comfort rather than of disappointment. Each little encounter, each small conflict faced or averted, each moment of gratitude, calls into being faint harmonics, resonating with a long history of earlier moments in the relationship. American psychologist Carl Rogers wrote movingly in similar terms of the meaning sex had for him as an older man. Now, he said, his delight was not in intensity of physical sensation, or in the heady emotions of shared passion, but in a ritual of mutual understanding and mutual responsiveness, repeated many times, its very familiarity breeding, not contempt, but enhanced depth and subtlety.[9]

It is the same with the music we listen to again and again, the movies we return to, the holiday place we come back to year in and year out: all of them are the means by which we rediscover what we know, reconnect with what is most important to us, reaffirm who we have become – and feel a sense of tranquility and reassurance as a result. By late adulthood, hopefully, we have ceased to struggle against ourselves, as hopefully we have ceased to struggle against our parents and our children. We accept them, as we accept ourselves.

Taking in and giving out

Most of us do not lead armies or nations, and our material resources in the years between 45 and 65 permit the construction of no mansions, cities or tombs. Yet typically we find that our external 'boundaries' reach their greatest extent somewhere between middle and late adulthood. We may extend our house to accommodate all of our growing children, or an ageing parent. We may have sufficient money set aside to purchase a beach house or a caravan, or a block of land to which we promise ourselves we will one day retire. If we collect things, a habit some acquire during middle childhood, our collections will have burgeoned, forcing us to convert an attic or build a large shed to house them properly. Since our incomes will most likely have reached their peak, we eat and drink well, and our bodies show it. If we tend to put on weight as we age, this will probably be the time when we will reach our greatest girth. Our addictions become more important, and we will not normally alter them, even when they put our health and life expectancy at risk. Freud continued to smoke his beloved cigars even after he developed a mouth cancer that led to a succession of painful operations, and the wearing of an ill-fitting prosthesis that hurt, and clicked irritatingly every time he spoke.

We do what we have always done. Indeed, we may do more of it, because as the excitements of sex, romance, ambition or childbirth recede we fall back on older, simpler satisfactions: eating, drinking, buying things (if we can afford them), talking with trusted intimates. Food, in particular, becomes many older adults' substitute gratification, the one pleasure that cannot be taken away and one that is always under our control. 'What the hell, you only live once', we say, and take another chocolate. As we turn back to such pleasures, as our displeasure with the changing world around us increases, so too do we fall back on the values and teachings of our childhood – even, paradoxically, on those rules, restrictions, disciplines and observances that we once resented, or failed to understand. Even the icons of our own culture, which we may have learned about at school with no great enthusiasm, now take on a new lease of life. Deploring the denigration of the great explorers by modern intellectuals, an 84-year-old former high school teacher said indignantly of Captain James Cook, 'he wasn't an "imperialist oppressor", he was a *hero!*' The rituals that we may have resented at school and discarded as young adults creep back into our lives as, faintly uncomfortable, we find ourselves speaking like, feeling like and even *looking* like our own parents or grandparents. My father, brought up in an era when one wore one's best clothes to church every Sunday, and for every formal occasion, had always worn a suit to work – but asserted his individuality by refusing to wear a hat at a time when nearly everyone did. As a young adult, I never wore a suit except for the occasional funeral. Between the ages of 23 and 40-odd, jeans were my preferred attire for work. In my late forties, I somehow found myself wanting to look less 'scruffy', and by 60, I regularly wore a jacket and tie except in high summer. I even bought a suit and quite enjoyed wearing it on more formal occasions. Yet there was one remaining way in which I preserved my youthful wish to be different from my father: I wore a broad-brimmed straw hat that he would have been acutely embarrassed by (and would probably have told me to take off!).

The grave of pathology?

When I was first training as a psychotherapist, back in the late 1970s, lecturers told us that schizophrenia 'burnt out' as people aged. Fifty-plus was the age that was mentioned. As they grew older, I was told, patients no longer displayed the symptoms of florid psychosis, and instead exhibited the sadly predictable consequences of having lived 'half a life' for so many years – rigid habits, oddities of behaviour and a general dulled-down quality, the result of long use of the major tranquillisers then prescribed for psychosis. Of course, those were the days when the norm for people with serious mental illnesses was still 'hospitalisation for life', and sufferers could be observed by doctors and research workers as the decades of their lives slid past, still within the walls of the institution. Since then, de-institutionalisation, combined with new anti-psychotic medications, have changed all that, and the literature no longer offers much support for the notion that schizophrenia, or any other mental illness for that matter, has a 'use-by date' after which a person might be free of his or her suffering.

Yet maybe there was a *degree* of truth in the anecdotal wisdom that was passed on to me. Schizophrenia may not 'burn out', but some other problematic conditions do seem to lose their 'sting' as humans move into their fifties and sixties. Problem drinkers – those who have repeatedly failed to quell their addiction earlier in their adult lives – report that they 'just can't drink much anymore'; alcohol seems to lose its appeal to them, probably because after long years of misuse and damage to liver, brain and other organs, their bodies simply refuse to tolerate any more of what has slowly poisoned them. Previously 'hyper-active' individuals seem to calm down. Impressively, a substantial proportion of 'borderline personalities', when contacted ten to 30 years after their initial diagnosis, were leading far more functional lives, and only one in four would still have merited the diagnosis of Borderline Personality Disorder at follow-up.[10] What does this mean?

Just as the body of the ageing adult is no longer capable of intense or prolonged physical exertion, just as a high-conflict couple come to a point where they begin to weary of the emotional bloodbath, many of the things that we felt so acutely and painfully in youth – betrayal by a partner who has an affair, the unfairness of accident, injury or life-threatening illness, the shame of a nose that seems too big, or hips that seem too wide – no longer seem so intolerable. It is as if we simply don't have the physical or emotional resources to pour into these feelings any more, and so, in effect, they pain us less. To paraphrase Margaret Thatcher's victory speech, where there was shame, we bring self-acceptance, where there was defensive anger, we bring empathy, and where there was hurt, we bring detachment. No conscious decision may be involved in these shifts: rather, our ageing bodies respond in accordance with their own diminished capacities.

Yet it isn't just that our bodies 'care less' than they once did: our brains may also play a part. Having gradually pushed forward the age at which the neuronal tissues are fully myelinated – first to the early thirties, then into the forties – neurologists are now saying that the process may not be complete (at least for some people) until the fifties.[11] This final stage involves the sheathing with fatty tissue of the areas that connect the brain's right hemisphere with the older, limbic areas that lie beneath the cortex. What this seems to mean is that it may not be until our fifties or sixties that some of us (I would guess, the high-reactives!) gain real control over the primitive impulses that have caused problems for us all our lives – explosions of rage, dramatic mood-swings, inability to think ahead or factor in the probable consequences of our actions. Finally, at this advanced age, our brains enable us to do what others' brains have long enabled them to do: to inhibit our survival-geared, 'irrational' impulses, to regulate our own behaviour and to 'self-soothe' when in distress instead of enacting our pain upon others. Surely this is the beginning of 'wisdom'?

In the previous stages of life, we may have accumulated a great deal of knowledge, but (as we've repeatedly seen in this book), what we 'know' (i.e. what the left hemisphere knows) does not necessarily prevent us from making the same mistakes, or necessarily help us to lead better, more fulfilling lives, because the compelling feelings 'conducted' by the right hemisphere can override our rational faculties. Now, however, we begin to fuse our personal experience with our awareness of wider patterns. As we come closer to death, we start to withdraw some of the intense emotional investment (Freud's 'cathexis') that we once had in our partners, our children or our careers. We see the significant others in our lives for who they are, rather than for who we wish, or need, them to be. We see ourselves more realistically too. As so often throughout our lives, biologically determined changes like ageing and brain maturation interact with external experiences – experiences of people, relationships, ideas, travel, illness or loss. The biological developments enable us to construe the experiences in a fuller, richer way than we might have done earlier in life; yet crucial life experiences may also potentiate the biological developments.

The coming of 'wisdom' is a key example of this principle, and it is psychologists, psychotherapists and teachers – as much, or more than the rest of us – who most need to learn that wisdom. When we are younger, we often believe that we can influence others simply by *telling them things* (the preferred mode of the left hemisphere). Only repeated experiences of failure can convince us that often, this does not work. We may be persuasive communicators and we may have much deep understanding to share with others, but we cannot *make* anyone else change, unless the change comes from within them. As we move into the late adulthood, we find it easier to accept that our role may not be to *tell*, but to *show*. The official role of the United States Senate is to 'advise and consent' to legislation; the wisdom of our advancing years is not so much to *advise*, but certainly to *consent* (in the sense of 'accept the things that can't be changed', to use the words of AA's Serenity Prayer). It is easier to put aside our own needs to feel valued, or influential or well-informed, and to focus on what the *other* person needs. Paradoxically, when we are able to do this, we often find that changes happen 'by themselves'. We do not have to 'do things' in order to help another person change; it is more a question of *getting out of the way*, while that other person does what they need to do, travels the road they need to travel and comes, in their own time – which may not be ours – to their own wisdom.

A torch to pass on

Most of us need to leave our mark on the world somehow: 'I have four children, and 13 grandchildren!' Mainly women, but some men too, speak this way, revealing that, for them, the satisfaction of raising new human beings and seeing them off safely into the world *is* their legacy. Some will even boast of the number of their grandchildren and great-grandchildren, while not in fact having a particularly close or affectionate relationship with any of them. For both men and women, there can be a sense of satisfaction in having successfully reproduced themselves, but that satisfaction is likely to run deeper if at least one of their offspring has 'followed in their footsteps', by taking over the family business, entering the same job or profession, or working the family farm. Men, typically, seem to need 'something to show' more than the 'mere' existence of children to prove that their lives have had meaning. If they have put their life energies into building up a business or a career, it may trigger existential loneliness and despair to think that no son or daughter will carry it on after they are gone. Yet sometimes the fact that their children reject the farm, the business, the profession or the trade primes men to turn decisively to service and mentoring. Thus they can replace their biological children with surrogates who may be more responsive, and with whom they can experience more of a feeling of having influenced and 'embodied' themselves in another human being.

It is in late adulthood that many people, of both sexes, turn to roles that involve the passing on of their own experience to a new generation. The writing of autobiographies and reminiscences is often an attempt not only to reflect on one's life, but also to preserve some of its accumulated experience for a new generation, to 'place it on record'. The supervising and training of younger people in the skills one has mastered oneself can be a source of enormous satisfaction, even to people who have not previously felt any wish to teach in a formal sense. Many athletes and sportspeople successfully make the transition from competitor to coach or trainer. The older tradesman passes on his skills to youngsters in technical colleges.

In early adulthood, our insecurities can cause us to be hard on our pupils – and our children. We are learning as we go along, and we reproach ourselves cruelly when we make mistakes or, worse, turn the reproach on those in our care, and blame them instead. When we teach or parent in late adulthood, we are more likely to be more confident, and more generous. Because we care less on our *own* behalf, and more on theirs, we do a far better job. For many of us, being a grandparent 'completes the circle' in a far more profound way than simply knowing that we have successfully reproduced. It gives us a second chance to be a parent, but this time informed by the wisdom of hindsight, and to feel (we're only human!) comfortably superior sometimes to our own children, whose anxieties are getting in the way of *their* parenting ('been there, done that!'). And hence it is hardly surprising that in our own culture, as in many others, the bond between grandparent and grandchild can be a very special one.

Grandchildren remember their grandparents with affection for many reasons. Grandparents can more easily be idealised, because they appear more balanced, more tolerant, more giving, less driven. They have time and energy to spare for the cultivation of their grandchild. Most important of all, grandparents can model a way of life, a career or a set of values that differs from that displayed by the child's parents, and may more closely resemble the temperamental aptitudes of the child itself. By modelling herself on a grandparent, a child can achieve a sense of difference from her parents while still feeling that her pattern of life is validated within her own family. As we saw in Chapter 6, each generation seems to need to achieve individuation by reacting against at least some of what its parents stand for. What could be more natural, then, than for the next generation to gain *its* sense of separateness and independence by 'swinging back' to the model that the previous generation rejected?[12]

Thus over three generations, families 'repeat themselves', difference leading very often back to sameness, independence to conformity, and then back to independence. My parents grew up in homes full of old, dark late-Victorian furniture, elaborate floral fabrics, saturated colours and open fireplaces. They opted for light, space, pastel-coloured paint, good modern furniture and 'clean' oil and electric heat. In my turn, I wanted to re-create the Victorian and Edwardian ambience that they had shunned, choosing older houses and filling them with William Morris fabrics and the heavy, dark-stained furnishings that I remembered with affection from my grandmother's home. I even re-opened bricked-up fireplaces and lighted wood fires in them, overriding the environmentalist scruples I had acquired in young adulthood. In their turn, my daughters have opted for a lighter, more 'modern' look, and my devotion to wood fires has not been reproduced!

In its ideal form, the grandparent–grandchild relationship is the model for how knowledge should be passed on. It is not coincidental that many tribal societies entrust older men and women with the task of initiating the young. But, of course, the transmission of knowledge across the generations is not necessarily smooth or successful. As we saw earlier, we seem, in youth or even as late as middle age, compelled to offer knowledge that others are not equipped to receive. 'Relationship education' programmes often fail. Why? Simply because when you are young and in love, you do not want to know (you are not ready to know) what may lie in store later. Wisdom produced by experience cannot usually be 'passed down' by one generation to the next through conscious teaching, only by example – and then its effects are often long-delayed.

Similarly, our society has (at least until recently) decreed that youth is the time for the study of abstract and subtle matters. And so our universities still feature attempts to teach young men and women, at the very threshold of adulthood, the deep principles of both the human and the natural worlds. Universities teach mathematics, philosophy, sociology, genetics, literary theory, mathematics, psychology, history – with scant success. Just as most people remember little of what they learned in high school, so those who go on to tertiary study at 19 remember even less of the impressive theory and technical language they are taught, except for the parts of it that they then employ directly, in a professional occupation. Even now, when universities offer more obviously 'relevant', 'practical' subjects – nursing, business management, marketing, information technology – much of what is taught still fails to make much impression. Why does university education so signally fail for this age group? Because once again, *knowledge is being offered at the wrong stage of life*, and (I suspect) because left hemisphere 'cleverness' is too often substituted for right hemisphere 'wisdom'.

The task of young adulthood, appropriate to its bodily capacities, is to master skills, to carve out territory, to *do* things. In the traditional Hindu model of the ideal life, the age of the soldier (action) came long before the age of the sage (wisdom). Understanding the whys, the processes and the principles is not of high interest to the majority of young adults. So they engage with such things, if at all, only superficially and, once the examinations and assignments are over, discard their 'knowledge'. At 30 or, better still, at 40, a much higher proportion of students are ready to look deeper, for by then they have lived enough to have a solid, experiential basis against which to measure the theories. It is doubly unfortunate that our society is so arranged that the young are kept away from the world of work and achievement by a curriculum they often perceive to be almost pointless – when the same curriculum could strike them as revelatory 20 years later.

Shirtsleeves to shirtsleeves

Once, the ageing rulers of our human kingdoms devoted most of their energy and resources to ensuring that their souls would be well cared for in the next life. The pharaohs and their nobles built massive tombs, lavishly furnished with food, material objects and even statues of servants, to supply their needs in the other world. Fifteenth-century English gentry paid large sums to monasteries so that masses could be said for their souls for many years after their deaths, sparing them a long sojourn in Purgatory. As humans have gradually come to dwell less on the next world and more on this one, the question of what we leave behind for our descendants has come to carry an urgency once reserved for things of the spirit. Both Patton and Stilwell, conscious of their place in history, preserved not only their diaries and letters, but every scrap of paper they ever scribbled a note on. So, too, did the Brontë sisters, and many other writers. Land was what many people once bequeathed to their offspring – the peasant's pitiful few acres, or the broad estates of the lord. Those who owned no land left a family business, or money. Those who owned neither land nor commercial interests left their best coat, or the bed in which their children had been conceived and born. Whatever the legacy, it raised issues of choice, and favouritism.

What an adult had built up, through inheritance, through marriage, through initiative and hard work, had on his (sometimes her) death to be dismantled and divided, unless there was a single heir to leave it all to. Customs in which everything was divided equally between surviving children rapidly destroyed accumulations of property or wealth. Customs in which the eldest son inherited everything automatically created dissention and jealousy. And what if the eldest proved to be immoral, incompetent or mentally unstable? 'There was once a King who had three sons', begins fairy tale after fairy tale; we all know what will follow. The youngest son will have to win by boldness, cleverness or 'magic' what his brothers expect to achieve simply through being born earlier. 'Born to rebel? Born to innovate?'

We have not solved the problem of legacies. Families which own land probably exhibit the old pattern in its most persistent form. Land that has been in the family for generations exerts a powerful hold on all who have worked on it, grown up on it and felt part of it. Landed families are often relatively isolated, making it easier for feelings around property division to become corrosive. To be forced to leave the family property, or to see a disliked sibling inherit the best part of it, can be an embittering experience. The same broad pattern applies, however, to almost any family where children have grown up with the expectation of inheriting wealth, or particular material objects. The more importance the family has placed on the *things* – as opposed to the *relationships* between family members – the more the physical objects come to *represent* relationships, to *stand in* for feelings. American novelist Henry James wrote memorably about it in his short novel *The Spoils of Poynton*. Thus a parent in late adulthood who, for whatever compelling reason, leaves more to one child than to another risks giving the impression that she *loves* one more than the other. When an ageing parent changes his mind, and reallocates what the children have previously come to expect as their share, this can strike a powerful blow at family stability. Shakespeare's *King Lear* (brilliantly transposed into the context of a mid-western American farm family by Jane Smiley in *A Thousand Acres*) is the ultimate exploration of just such a tragedy. Starting to slide into dementia and blinded by his own ego, Lear prefers his elder daughters Goneril and Regan to the one daughter who actually loves him – Cordelia. Like Cinderella's ugly sisters, Goneril and Regan plot, scheme and lie to gain yet more power, while only

Cordelia remains faithful to her father, despite his failure to 'see' her (as we might say these days).

In my experience, adult children who are secure in their selfhood, and who have a realistic view of their parents' strengths and weaknesses, cope better with unequal legacies than those who have retained into adulthood a child's eye view of their parents, those whose own sense of self is still bound up in childhood alliances. Sometimes adult children, angry about being 'left out' or 'treated unfairly' in a parent's will, allege that one of their siblings, or a much younger spouse, has 'got at' a parent in his or her dotage, and 'manipulated' him or her into altering the previous intentions. As in *King Lear*, it does sometimes happen that way – but not nearly as often as families think. Rather, it is as if family members simply cannot cope with the thought that their loved parent has temporarily weakened an earlier resolve, or felt the momentary pull of another allegiance. *When love can't be shared . . .*

My paternal grandfather, Albert, left his youngest daughter a larger share of his property than either of her two sisters. She herself must have decided that this was unjust, for she actually divided her legacy equally with her older siblings, yet despite her generous act at least one of her sisters was unable to accept that their father could somehow have preferred her younger sister to her. It took her years to get over the implied disfavour for, like all of them, she was temperamentally extremely sensitive. Albert would have been able to convince himself that there were good reasons for leaving more to his youngest, for she had been a frail baby, with numerous childhood illnesses, and for a long time there seemed no expectation of her marrying. But the real reason it came naturally to him to prefer his youngest child was rooted a generation back. He *himself* had been the youngest surviving child in his family, and he, too, had been treated as a special case in his father's estate, causing lifelong resentment and discord between himself and his older brother. As our parents do to us, so we (too often) do to our children, acting on instinct, not reflection, sure that what we are doing is right because it 'feels natural'. And in so doing, as Emily Brontë understood so well in *Wuthering Heights*, we write the script for a repeat performance in the next generation.

'Shirtsleeves to shirtsleeves in three generations' said the old adage. 'It takes one to build it up, one to maintain it, and one to lose it', said another. Such sayings referred to wealth and property, but in fact the 'three generation cycle' applies to just about any quality, talent or asset that human families can possess, including even things like intelligence, sporting prowess or creativity. The first generation 'builds' it, often from scratch, because that is how mastery and individuation are acquired; if the second generation cannot individuate by surpassing the first, then their route to selfhood becomes *maintaining* their inheritance (the prescription of the average eldest child) or turning their attention to other goals ('and so the youngest son rode out to seek his fortune'). The third generation, too far from the first to appreciate the struggle that built the legacy, simply takes it for granted and often squanders it. Then, in the fourth generation, a child is born who, possibly temperamentally similar to the great-grandparent who built the family fortune or developed the family talent, and driven to build a different life from her wastrel parent, adopts it as her mission to start all over again.[13]

Notes

1 See Ernest Hartmann, *Boundaries in the Mind: A New Psychology of Personality*, NY, Basic Books, 1991; Jerome Kagan, *The Temperamental Thread: How Genes, Culture, Time and Luck Make Us Who We Are*, NY, Dana Press, 2010.
2 See Frank Sulloway, *Born to Rebel: Birth Order, Family Dynamics and Creative Lives*, Boston, Little, Brown, 1996: 315–318.
3 Carlo D'Este, *A Genius for War: A Life of General George S. Patton*, NY, HarperCollins, 1995; Robert K. Wilcox, *Target Patton*, Washington, DC, Regnery Publishing, 2008 [reprinted in 2014].
4 See Hugh Crago, 'A Family in Time' (unpublished, 1993).
5 The original 'The Stages of Life' painting hangs in the Museum der Bildener Künste, Leipzig.
6 See Silvan Tomkins, 'The Right and the Left: A Basic Dimension of Ideology and Personality' in R. W. White (Ed.), *The Study of Lives*, NY, Atherton, 1963: 389–411.
7 See Michael E. McCullough, *Beyond Revenge: The Evolution of the Forgiveness Instinct*, San Francisco, Jossey-Bass, 2008.
8 Ronald Blythe, *The View in Winter: Reflections on Old Age*, London, Allen Lane, 1979.
9 Carl R. Rogers, *Becoming Partners: Marriage and its Alternatives*, London, Constable, 1973.
10 See Michael H. Stone, *Abnormalities of Personality: Within and Beyond the Realm of Treatment*, NY, Norton, 1993: 134–142.
11 See Kurt W. Fischer and Ellen Pruyne, 'Reflective Thinking in Adulthood', in Jack Demick and Carrie Andreotti (Eds), *Handbook of Adult Development*, NY, Springer, 2003: 169ff.
12 See Edwin H. Friedman, *Generation to Generation: Family Process in Church and Synagogue*, NY, Guilford, 1985: 58–64.
13 See Michael E. Kerr and Murray Bowen, *Family Evaluation: An Approach Based on Bowen Theory*, NY, Norton, 1988: 221–255.

10

'THE CLOUDS THAT GATHER ROUND THE SETTING SUN'

Sigmund Freud was forced to leave Vienna in 1938, after the German army incorporated Austria into the Third Reich. The Gestapo, treating this world-famous Jew with a mixture of awe and scorn, asked him to certify in writing that he and his family had been well treated. Freud, old and ill, but never averse to seizing an opportunity for irony, wrote, 'I can heartily recommend the Gestapo to anyone'. He and several of his family travelled to London, and there set up house. In constant pain from his mouth cancer, Freud pushed himself to write almost to the end. Until his last weeks of life, he continued to see a handful of analytic patients. It seems that he had a contract with his physician that when he could no longer see a reason for keeping up the struggle, Dr Schur would give him a lethal overdose of morphine. In the novel based on his fine television series *Freud*, scriptwriter Carey Harrison makes a dying Freud whisper to Schur, 'Frightened all my life. And now it's easy'. He may well have said something very like it.[1] He was 83 years old.

With few exceptions, we age and die as we have lived. Our personalities do not usually alter radically as we approach the end of our lives. Rather, what happens is a kind of thinning out, a paring down, so that who we are in old age reveals the essence of who we have always been. As the face loses much of its fat and the bones of cheek and jaw stand out gauntly, so the bone structure of our personalities emerges too. At their best, very old people display a vital honesty, a calm sense of knowing what really matters and an impatience with the superficial and the evasive.

The speech of adolescents resembles a slightly rusty tap suddenly turned full on: their words come out in rapid, intermittent bursts, their laughter, unneces-sarily loud, has a forced quality to it. By middle adulthood, speech flows more smoothly, and laughter is more wholehearted; we 'own ourselves', and the words that come out of our mouths reflect that ownership. In old age, the tap may only manage a trickle. The slow, considered phrases and lengthy pauses of old people's speech probably contribute to the image of 'wise old age'; yet sometimes these things reflect not weighty deliberation, but an internal struggle to locate a particular word, or to keep on track when memories from the past flood in, unasked. The 1984 movie *Un Dimanche a la Campagne* ('A Sunday in the Country') sensitively portrays the way that past and present flow together for an ageing artist as his adult children and his grandchildren gather around him for their accustomed weekend visit.

Asked a specific question about something in their past, older people will often veer off onto a personally significant tangent, to the frustration of a questioner who has not learned that old age has its own agenda. The tracks of memory are very deep, now, and with repeated travel over the same path, it is harder (though not impossible) for old people to move into new territory. My father had always believed that his own father was a poor man – my grandfather had constantly worried about being 'ruined'. When I told Dad what I had discovered about the extent of his father's property – not great wealth, but substantial by country town standards – he simply repeated the version he had always believed, and passed on to me. It was as if he didn't want to know. For the same reason, it is difficult for elderly people to adjust quickly to new patterns of life: the routines and timetables they have followed for years help to remind them of who they are, and of what comes next. No wonder so many old people go downhill rapidly when they are moved, even with the best of intentions, from their own homes to an aged care facility.

Holding on and letting go

At 70 and 80, our bodies are no longer reliable: limbs fracture more easily, and mend slowly; eyesight and hearing deteriorate; our hearts no longer beat as regularly and strongly; our brains shrink in volume; and our hair, if it has not already done so, silvers and thins. Our bodies fail to bounce back after brief exertion, leaving us with shortness of breath, or with a pervasive sense that our daily lives are a series of small struggles – to get up, to sit down, to hang the washing on the line, to lay the table, to cook a meal, to clear it up afterwards. Everything can become an effort: we ache, we sigh and we grumble. Just getting through each day can feel like a triumph over adversity. 'Dour' was the word people once used to describe their ageing relatives – well, as I approach 70 myself, I can see how that word fits, and why we become 'dour'. Despite my generally optimistic temperament and my lifelong interest in new ideas, I hear myself increasingly sounding like a 'grumpy old man', critical of the many changes (both technological and social) that have risen like a tide around me and obliterated much of what once defined me and gave me a sense of achievement.

A lot of what I prided myself on learning at school and university 50 years ago is not taught anymore: Latin and Greek (along with the scientific names of animals and plants that are derived from them), the fascinating history of the

English language, how to consult a dictionary, how to speak or sing in public without a microphone, how to add and subtract without a calculator. The flat prose of the modern Bible has replaced the sonorous (if occasionally inaccurate) King James version, and couples getting married no longer say, 'With my body I thee worship'. Young people struggle to read with understanding (let alone enjoyment) anything written before 1900, leaving the work of Shakespeare, Milton and even Dickens in the category of 'boring books by dead white males'. Instead, they have 'friends' on Facebook, the possibility of becoming an international star via homemade videos that 'go viral', and of course they have *Harry Potter*. Worst of all, in my view, we have almost completely lost a sense of how to place ourselves in the context of history. We have little to compare ourselves with, and little to help us assess our values. We fail to recognise when our society heads down the same self-destructive paths as those taken by past civilisations. We boast of our digital revolution, without awareness that a century and a half ago, the telegraph and the telephone seemed equally revolutionary (and to some, equally frightening).[2]

Ageing readers of this book will have other things to lament, and different gripes about the present. I offer mine simply as a personal example of how different the world can look when you see so much of your own past simply disappear. Declining physical capacities almost inevitably affect how we *feel* about our own lives – and the life of the world around us. The aged have always felt this way – at least as far back as the Greeks of fifth-century BCE Athens (who famously complained about the manners, entitlement and lack of respect shown by the young people of their day).[3]

To some old people, all of this is simply frightening: 'old age is a terrible thing', they say. To others, there is a kind of relief, as if the end of the struggle is in sight: 'I'm not afraid to die', said my father once, about a year before his death, 'you get – [he fumbled for the right word] *tired*'. Some old people face the decline of the body with cheerful acceptance: 'I can't drive any more, my eyes are too bad, and you know what, Hugh, I *don't miss it!*', said my mother's old friend Nell, then in her eighties. Younger adults naturally view ageing as loss and decline, and don't like thinking about it, but there was no defiant bravado in Nell's remark, no bright, false 'think positive' rhetoric. She was saying what she knew to be true: lots of things that once bothered us simply don't matter anymore.

Even illness, accidents and operations can sometimes be viewed in the same matter of fact way. 'Oh, I'm living on borrowed time – they're keeping me alive with tablets!', remarked my wife's old headmaster, insisting that he had better stay in a motel rather than with us, because he would need to be 'up and down to the bathroom' all night. Of all the indignities old age imposes upon us, those involved with such basic bodily functions may well be the worst. Yet while we must give up some of our dignity, we gain something else in its place. When we know our remaining time is short, we value it too highly to waste it complaining. As my father was wheeled into the operating theatre for the heart operation from which he knew he might not recover, he grinned and waved to my brother and sister. He was less worried than they were. He didn't recover, and I suspect he would have preferred it that way.

Going home again

The medical texts speak of a 'blunting of affect' (that is, of emotion) that can occur in old age, and perhaps this is part of the laconic quality old people often display, but as humans feel death draw nearer they are still perfectly capable of feeling a whole range of feelings. Nor do we need expensive university studies by gerontologists to establish that many old people still value sex, and yearn for the comfort of physical intimacy. Visits from loved ones are prized more highly, and previously taciturn men are sometimes seen with tears in their eyes as they wave goodbye for what may be the last time. It becomes more and more important to get yourself to another reunion of the mates you went to war with 50 years ago, or another gathering of the schoolgirls you taught in your twenties, more vital to revisit the country you grew up in, but have never been back to since. Each of these things can provide an emotional high – 'wonderful', like 'terrible', is a word the aged use a good deal. Both are global words, words that evoke the intense, unqualified vision of early childhood, the total immersion characteristic of the unaided right hemisphere. The wheel has come full circle.

Even individuals who have spent most of their adulthood denying their emotional roots sometimes find it possible in old age to complete their lives in ways they would never have dreamed possible earlier. A retired man in his late sixties once came to see me complaining of 'worry troubles'. All his life he had been a man's man, living for sport and career, blithely pursuing other women, cut off from his sons for some 20 years. Somehow he had been able to live comfortably with all of this. Now, alone in a big, empty house, he could not sleep. Therapy with this man was not much different from the granting of a kind of secular absolution. Gradually, he began talking of regrets, fears and long-past hurts from childhood. He initiated contact with his sons, and found, to his surprise, that they did not reject him. He began to accept some responsibility for the breakdown of his marriage. In his final years, he began to do the moral 'growing up' he had somehow managed to avoid all his life.

The heroic journeys of young adulthood in which we proved our selfhood and asserted our independence are now balanced by emotional and spiritual pilgrimages back to our personal or collective past. Having left our families – and particularly if we left them in a way that was painfully incomplete – we are now compelled to come back to them. We may have had little contact with siblings for many years, but now we seek them out and re-build a relationship that was once important. After all, as developmentalists remind us, sibling relationships last longer than our relationships with our partners, and with our own children. Our siblings shared our childhood world, and revisiting memories with them can provide a deep satisfaction. And no matter that our parents and grandparents are long since dead, we can return to them in spirit and, in a sense, make our peace with them. Near the end of his life, a drug-sodden, increasingly desperate Elvis Presley would drive at night back to Tupelo, Tennessee, claiming that he needed to look under his parents' house for a marble he had lost as a boy. 'It's always important to visit the place where your Mama birthed you', he would explain. He had lost far more than a marble.[4]

Following her ousting as Prime Minister in 1990, Margaret Thatcher confessed to 'dark thoughts'. She commented,

> I am not by nature either introspective or retrospective: I always prefer to look forward. Now there was far more opportunity for reflection . . . and, painful as it was, perhaps for the first time I felt an inner need to ponder on what I had made of my life.[5]

Despite being elevated to a life peerage, Baroness Thatcher, like many former political leaders, seemed to find that her enforced 'retirement' had removed much of the meaning of her life. The death in 2003 of her husband Dennis, on whose quiet support she had always relied, was a major blow. Her drinking increasingly became a problem, and, following a series of small strokes, she started to show signs of dementia at the age of 75. She could not retain the memory of Dennis's death, and had to be reminded that he was no longer living. She had not talked of her childhood home in Grantham for many years, said her daughter Carol, 'until it started cropping up in sentences, and I realised that she now thought of it as her "home"'.[6] She died, aged 87, in 2013 and some of those who had suffered during her years in power openly rejoiced. Enid Blyton's descent into dementia followed a very similar course.

The emptying of the inside

I first realised that something had changed in my own mother when I found her reading with apparent enthusiasm a 'sex and violence' best-seller by Jeffrey Archer. She had always studiously avoided any novel with 'too much going to bed in it', and violence was not to her taste either. Now she seemed unperturbed by large doses of both. At around the same time, it was reported that she had said something offensive to my sister-in-law, and to an old friend. In my family, temperamental sensitivities are such that one doesn't have to say much to give offence, but my mother had usually kept her outspoken opinions within appropriate limits. I had to face it: she was in the early stages of dementia.

Alzheimer's type dementia (where no actual strokes are involved) is an apparently inexorable degenerative condition which may take ten or 12 years to unfold, and in which short-term memory becomes increasingly unreliable while, for a considerable time, long-term memory remains relatively intact. Most adults' memory begins to decline in efficiency from around the age of 40 ('That chap – what was his name? Damn it, it was on the tip of my tongue!'), but what distinguishes dementia from the sporadically unreliable memory of a non-dementing person is the total failure to recall what has been said and done *only minutes before*. This is what puts dementia sufferers at risk (they forget to turn off electrical appliances, forget where they have parked cars, forget instructions they have just been given and even forget the way home); it is also what removes so much of their dignity. Our ability to remember things forms the connecting tissue of our mental life. Our memory of the past, and our ability to retain information in order to plan for the future, makes us human.

Under Alzheimer's influence, we begin to live in an 'endless present' in which, as for a baby, everything seems new and different, even if the same thing has happened only a short time before. At the last, even well-known people and members of one's own family cannot be recognised, and are treated as strangers. To identify my father when he (her third son) visited her close to the end of her life, my grandmother Ethel had to count off the names of her sons in birth order (accessing long-term memory to make up for her inability to recognise him): 'Let's see. Dick, Ted, Ian. You must be Ian!'. Twenty-five years later, my father saw his wife go the way that his beloved mother had gone. Immersed in my own dismay at Mum's condition, I think I failed him in empathy then.

'She's just a vegetable', some people say of a person with advanced dementia (it is equally true of men, of course, but for some reason we do not understand, twice as many women as men develop Alzheimer's type dementia). 'Vegetable' is cruel, but there's a degree of truth in it: it is as if we become a 'body without a mind', an 'empty shell'. Yet until that final, saddest stage, and sometimes even then, dementia patients retain shreds and patches of their former humanity. They can still be reached with music, for example, singing along with hymns remembered from childhood, or moving their bodies to the hit songs of their adolescence – for 'procedural memory' endures when much else falls away.[7] Tears pour down their cheeks as they hear the melodies that once meant so much to them – a sure sign that while much of their left hemisphere functioning is now seriously impaired, the right hemisphere's instinctive recognition of patterns (auditory, visual or kinaesthetic) is still operating.

With the decay of memory comes disinhibition – the lifting of the controls most of us have exercised since early childhood on what we say and do. Like sufferers from schizophrenia at a much earlier stage of life, my mother and other dementing individuals do and say inappropriate things without realising it; the things themselves, however, may be truer and more sincere than their earlier 'polite hypocrisy'. Like little children, they say exactly what comes into their minds. 'Splitting' (which Melanie Klein associated with infancy) may reappear – a dementing mother angrily demanded of her daughter, 'Where is that nice lady who looks after me?'. The 'nice lady', of course, was the same daughter.

As dementia slowly worsens, another tragic parallel to early childhood can be seen. Dementia patients lose their linguistic, social and motor skills in a sequence that roughly reverses the order in which those skills were acquired years before, in early childhood. Sentences become simpler, complex words are forgotten and the dementing person struggles to make do with 'basic English'. Reading becomes impossible. My mother, a lifelong reader of detective novels, could no longer hold the developing sequence of facts in her mind long enough to make sense of a murder mystery. Fine motor control is lost: plates are dropped and broken; eventually, bowel and bladder control are lost as well, so that the dementing person becomes incontinent and must be cared for almost like a baby. Eventually, even the ability to feed oneself may go. 'Second childhood', is how Shakespeare's Melancholy Jacques describes it in *As You Like It*, in what must be the bleakest account of old age in all literature: 'sans ['without'] teeth, sans eyes, sans every thing'.[8]

Yet even in this inevitable descent into the shadows, there is a kind of balance, a kind of justice. The lifting of inhibition, and the blunting of emotion, brings with it the short-lived ability to recall long-distant feelings and to confess long-concealed secrets. In her last year of life, my mother spoke for the first time of things done to her as a child, and things she herself had done as a young woman. They were things which up until then she had been too ashamed to admit and, probably, was not even consciously able to remember any more. The revelations emerged only briefly, as if a spotlight had suddenly illuminated a particular patch of the past and then as suddenly been switched off, plunging the spot back into total darkness. My mother was able to retrieve these memories for a few minutes partly because she no longer feared the feelings they carried with them – the frontal lobes of her cerebral cortex, which for so long had acted as her censor and internal critic, had ceased to function. The long-saved files could at last be accessed – but it was only others who would remember what she had retrieved.

People often say that their ageing relative 'becomes a totally different person' as the result of the progress of dementia: in my experience, this is not so. What comes out now must once have gone in, sometime, somehow. Maybe family members cannot tolerate what they now see, so it is easier for them to tell themselves that there has been a 'change of personality'. It is unfair to judge the younger generation for this falsely rooted belief. No child ever sees his or her parent as anything but an adult. How can we be expected to know what our father or mother was like as a child – let alone know the secret fears and infantile fantasies he or she may have entertained then? When those early fears and fantasies emerge unexpectedly, *of course* they seem unrelated to the parent we have always known. The sudden panic or anger or tears that may shake the person with dementia may not be 'new', but they may well be unprecedented in the experience of other family members, particularly if their ageing parent has always exerted very strong control over his or her emotions. At times, dementia almost seems to be a process by which the repressed unconscious becomes conscious: a weird parody of psychotherapy. Unfortunately, however, this kind of 'therapy' brings no true healing. Absolution gained in one minute is lost in the next.

Alzheimer's is an observable condition: the actual degeneration of the brain is clearly visible when it is examined in autopsy. But what *causes* the 'plaques' and 'tangles' of decayed neuronal matter visible on the surface of the brain, the 'holes' in key areas of the cortex which are the outward and visible sign of a failing memory? Here experts differ widely. At one extreme is the view that Alzheimer's is inevitable if we live long enough, that it is simply one more example of the body breaking down, and that the only reason that there are more cases of Alzheimer's now than a hundred years ago is because so many more people are living to be 80 or even older. At the other extreme, some consider Alzheimer's to be entirely emotional in origin, the result of many years of repression, and a sort of 'overload' of undealt-with issues from the past.[9] Some point to the occasional patient who has been totally functional up to her death, with no signs of memory loss, and yet proves to exhibit the telltale Alzheimer's signs when an autopsy is held.[10] And, while Alzheimer's clearly 'runs in families' (as it does in my own), what is it that 'turns on' the genetic potential for dementia in some family members but not in others? Is it possible that the same genetic mechanism that leads to a functional 'pruning' of unused neuronal connections in early childhood (and continues for years thereafter) can somehow get 'turned on again' in old age, to produce a second, maverick 'pruning'?[11]

The fact that dementia of the Alzheimer's type appears to be far more common today than it was in previous centuries, coupled with evidence of its ever-earlier onset, points to the possibility that something more than just increased life expectancy may be involved. Alzheimer's has typically been relatively rare in non-Western societies – at least until Western dietary habits and other cultural changes began to affect those societies. Is it the pollution of the air, the increased consumption of processed meat products,[12] or simply the lack of regular physical exercise that turns on the gene that may otherwise have remained inactive? My own guess is that decreased blood flow to the brain may be a key cause of dementia of *both* the multi-infarct type (Enid Blyton's and Margaret Thatcher's) and the Alzheimer's type (Iris Murdoch's)[13] – one producing sudden, partial impairment as the result of a mini-stroke, the other a slow decline as arteries gradually harden.[14] The civilisation of the West is a particularly unhealthy one: we eat the wrong food (and too much of it); we breathe air that is laden with toxic fumes; instead of walking, we drive everywhere; we spend hours sitting in front of television sets or hunched over laptops and mobile phones; we are seriously addicted to sugar, salt, wheat, caffeine, nicotine, painkillers, antidepressants and many other substances; and we absorb unwanted and potentially damaging hormones from the water we drink and the food we eat. Have we really progressed beyond the crowded, filthy cities of the pre-modern era, with their vermin, open drains and constant threat of epidemic? I often wonder whether we have simply substituted one sort of degraded environment for another.

How is it that some individuals appear to be able to keep the mental effects of Alzheimer's at bay even though the physical symptoms are (invisibly) present? The only solution is to accept that mind and body are one organism and that while physical degeneration can and does affect the spirit, positive, emotionally healthy attitudes and habits of thought are still able to influence what is actually happening in the body. 'Use it or lose it' is the dictum commonly voiced in relation to the brain. Yet plenty of Alzheimer's victims were intelligent people, who continued in old age to 'use' their intellects on anything from scholarly pursuits to doing the daily crossword, and that did not prevent them losing their memory. Joseph Haydn was one of them. No longer able to compose, he kept himself busy in his final years collecting and notating the folk songs of Austrian peasants – simple activities that he could still carry out. Yet his memory continued to deteriorate.

Is it *emotional* health that is crucial, not intellectual 'exercise'? Recent research has reminded us that symptoms of depression can precede symptoms of cognitive decline in otherwise cognitively normal over-65-year-olds[15] (although of course this might simply indicate that depression is part of the prodromal phase of Alzheimer's). Or could it be that those who repeatedly deny, repress and even consciously lie about their emotional secrets are also those who most readily develop dementia? Could it be that those of us who have least tolerance for the truth about ourselves, and who cannot face the emotional pain and shame of our lives, are also those who are most likely to activate their genetic potential to develop Alzheimer's? As they have protected themselves in life, so now the organic decay of their brains protects them from the sharp awareness of hurtful memories. It is seductive to think so, and yet we lack the hard evidence to prove it. We simply do not know. What we can say with certainty is that dementia is a dark mirror image of healthy ageing. The 'paring down', the basic honesty of the old person who has come to terms with life, is parodied in dementia. Remember the individuals we discussed in Chapter 8, who underwent no crisis at midlife but who found that 'things happened to them' instead? In dementia, what we cannot do for ourselves ends up being *done to us*, in a way that seems cruel to the outside observer, yet which paradoxically is kind to the sufferers themselves.

What do we know about the difference between those old people who enjoy 'quality of life' and those who do not? The long-running Grant Study commenced with a sample of Harvard men in the 1940s and has continued ever since, with much-expanded samples representing both genders, and a far wider socio-economic and ethnic range. Evidence from this study suggests that those individuals who continue to create *meaning* in their lives have a more positive attitude to their situation, even in the face of physical illness or disability, than those who do not.[16] Meaning may come from religious beliefs, but does not necessarily depend upon them. Basically, it would seem that if we can experience our lives as purposeful, if we believe we have something to give to others, if what we do supplies us with satisfaction and fulfilment, then we will be far less likely to fall into the same depression and apathy that typifies the Alzheimer's patient. As always, human relationships play a key role. They 'give us something to live for', a simple phrase that says a great deal.

Holding on and letting go

As human beings approach death, they begin to 'let go' of many of the things that have previously bound them to life. This is Freud's 'de-cathexis' – the *withdrawal* of a personal emotional investment in something, or someone. It is a gradual process, and may extend over many years. As I approach the age of 70, my life is still full of work, rewarding activities and meaningful relationships. Yet I no longer care about some of the things that mattered intensely to me 20 or 30 years ago. Personal disappointments that once affected me keenly no longer cut so deep. Even some of my intellectual enthusiasms, maintained over much of my life, seem less important. I may not ever write that book that I dreamed of writing in my early twenties. Ideas and dreams count less, and people count more. Objects (furnishings, books, houses) remain important to me, but I can begin to imagine living without them. The endpoint of this process of 'letting go' is movingly charted by Leslie Moore in a little book called *Turn Right, Good Moon*, in which a grown-up family watch their beloved mother gradually relinquish her hold on life, in order (as she herself says) to 'die of death' rather than 'die of cancer'.[17]

The timing of death is something that is commonly talked of as outside our control. 'It's not for us to name the day or the hour', people used to say. And in some senses that is true. Accidents and wars cut us down in our prime, heart attacks strike suddenly, cancers grow insidiously until their presence becomes unmistakable. Most of those who die earlier than average do so because of poverty, malnourishment and poor hygiene (as was once the case for a very large proportion of the world's population, and still is for a great many). But in the affluent West, those who die prematurely also include, I suspect, a disproportionate number of those born temperamentally vulnerable, as we've seen in the case of the Brontës, van Gogh and Elvis Presley. Because these people became famous, we know enough to be able to trace the temperamental roots of their early deaths. But of course, there are hundreds of thousands of others who will never be famous, but who die early for the same reason. For every Keats or Mozart, who packs a lifetime's inspired creativity into a few brief years, there are hundreds of young adults whose lives are equally driven, but who leave no lasting record behind except in the memory of their friends: 'She really loved life', they will say at the funeral; 'I can't believe that someone so full of life could be dead'.

It is not that temperamental vulnerability necessarily predestines a person to early death: many such individuals live to a ripe old age. But 'thin boundaries' make individuals more vulnerable to trauma of all kinds, more sensitive to environmental stress and thus more prone to have accidents, succumb to illnesses or to develop the persistent, negative thought-patterns we associate with depression. Almost all of us, as we go on living, feel the 'hammer blows of fate'. For most of us, these blows can be endured for a long while. But for the temperamentally vulnerable person, each successive blow takes a heavier toll on health, optimism, willingness to keep going. Whether at 30, 40 or even 50, it can suddenly all seem 'too much'. Some take their own lives; far more simply commit 'passive suicide', as George S. Patton and Branwell Brontë did, heightening their vulnerability by risk-taking, abusing drugs or medication and failing to look after their bodies. There is a sense in which most of these people chose their own deaths – not by deliberate, conscious planning, but simply by living in a way which invited death to come sooner rather than later.

It seems hardly coincidental that not one of the Brontë children (even the resilient Charlotte) lived longer than their mother had. Gustav Mahler died just a year short of his mother's age at her death (the same mother he had idolised as a child, the same mother whose lameness he had seemingly 'imitated' in his own adult gait). Elvis Presley's mother had been 46 when she died. But Elvis *believed* that Gladys was four years younger than she actually was. Even after her death, he seemed unable to shake this conviction – and he himself died at 42. The internal calendars we run often tell us quite precisely that we must not outlive a parent – perhaps it seems a form of disloyalty? – or, conversely, that it is vital to outlive them – and so we do. Thus it is that our alliances with a parent, forged so early, continue to influence us long after their deaths, and even as we approach our own.

Even those of us who live to a ripe old age may choose the timing of our own deaths, albeit less spectacularly. It is no coincidence that so many aged people die within days of their birthday, Christmas or some other personally significant date. They 'hold on' long enough to see the day through one more time, and then 'let go'. Dennis Potter, who created the disturbing television dramas *Blackeyes* and *The Singing Detective*, was told that he had inoperable pancreatic cancer. Methodically, he planned a schedule of work that would enable him to complete two final screenplays. To do that, he would need to live until his 59th birthday. He died just weeks after that date, having completed *Karaoke* (about a dying writer who leaves his money to a young nightclub hostess) and the stark, uncompromising *Cold Lazarus*, set four hundred years in the future.[18] Perhaps he felt that he had successfully conceived his final two 'children'?

Emotionally significant reunions with family members or old friends also seem to 'release' people from life. Many old people die soon after a wedding anniversary, a family reunion or, even more commonly, the birth of a grandchild or great grandchild. Most degenerative illnesses are such that life can be prolonged – not indefinitely, but for a time – by sheer act of will. The sufferer makes the effort to keep struggling for breath, battling the pain, staying conscious at least part of the time, *because there is something to stay alive for*. When the goal is reached, it is as if the effort is no longer required.

'Deathbed scenes' used to feature prominently in literature – and in life. Before modern medicine and hygiene, most people died at much earlier ages than we typically do, and death came, on the whole, more swiftly, for there was no 'heroic medicine' to prolong life artificially. It was therefore quite feasible for a dying person to summon his or her family and dependents, give them a blessing, announce the provisions of a will or, on occasion, deliver a curse. Then, within hours or even minutes, the person would die. It seems melodramatic to us, but it probably happened in real life with considerable frequency. The administration of the Last Rites of the Church was another ritual to speed the dying on their way. It too could enable a person to 'let go' less traumatically. Even Charles, the unbelieving protagonist of *Brideshead Revisited*, is deeply moved by witnessing the dying Lord Brideshead accept the consolation of the Church in his final moments. The *idea* of forgiveness runs very deep indeed.

A sleep and a remembering?

In the 'twilight sleep' of coma, unable to speak and apparently unresponsive, people clearly retain some kind of mental life, and can register something said or done in their presence. Dying, my mother flickered in and out of consciousness, mumbling phrases and sentences that showed very clearly that she was reliving some part of her childhood. The names she called out were not ours – those of her family of procreation – but those of relatives she had known when she was a small child. She obviously sensed our attempts to touch her hand, or rearrange her blanket, but translated these small physical gestures in the present into parts of the long distant scene she was reliving in her mind. This is very much the same as what happens in normal dreaming, where a sound in the sleeping person's room, or a touch that does not actually wake them, will nevertheless be registered and represented as an event consistent with the dream the person is immersed in.

My father suffered a fatal stroke while still under the anaesthetic during the course of his final heart operation. He remained in an induced coma for a week, as if sleeping peacefully, not speaking at all, but responsive to handclasps and even, to a degree, to a nurse's requests for a change of position, or to open his mouth so she could moisten his parched lips. Clearly, he was not 'unconscious'. It was not possible to tell what was going through his mind, as it was with my mother, for he did not speak. Always, Dad had kept his deepest feelings to himself, and he did so still. Yet his eyelids moved as if he were dreaming, and when we spoke the name of his favourite sister, a sudden flicker of movement catalysed his body, and he briefly squeezed my hand. At some level, perhaps he understood what had been said and fitted it, somehow, into whatever landscape he was silently traversing. *We take in, even when we can no longer give out.*

Anyone who has sat with a dying relative, or has nursed a dying patient, will also be familiar with the patient's apparent awareness of who is in the room. I had spent about 12 hours with my father and, his condition unchanged, had gone out for a meal and a break for an hour, leaving him with my brother-in-law. My father died during that absence. It is often thus: the dying seem to wait until they no longer sense the presence of particular loved ones, and then slip quietly away, or die only after loved ones who have been long awaited reappear in the room. There may not be full consciousness during a coma, but there is some degree of volition. At least some of what we say to a person in a coma can be taken in and, perhaps, make a difference.

'An eye that hath kept watch o'er man's mortality'

We die as we have lived. Those whose whole selfhood has been bound up with their work struggle to work to the last — as Sigmund Freud and Dennis Potter did. Those fixated on the right way to look and act cling to those (my Aunt May's last words to her son were 'Nice trousers, Richard!'). Those for whom life has been turbulent and painful often die in similar turbulence, fighting to stay alive, yet simultaneously fighting their own efforts: 'Rage, rage against the dying of the light',[19] wrote Dylan Thomas, an alcoholic who himself died young. Emphysema patients, warned for years that smoking will kill them, hang on to life so they can have one more cigarette. The heroes of medieval Icelandic sagas uttered laconic remarks like, 'I see they're making broad-bladed ones now' as the arrow that had penetrated their heart was withdrawn. Those who have hated long and well try to make their final words carry an extra weight of corrosive poison. Those who are sure of an afterlife often carry their serenity with them as they go; others, who may have mouthed the creed without ever fully believing it, now face their fear of the end.

When people are revived just short of death, or even after clinical death has already occurred, they sometimes say that as they experienced what they thought were their final moments, their whole life 'flashed before their eyes'. There is no particular reason to doubt them. All of us are meaning-making creatures, and we will surely make meaning to the very end. A 'fast forward' or 'fast rewind' through a lifetime of memories, pleasant and painful, is eminently possible; perhaps, indeed, something in the chemistry of the failing brain specifically encourages it. Potter's *Cold Lazarus* ends with such a sequence, the author 'writing his own death', in advance of the event. And, as we saw in Chapter 1, many dying people experience variants of a predictable series of images: the tunnel, the darkness, the emergence into light, the meeting with 'wonderful beings', the sense of calm and peace. That these final images might draw upon the experience of birth, registered but 'forgotten' so many years before, is hardly surprising. But the images seem most often to come in the *reverse* of the order we would expect if they were simply replaying a long-ago recording of the birth process. The sequence often ends, not with bright light and discomfort, but with warmth and euphoria.[20] The fact that many have experienced such image sequences may or may not validate the hope of the survival of the spirit after death; but it certainly points to the ability of the brain to store, for an entire lifetime, impressions from its earliest awareness, and to recast them into meaning for one final time. If we needed any further proof of the existence of an 'unconscious', the process of dying supplies the strongest yet.

As the circle of our individual lives reaches completion, so our deaths form part of a wider circle. Somewhere, close or distant, combinations of genes similar to our own are coming into existence. Somewhere, in the room with us, or being born hundreds of miles away, a grandchild, a niece or a nephew is starting on a life course that will differ from ours in many respects, but which may well end up sharing the pattern of our own. With our death, we make space for our own replacements, we step off the stage so that others can perform – almost certainly influenced by our performances, even though they may never have met us. The show goes on, though we are no longer there to see it.

Deaths ripple through families in mysterious ways that rationality cannot explain. Thousands of miles away, on the other side of the world, people will 'know' of the death of a relative, even though they have had no news of it, and may not even be aware that their relative was ill, or close to death. Pre-industrial peoples, who preserved kin connections much more strongly than we do, experienced such things routinely, via dreams or visits from what they took to be the spirit of the dead person. How can these things be explained? Once again, we are forced back on 'biological knowing', on the fundamental connectedness of animals who were raised together, or who share common genetic material. *We know before we know.*

Humans fear death, in part, because they have invested so heavily in a personal self, a personal consciousness. When that consciousness comes to its end, it seems the greatest loss, the greatest tragedy. Yet if our selfhood has been secure from the beginning, or if we have been able to 'grow into' that security later in life, it is probably easier for us, as death draws closer, to let go of our infantile belief that the universe revolves around us, to recognise that we are simply grains of sand on the furthest shore. For many centuries, it was thought that one's great task in life was to die well. In this secular, youth-worshipping time in the world's turning circle, we shun death. But when we turn the aged over into the care of 'professionals', we deny ourselves the experience of participating with them in their dying. In so doing, we deny the importance of the last act of meaning of which they are capable, and we deny ourselves the inspiration and deep sense of completion that comes from witnessing a 'good death'. Our society's love affair with technology and professional expertise need not stop us from participating in what used to be called 'holy dying'. And as we help others to die well, we complete the circle for ourselves, as well as for them.

I've allowed William Wordsworth the chance to say the last words of this book; they are simple, heartfelt words that acknowledge what a privilege it can be just to have lived – at least for those as fortunate as he:

> The Clouds that gather round the setting sun
> Do take a sober colouring from an eye
> That hath kept watch o'er man's mortality;
> Another race hath been, and other palms are won.
> Thanks to the human heart by which we live,

Thanks to its tenderness, its joys and fears,
To me the meanest flower that blows can give
Thoughts that do often lie too deep for tears.[21]

Notes

1 Carey Harrison, *Freud: A Novel*, London, Weidenfeld and Nicholson, 1984; Peter Gay, *Freud: A Life for Our Time*, NY and London, Norton, 1988: 628, 651.

2 See Carolyn Marvin's fascinating study, *When Old Technologies Were New: Thinking about Electric Communication in the Late Nineteenth Century*, NY and Oxford, Oxford University Press, 1988.

3 Such sentiments are most often attributed to Socrates, but may represent the views of his pupil, Plato, and can also be found in Aristophanes' comedy *Clouds*.

4 See Peter Whitmer, *The Inner Elvis: A Psychological Biography of Elvis Aaron Presley*, NY, Hyperion, 1996: 421.

5 Margaret Thatcher, *The Path to Power*, London, HarperCollins, 1995: 466.

6 Carol Thatcher, quoted in *The Telegraph*, 24 August 2008 (www.telegraph.co.uk/news/politics/conservative/2614020/Margaret-Thatcher-mental-decline-revealed-by-her-daughter; accessed 15 September 2015).

7 See A. M. Brickman and Y. Stern, 'Ageing and Memory in Humans', *Encyclopedia of Neuroscience*, Vol. 1 (2009): 175–180.

8 William Shakespeare, *As You Like It*, Act II, Sc7 ll. 140–167.

9 In general, psychoanalytic scholarship has had little to say on dementia. However, see Joel Sadavoy, 'Psychodynamic Perspectives on Alzheimer's Disease and Related Dementias', *American Journal of Alzheimer's Disease and Other Dementias*, 6, 3 (1991): 12–20; see also Ann M. Kolanowsky and Ann L. Whall, 'A Life-span Perspective of Personality in Dementia', *Image: The Journal of Nursing Scholarship*, 28, 4 (1996): 315–320.

10 The remarkable case of Sister Bernadette can be found in Donald Snowdon, *Ageing with Grace: The Nun Study and the Science of Old Age; How We Can All Live Longer, Healthier and More Vital Lives*, London, Fourth Estate, 2001: 133–134.

11 See W. T. Greenough, J. E. Black and C. S. Wallace, 'Experience and Brain Development', *Child Development*, 58 (1987): 539–559; W. Greenough and J. Black, 'Induction of Brain Structure by Experience' in M. Gunnar and C. A. Nelson (Eds), *Developmental Neuroscience*, Minnesota Symposium on Child Psychology 24, Hillsdale NJ, Erlbaum, 1992: 155–200.

12 This controversial thesis was proposed by Murray Waldman and Marjorie Lamb in *Dying for a Hamburger: The Alarming Link between the Meat Industry and Alzheimer's Disease*, London, Piatkus, 2004.

13 For more on novelist Iris Murdoch's dementia, see John Bayley, *Iris: A Memoir of Iris Murdoch*, London, Duckworth, 1998; a fine feature film, *Iris*, was based on this account.

14 Reduced blood flow to the brain is discussed by Daniel L. Schacter in *Searching for Memory: The Brain, the Mind and the Past*, NY, Basic Books, 1996: 285ff. Schacter's view is that the effect of this is greatest in the key areas of the frontal lobes of the cortex.

15 Leigh A. Johnson, Hamid R. Sohrabi, James R. Hall, Taddei Kevin, Melissa Edwards, Syd E. O'Bryant and Ralph N. Martins, 'A Depressive Endophenotype of Poorer Cognition among Cognitively Healthy Community-dwelling Adults: Results from the Western Australia Memory Study', *International Journal of Geriatric Psychiatry*, 30, 8 (August, 2015): 881–886.

16 See George Vaillant, *Ageing Well: Surprising Guidelines to a Happier Life from the Landmark Harvard Study of Adult Development*, Boston, Little, Brown, 2002.

17 Leslie E. Moore, *Turn Right, Good Moon: Conversations with a Dying Mother*, Sydney, Tonewood Knoll, 2014.

18 See Hugh Crago, *Entranced by Story: Brain, Tale and Teller from Infancy to Old Age*, London and NY, Routledge, 2014: 206–208.
19 See Dylan Thomas, 'Do Not Go Gentle into that Good Night', *In Country Sleep and Other Poems*, London, Dent, 1952.
20 See Yvonne Kason and Teri Degler, *A Farther Shore: How Near-Death and Other Extraordinary Experiences Can Change Ordinary Lives*, NY, HarperCollins, 1994.
21 William Wordsworth, from 'Ode on Intimations of Immortality from Recollections of Early Childhood' (early version first published *Poems in Two Volumes*, 1807, later revised in its present form, 1815).

FURTHER READING

Note: Intending counsellors, psychotherapists and clinical psychologists should read *novels*. Good novelists are as intensely interested in human personality and behaviour as helping professionals, but novelists have learned how to write, while many experts, particularly academic ones, have merely learned how to write obscurely. Many of my own professional colleagues do not read much at all, and if they read novels, they look only for escape and entertainment. It's a pity that so many of us fail to see what we could learn (painlessly!) from literature.

Even if we don't read novels much, those of us who engage deeply with human lives and human distress should certainly read *biographies*. It doesn't really matter who the biographies are about – actors, pop stars, politicians, business moguls, sports heroes, musicians, scientists, authors, media personalities – the life story of any individual in whom we are interested can add to our knowledge of human beings, the patterns of their lives and the causes of their pain. Good biographers, like good novelists, look deeply into their subjects, writing in depth and detail – we see the influence of genetics in the way people reflect the patterns of the generations before them; we see the influence of historical and social contexts on the choices and values of individuals; and if we read biographies frequently, we see the predictable regularities of human life unfold again and again, leaving us with a secure grasp on the patterns of growth and ageing that govern all of us. Like novels, biographies should be painless to read, but they offer far more than simply entertainment.

Fortunately, there are some professional experts who know how to write as compellingly and accessibly as biographers or novelists. I have tried wherever possible to choose such authors for the list that follows.

Blythe, Ronald, 1987, *The View in Winter: Reflections on Old Age*, 1st edn 1979; repr. Harmondsworth, Penguin.

Brumberg, Joan Jacobs, 1988, *Fasting Girls: The Emergence of Anorexia Nervosa as a Modern Disease*, Cambridge, MA, Harvard University Press. [How anorexia was seen prior to our own era – a compelling lesson on how differently 'problem behaviours' can be seen in different societies and at different times in history.]

Crittenden, Patricia McKinsey, 2012, *Raising Parents: Attachment, Parenting and Child Safety*, NY/London, Routledge. [A courageous attachment-oriented look at why parents abuse or neglect their children, with massive implications for those working in child protection.]

Davies, Douglas, 2010, *Child Development: A Practitioner's Guide*, 3rd edn, NY, Guilford. [One of the few texts that truly integrate clinical and developmental perspectives, with excellent case studies of common childhood problems and how they are addressed in treatment.]

Dunn, Judy and Plomin, Robert, 1990, *Separate Lives: Why Siblings Are So Different*, NY, Basic Books.

Gerhardt, Sue, 2004, *Why Love Matters: How Affection Shapes a Baby's Brain*, London, Routledge.

Hargrave, Terry and Anderson, William, 1992, *Finishing Well: Ageing and Reparation in the Intergenerational Family*, NY, Brunner/Mazel.

Hartmann, Ernest, 1991, *Boundaries in the Mind: A New Psychology of Personality*, NY, Basic Books.

Jamison, Kay Redfield, 1993, *Touched with Fire: Manic-Depressive Illness and the Artistic Temperament*, NY, Free Press.

Kagan, Jerome, 2010, *The Temperamental Thread: How Genes, Culture, Time and Luck Make Us Who We Are*, NY, Dana Press.

Karen, Robert, 1998, *Becoming Attached: First Relationships and How They Shape Our Capacity to Love*, NY, Oxford University Press.

Levinson, Daniel, with Darrow, Charlotte N., Klein, Edward B., Levinson, Mariah H. and McKee, Braxton, 1978, *The Seasons of a Man's Life*, NY, Ballantyne.

Levinson, Daniel, with Levinson, Judy D., 1996, *The Seasons of a Woman's Life*, NY, Ballentine.

McGoldrick, Monica, Gerson, Randy and Petry, Suellen, 2008, *Genograms: Assessment and Intervention*, 3rd edn, NY, Norton.

Miller, Jane, 2010, *Crazy Age: Thoughts on Being Old*, London, Virago.

Napier, Augustus and Whitaker, Carl, 1978, *The Family Crucible*, NY, Harper.

Nathanson, Donald, 1992, *Shame and Pride: Affect, Sex and the Birth of the Self*, NY, Norton.

Neuland, Sherwin B., 1994, *How We Die*, 1st edn 1993; repr. London, Chatto & Windus.

Schacter, Daniel, 1996, *Searching for Memory: The Brain, the Mind and the Past*, NY, Basic Books.

Schivelbusch, Wolfgang, 1993, *Tastes of Paradise; A Social History of Spices, Stimulants and Intoxicants*, NY, Vintage. [First published in German in 1980. Fascinating history which sets the whole issue of addictions in a far wider context than most mental health professionals are aware of.]

Smith, Matthew, 2012, *Hyperactive: The Controversial History of ADHD*, London, Reaktion Books.

Stern, Daniel, 1990, *Diary of a Baby*, NY, Basic Books.

Sulloway, Frank, 1996, *Born to Rebel: Birth Order, Family Dynamics and Creative Lives*, Boston, Little, Brown.

Terr, Lenore, 1994, *Unchained Memories: True Stories of Traumatic Memories, Lost and Found*, NY, Basic Books.

Vaillant, George E., 1995, *The Natural History of Alcoholism Revisited*, Cambridge, MA, Harvard University Press. [Detailed *longitudinal* study of alcoholism across the lifespan of individuals.]

van der Kolk, Bessel, 2014, *The Body Keeps the Score: Mind, Brain and Body in the Transformation of Trauma*, London, Allen Lane.

Wright, Lawrence, 1997, *Twins: Genes, Environment and the Mystery of Identity*, London, Weidenfeld & Nicolson.

INDEX

Printed in Great Britain
by Amazon